Praise for RESET

"Must reading for parents, policy-makers and pundits."
–Bing Gordon
Chief Creative Officer, Electronic Arts

"As your son or daughter would no doubt put it, Rusel DeMaria 'gets it.' He combines an insider's understanding of how the games industry works, a fan's vantage point on what's exciting about this emerging medium, a concerned citizen's perspective on the social and educational impacts of games culture, and a visionary's take on where this might all be leading. It's a potent combination—all the more so because he pulls it off with common sense and accessible, even engaging prose. This is a book parents and educators should read before they make any final judgments about the place of games in the lives of young Americans, and young people should read *Reset* if they are looking for arguments about why playing games doesn't rot the brain."

–Henry Jenkins, author of *Convergence Culture: Where Old and New Media Collide*

"Rusel DeMaria has long been a unique and insightful voice inside the games industry. *Reset* is the first book about video games that covers the whole area, in a completely lucid and entertaining way, for a wide audience. Anyone can now get up to speed on a controversial topic of vital concern to our culture and our economy."

–James Paul Gee, Tashia Morgridge Professor of Reading, University of Wisconsin-Madison, and author of *What Video Games Can Teach Us About Learning and Literacy*

"Rusel DeMaria opens the eyes of the reader to rethink and reshape the notion of videogames from something to be feared to something that is a vital agent for social change, creativity and innovation in the 21st Century.... An absolute must for parents, students, policymakers, educators, or anyone who wants to be enlightened about how learning itself will forever change because of the influence of videogames."

–Corey P. Carbonara, PhD, Professor, Film and Digital Media Director, Digital Communication Technologies Project, Baylor University

MORE PRAISE FOR *RESET*...

"Rusel DeMaria's book is valuable and refreshing. He speaks directly to the non-gamer without recourse to academic jargon, yet manages to distill key concepts and theories from academia, the game industry, and popular culture through his research and interviews in multiple disciplines. This is a must-read for parents, teachers, and non-gamers who want to know what all the fuss is about with games. Academics and game developers will find the text useful as well."

–Richard Van Eck, Associate Professor, Graduate Director, Instructional Design & Technology, University of North Dakota

"DeMaria has written a book I can wholeheartedly recommend to parents to understand the entire gaming experience! While there are many other books that cover elements of kids and gaming, he has given the comprehensive context for those who don't currently understand this entertainment medium."

–Gordon Walton
Co-Studio Director, BioWare Austin

"DeMaria has taken his game to a new level. Always insightful about games and technology, his new book is a smart and thought-provoking new take on why we play in these new ways, and why we should. There is proof here for the long overdue acceptance of video games by mainstream society."

—Trip Hawkins, Founder, Electronic Arts and CEO, Digital Chocolate

"I hand-picked Rusel DeMaria (a video game veteran) to work with me researching my *Game Designer's Reference Book*. Over those two years of working together his deep knowledge of video games was incredibly helpful. Now he takes that knowledge and combines it with his personal passion for the positive role of video games in society. The result is a vision of games that entertain while they inspire the best in all of us."

–David Perry, Video Game Pioneer, Founder Shiny Entertainment, CEO, GAMECONSULTANTS.COM

"FINALLY! Rusel DeMaria shatters the preconceptions of video games with a long overdue and thought provoking reality check. Forget the nightly news spewing us with the latest ambulance chasing attorney seeking the new 21st century insanity plea. *Reset* reveals a deeper understanding of not only the chemistry of gaming and the insights of game designers, but also the culture of gamers and the all-too ignored positive impacts that games already play in our lives and especially in our future. The medium of gaming has just begun—and DeMaria has done an excellent job in revealing why there is a great deal to be gained from embracing our inner demons in the gaming world."

–Lorne Lanning, Video Game PioneerCo-founder & Creative Director, Oddworld Inhabitants

Reset

Changing the Way We
Look at Video Games

RUSEL DeMARIA

BERRETT-KOEHLER PUBLISHERS, INC.
San Francisco
a BK Currents book

Berrett-Koehler Publishers, Inc.
235 Montgomery Street, Suite 650
San Francisco, CA 94104-2916
Tel: (415) 288-0260; Fax: (415) 362-2512 www.bkconnection.com

Ordering Information

Quantity sales. Special discounts are available on quantity purchases by corporations, associations, and others. For details, contact the "Special Sales Department" at the Berrett-Koehler address above.

Individual sales. Berrett-Koehler publications are available through most bookstores. They can also be ordered directly from Berrett-Koehler: Tel: (800) 929-2929; Fax: (802) 864-7626; www.bkconnection.com

Orders for college textbook/course adoption use. Please contact Berrett-Koehler: Tel: (800) 929-2929; Fax: (802) 864-7626.

Orders by U.S. trade bookstores and wholesalers. Please contact Ingram Publisher Services, Tel: (800) 509-4887; Fax: (800) 838-1149; customer.service@ingrampublisherservices.com; or visit www.ingrampublisherservices.com/Ordering for details about electronic ordering.

Production Management: Michael Bass Associates
Interior design and page layout: Rusel DeMaria
Copyediting: Laura Larson

Library of Congress Cataloging-in-Publication Data
DeMaria, Rusel, 1948-
    Reset : changing the way we look at video games / by Rusel DeMaria.
      p. cm.
    Includes bibliographical references and index.
    ISBN-13: 978-1-57675-433-7 (hardcover)
    1. Video games--Social aspects--United States. 2. Video games--United States--Psychological aspects. 3. Video games--Economic aspects--United States. 4. Video gamers--Education (Higher)--United States. I. Title.
    GV1469.3.D455 2007
    794.8--dc22
                                            2007001449

First Edition
11 10 09 08 07   10 9 8 7 6 5 4 3 2 1

Dedicated to all future video game designers.
May you know the joy that comes from
contributing to a better world through your art.

CONTENTS

v

ACKNOWLEDGMENTS

This book owes its existence to the pioneers of video game design whose work has inspired me to know that there is more to games than literally meets the eye. To that end, I want to express my thanks especially to those pioneering designers who provided me with the most memorable video game moments and personal insights, notably Dani Bunten Berry, Nolan Bushnell, John Carmack, Noah Falstein, Richard Garriott, Trip Hawkins, Larry Holland, Lorne Lanning, Jordan Mechner, Sid Meier, Shigeru Miyamoto, Brian Moriarty, David Perry, John Romero, Warren Spector, Jon Van Cannegham, Will Wright and countless early arcade game pioneers too numerous to list.

Many people encouraged me during the writing of this book, none more than James Paul Gee, Ian Bogost, Corey Carbonara, and Gordon Walton. To them, I owe a great debt for their unfailing support and insightful comments. And many thanks to the guinea pigs for the first draft, who commented with sometimes brutal honesty: Robert Clegg, James Gee, Meadow Martell, Jeevan Sivasubramaniam, Troy Voelker, and Gordon Walton.

My editor, Johanna Vondeling, pushed me constantly to do my best. There is no doubt in my mind that whatever is right with this book owes a lot to her efforts. Similarly, Jeevan Sivasubramaniam was always there to answer my questions and support me during the inevitable crises.

Finally, my family: Max has been an inspiration to me, both as a young man and as a video game "natural." Watching him play the hardest games and make them look easy, running around with him in online games, and discussing video games from his perspective have all been a joyful and invaluable service to my vision. And for my wife, Viola, there is too much to say—simply put, thanks for putting up with me, for keeping me healthy, and for appreciating video games from afar.

Introduction

TO THE CONTRARY

Learning is what most adults will do for a living in the 21st century.

—S. J. Perelman

Video games are the "misbehaving teenagers" of the media, often seen as breaking, bending, or mangling the rules and conventions of society. At best, the term *video game* inspires thoughts of triviality and childish obsessions. At worst, video games are attacked in politics and billed in the media as violent, antisocial, corrupting, and dangerous to our youth. Public discourse dwells almost exclusively on the negative, "misbehaving" side.

A growing but less commonly discussed view of video games is that they may represent one of the most powerful learning technologies ever invented, a sentiment echoed by video game supporters and critics alike. Is it possible that the much-maligned video game could be as powerful for positive purposes as it appears to be negative?

Although this book begins with an examination of the most prominent charges against video games, the majority of its discussion is devoted to exploring their real positive potential. What "magical" qualities do they possess, and how do we harness those qualities? How can mere games be "powerful teaching tools," and what do they teach? More important, what *can* they teach and how?

I started asking myself such questions around 1994 when I began my first video game design project. I had already been playing video games for nearly thirty years, but I quickly found that playing and designing were very different. Playing is like

1

walking through a door into a different universe and learning its rules, its challenges, and its opportunities. Designing is like being the architect of that universe and the door leading to it. The designer is in charge of every detail: every event, every puzzle, and all possible paths through the game. I immediately realized that anyone who walked through my door would be voluntarily entering my universe. They would be affected by the kind of world I created.

When Madame Curie said, "You cannot hope to build a better world without improving the individuals," she might have been speaking to me at the moment I began to envision my first game world. The video game world I wanted to create was one that enriched the players' lives in some way, whether by helping them learn something, improving their skills, or challenging and inspiring them to grow as human beings.

When I expressed such ideas and thoughts about games to gamers and to people in the game industry, I got a variety of reactions. Some stated that it was a good idea, but they couldn't really see how it would work. Commonly I heard that the purpose of video games was to have fun, and anything else would interfere with that primary goal. Some people shrugged indifferently, while others asked me, "Why bother?"

I couldn't answer the question "Why bother?" I simply saw the opportunity to do something more than produce a piece of "ordinary" entertainment or clone an existing game. To be sure, the video games that I found most memorable were those that surprised me, challenged my thinking, provided ethical dilemmas, or in some way offered me a chance to know myself better. I wasn't the first to consider the impact of the game on the player, and a handful of my favorite games provided the inspiration for my vision of more humanly relevant video games.

As for the critics who didn't believe you could or should try to combine "meaning" and "fun," I was unconvinced. Theodore Sturgeon, my writing mentor, used to say, "Ask the next question," and that mantra has remained with me to this day. By asking the next question, I can always find a way to add deeper human relevance to a video game concept. There's no need to sacrifice fun for meaningful experience. In fact, I believe the more meaningful the game experience is, the more fun it really is—a thought suggested by the great video game designer Sid Meier, who told me, "We found that people like to learn, especially when the learning is not forced on them."

Why does any of this matter? To begin with, video games are played by millions of people all over the world. More people in more countries are discovering video games every year, and many of them are children and teenagers. Obviously, the effect these games have on young people is of great concern to parents, legislators, and educators everywhere, yet most video game dialogue focuses on what's wrong with or dangerous about video games, not what they may offer or how to get the most benefit from them.

But video games are just games, aren't they? True, video games are games, but they are not "just" games. It's like saying "novels are just books" or "movies are just movies." In fact, the art of writing good novels is quite complex and requires a great amount of skill. The art of making movies is arguably even more complex, involving the skills, both technical and artistic, of a small army of people. Moviemakers know their craft, and they know very well how to engage audiences and affect their emotions.

Video games are in some ways like movies, in that they combine a variety of technical and artistic talents, and while moviemakers can tug at your emotions and thrill you with camera techniques and car chases, video games do even more—they motivate. They motivate players to take action. They motivate players to think, plan, and do. They motivate players to seek results, to assess situations, and to act to achieve goals.

Although I sometimes think of video games as "just games," I also think of them as a technology of entertainment and learning. The idea of video games as a technology will become clearer to you as you read this book because it turns out that video games combine several powerful tools that can be used effectively to present information in a variety of ways, motivation being just one. As it is with any new technology, it is people who decide how to use it. The technology is neutral. How we currently view video games, and how we will view them in the future, depends largely on how they are used.

If video games do have the potential to have a positive impact on players, perhaps it is in part up to us to realize that potential, to encourage it, and even to demand it. If video games are as powerful a learning tool as many experts believe them to be, then we owe it to ourselves and to our children to find and utilize their power to spark imaginations, make learning fun and creative, and offer the best we have to our kids and to all gamers around the world.

My focus is on commercial, off-the-shelf, and Internet games—video games that I believe can entertain and teach in various ways. In this book, I offer you a chance not only to see video games in a new light but to understand their relationship with human concepts of play and learning and some of the ways they can facilitate learning. I also suggest some guidelines that parents and other family members might find helpful when interacting with video gamers, along with a short list of games that offer positive experiences. At the end, I will offer you a chance to advocate for the types of games you want to see, with some tips, talking points, guidelines, and contact information for some of the top video game companies.

Chapter 1

DANGEROUS GAMES

"The disturbing material in Grand Theft Auto and other games like it is stealing the innocence of our children and it's making the difficult job of being a parent even harder." [1]

—Hillary Rodham Clinton, 2005

It is pleasant at times to play the madman.

—Seneca (5 BC–65 AD)

In 1982, the U.S. surgeon general, C. Everett Koop, sounded a national alarm. Stating that video games caused "aberrations in childhood behavior," he warned that kids were becoming addicted to video games "body and soul." He also said, "There is nothing constructive in the games. . . . Everything is eliminate, kill, destroy."[2] Koop later retracted that statement, claiming it was an off-the-cuff response to a question. Retracted or not, his opinion gave voice to common beliefs of the time. Also in 1982, National PTA president Ronnie Lamm stated, "We've taken away their guns and holsters and cowboys and Indians, and we're now giving them a cartridge with the same kind of violent themes."[3]

In the early 1990s, Senators Joseph Lieberman (D-Conn.) and Herb Kohl (D-Wisc.) conducted a campaign against video games. During one of the 1993 hearings, in a harsh attack on video game makers, their colleague, Senator Byron Dorgan (D-N.D.), said, "Shame on the people who produce that trash. . . . It is child abuse in my judgment."[4]

In fact, for most of the first thirty years of video game history, the predominant messages in the press and from politicians were almost universally negative and fearful. At best, video games were seen as a colossal waste of time; at worst, a threat looming over our youth and society. In fact, one guest on the

MacNeil/Lehrer NewsHour in 1982 stated, "It is my concern that 10, 20 years down the line we're going to get a group of children who then become adults who don't view people as human beings, but rather view them as other blips to be destroyed—as things."[5]

Based on such alarming statements and the fact that video games have become more and more popular over the past decades, we might expect our society to be overrun by soulless video game zombies. As far as I can tell, the first video game generation, now those predicted adults, are just like other citizens. For better or worse, they do not view people as "blips."

ONGOING CONTROVERSY

The controversy rages on, however, and predictions made a quarter of a century ago are long forgotten. New predictions and concerns arise every few years, and new sound bites fill the media. We can't help but worry: Are they correct this time? Are today's video games going too far?

The people who make video games play a part in the ongoing controversy, too. They have often demonstrated a talent for testing boundaries and violating social conventions, almost from the very beginning. Though certainly not the first time video games came under fire, one of the most pivotal events occurred in 1992, when Mortal Kombat broke new ground by depicting realistic human figures in one-on-one battles. The human realism concerned many critics, but the game didn't stop there. Blood flew as the blows landed, and the famous "fatality" moves depicted such horrors as someone pulling out the defeated enemy's heart or spine. Kids loved it. Parents didn't.

Another game, Night Trap, caused controversy around the same time for sexual themes and scantily clad actresses in what appeared to be a voyeuristic context. Although the actual context was for the player (as the hero) to watch over the characters and protect them from a killer, the game's sexual implications concerned many critics, despite the fact that, unlike Mortal Kombat, Night Trap was not wildly successful.

A few years after Mortal Kombat, a game called Doom popularized a type of entertainment that ultimately came to be called the "first-person shooter." First-person shooters occur from the point of view of the player, something like the clichéd "stalker" view used in movies to show a victim from the killer's perspective.

Doom was a sensation among video gamers, and once again a game raised a red flag of concern. What was behind this immensely popular game that seemed to immerse players in a world of intense and graphically realistic violence? What adverse effects would it have on the people, particularly young people, who played it?

Then came the tragic shootings at Columbine High School. This complex tragedy shocked the nation, and naturally people sought to understand what had happened and why. Doom turned up as part of the story, and for a while some people attempted to link the school shooting with the video game, but the links were fragile at best, and the causes of the tragedy far more complex. In the end, video games were not seen as the proximate cause but rather one of several symptoms of two young men's deepening obsessions, isolation, and alienation.

In time, the news media and the political rhetoric about video games seemed to taper off, as the world presumably got used to first-person shooter games like Doom. The relative peace, such as it was, did not last. Once again, a game burst on the scene that shattered boundaries and reignited controversy: Grand Theft Auto 3. In Grand Theft Auto 3 and its sequels, players have free reign over a huge 3D world. They can do virtually anything, but among the most commonly publicized activities are stealing cars, beating up and killing random people, participating in gang wars, shooting police, running a prostitution ring, engaging in sexual acts, and driving recklessly. Of course, there is a lot more to the game, but its most publicized activities have outraged a lot of people, in part because the game draws high praise from players and was the most sought-after game of 2001.

Senators Kohl and Lieberman hauled the industry over the carpet after Mortal Kombat and Night Trap, prompting the video game industry to create a voluntary independent rating system, managed by the Entertainment Software Ratings Board (ESRB). Now printed on all retail game boxes, ESRB ratings are intended to help regulate the sale of "inappropriate" games to minors and at the same time inform parents and other buyers of the kinds of content included in the games. The ESRB ratings are intended to work like movie ratings, which inform parents about whether specific movies may be appropriate for younger viewers.

For a variety of reasons, the ESRB ratings have not quelled criticism of video games, which in any case tends to focus almost entirely on certain high-profile games such as the Grand Theft Auto series and a far less popular game called Postal 2, which allows players to engage in acts of brutal violence against innocent victims. What we learn from politicians and from the news is still largely negative and disturbing. Unfortunately, we rarely hear the whole story.

Reporting on video games in general, and on highly visible ones in particular, is often sensationalistic and simplistic. For instance, it's generally easier to classify all video games under one label. Sound bites do not lend themselves to subtle distinctions. Meanwhile, many scientists and researchers present evidence to prove the effects of video games and establish causation between these games and later antisocial behavior. Other scientists and researchers dispute these assertions, but their findings are less often part of the public discourse.

Unfortunately, in politics and the media, it's easier to state such results in simple, absolute terms in support of a specific agenda than to deal with the fact that much of the research is unproven or, at best, disputed. Even statements by some of the most ardent video game critics are taken out of context, and their qualifications and disclaimers that these games do not represent the whole set of video games are ignored in favor of a more definitive and easily digestible message. Lost in the discussion is the fact that most video games do not feature excessive violence or glorify criminal and antisocial activities, as we will see in Chapter 2.

SHIFTING PERCEPTIONS

Even though high-profile video games have grabbed much of the attention with their violence and antisocial themes, little by little people are beginning to recognize that these games do not tell the whole story. While concern over the effects of video games, especially on children, has not gone away, the ever-increasing number of articles exploring the positive aspects of video games reveals a slight shift in perception. Why is coverage of video games changing?

Perhaps attitudes are shifting because people are beginning to look past the obvious criticisms and concerns to recognize video games in a more complete context, a context that realizes their positive aspects and potential for good. Even some of the harshest critics of video games today see this potential. Dr. Elizabeth Carll, who chairs the Interactive Media Committee of the American Psychological Association's Media Division and is a former president of the Media Division, has been an expert witness at various governmental hearings and is concerned about the effects of some games on children. Yet in an interview she told me, "Many video games are positive and teach children important skills. However, it is the groups which are violent, particularly those which reward violent and antisocial behavior and may teach violence as a means of resolving conflict, which are of concern."[6] She is not an opponent of video games but only of certain problematic content that she believes is not appropriate for children.

My focus in this book is on the positive side of games, not because there isn't a negative side and not because video game criticism is necessarily invalid. I choose to present the positive side because it is far more powerful and prevalent than most people think, and because it offers a tremendous gift to society if we decide to accept it. Despite my positive focus, I have not ignored the criticisms of games. In fact, I have immersed myself in those criticisms through books, articles, court cases, congressional testimony, and personal interviews with more than a dozen experts on different sides of the debate.

Among the most significant charges leveled against video games are that they promote antisocial behavior—most specifically violence and criminal activities—and that they are addicting. In addition, some people fear that video game playing can pose various health risks. Are these charges true? What kinds of effects are video games having on people who play them? Should the video game industry be "cleaned up"?

I can't answer all of these questions, but I can at least attempt to clarify the issues and present information that I hope will allow you to make up your own mind. Obtaining definite and universally accepted data and conclusions about media effects is almost impossible, as I have discovered in my research, and all we can do as reasonable and concerned people is look, listen, and decide for ourselves. We will each apply our own standards of decency, morality, and appropriateness to the media we and our children consume. Ultimately, we will weigh the positives and negatives of video games, as we do for every technology and entertainment medium, according to those standards.

The studies, the research, and the various testimonies of experts are, therefore, less important in the long run than our own sensibilities, especially where, as you will see, there is so much debate and so little universal agreement among experts.

DO VIDEO GAMES PROMOTE ANTISOCIAL BEHAVIOR?

Most people today believe that violent media contribute directly to real-world violence. According to the American Academy of Pediatrics, "Playing violent video games has been found to account for a 13% to 22% increase in adolescents' violent behavior."[7] According to Craig Anderson of Iowa State University, "high exposure to media violence is a major contributing cause of the high rate of violence in modern U.S. society."[8] Other people have called video games "murder simulators,"[9] while the players of these games have been labeled as "emotionally unhealthy and mentally unstable."[10]

What are the roots of these beliefs, and why are so many people absolutely certain that video games pose such a real danger, particularly to young people?

OUR TASTE FOR VIOLENCE

As easy as it might be to represent modern media, including video games, as the epitome of violence, the recent history of Western civilization reveals an uncomfortable truth: specifically, that people's prurient taste for violence is not only common but among our most compelling, if also disturbing, interests.

In *Savage Pastimes*, Harold Schechter offers an often grisly history of our fascination with violence and crime, asserting, with plenty of lurid examples, that what we have today is tame by comparison. He maintains that contemporary society and media are far less violent than in the past, even our most controversial programs and video games. "Those who deplore the current state of American society and accuse media of pandering to, if not actually creating, an unwholesome obsession with violence would do well to learn something about cultural history."[11]

Schechter points out that, in contrast to modern life, where most of our exposure to real violence, crime, and death is via news and entertainment fictions, past societies were far more accustomed to violence in their real-life worlds. Livestock was regularly slaughtered by family members, hangings and beheadings were social events, and corpses of criminals were often displayed publicly following execution. Yet, based on the evidence of more than a century of consistent and phenomenal sales of various dime novels, broadsides, periodicals, "penny dreadfuls," and paid admissions to wax museums full of horrors—not to mention grisly and violent fairy tales—our ancestors were also avid consumers of sensationalized horror, violence, and crime.

By no means is this necessarily a happy fact, but it is a fact nonetheless. Violence fascinates people, yet the question remains: Is it causing us to be more violent? Schechter points out that whereas people had thought television violence would inevitably turn a generation into psychopaths, baby boomers, most of whose male children spent their early days with toy guns in their hands, "grew up to be the generation that preached (however sanctimoniously) peace, love, flower power, and believed we could end the Vietnam War by surrounding the Pentagon and chanting 'Om.'"[12]

Our attraction to violence—fantasy or real—seems to be a common human trait found in most "civilized" societies, but does the consumption of violent entertainment make people more violent? Putting aside our past cultural history, today's beliefs about video game violence hinge to a large extent on studies of television viewing. There is a widely accepted belief that watching violent television causes violent, even criminal, behavior. How did we come to this belief, and is it true? Does watching violent TV turn people violent and cause them to become criminals?

DOES WATCHING TELEVISION CREATE CRIMINALS?

One of the chief arguments against violence in video games is based on studies of television violence between 1960 and 1981 involving 856 third graders, many of whom were tracked at various points in their lives up to age thirty. Five years after the study concluded, L. Rowell Huesmann, one of the primary researchers in this study (with Leonard Eron), testified before the Senate Judiciary Committee, claiming that there was a "strong relationship between early violence viewing and later adult criminality."[13] He used a bar graph to demonstrate a correlation between children who had viewed a lot of violent television as eight-year-olds and subsequent violent criminal records.

Huesmann's testimony and his bar graph convinced both the U.S. Senate and the media that television violence was dangerous and that it was a serious contributor to a later life of crime. This view and the study that promoted it have been treated by researchers, politicians, and social agencies as incontrovertibly factual ever since, and both are repeatedly cited in literature that argues against violence in video games.

The problem is that these studies were not as clear as Huesmann's testimony might have suggested. In his book *The Case for Television Violence*, Jib Fowles examines the published results of the long-term study and reveals that the researchers in fact ignored many findings that did nothing to prove their point and only relied on weak correlations in one out of six criteria. Moreover, he states, their final published paper never mentions the word *television* once. "Instead of highlighting the learning of aggression from television, the authors pointed to other instigators of aggression—familial, neurological, genetic—and in doing so undermined their previously exclusive focus on television violence."[14] In fact, Fowles goes even further, stating in an interview, "It's quite clear when reading their 1984 publication, they are shying away from their own previous explicit statement about television violence."[15]

In the November 23, 2000, issue of *Rolling Stone* magazine, Pulitzer Prize–winning author Richard Rhodes revisited the case against media violence and through correspondence with Huesmann was able to ascertain that the famous bar graph displayed in the Senate hearing represented only three individual cases out of a sample of 145 boys. I also spoke with Huesmann, and he confirmed this fact. He defended his position by noting that he had conducted two different long-term studies and had obtained results from the second, which confirmed his theory of the effect of television violence on people's later tendencies toward violence. However, he admonished in the interview, "No social scientist would say that even these two studies together are by themselves a convincing picture without further evidence."[16] He believes that, when combined with laboratory studies, in which the variables of the situation can be more controlled and which show short-term effects of aggression in people who watch violent television, the long-term studies are meaningful.

Jonathan Freedman, author of *Media Violence and Its Effect on Aggression: Assessing the Scientific Evidence*, also questions the research on television violence. Freedman has examined all of the available studies of media violence for both television and video games. In the case of the long-term television studies, he has no problem with the methodology. "This is not bogus science. It is well done," he told me. "What is debatable is the interpretation of results."[17]

The problem with these long-term studies, Freedman says, is that they do not take into account the many factors that could influence the results, such as the fact that perhaps more aggressive kids might have fewer friends, or the friends they do have might exert poor influences on them or reinforce aggressive tendencies. We know little about their neighborhoods or how their parents treat them. In short, without knowing a lot more about these kids and the lives they have led for thirty years, the end result of these studies leaves more questions than it answers. In addition, Freedman told me, the results of such studies are not consistent, and where they do show the kinds of positive correlations the researchers claim, the effects are very weak.[18]

Huesmann defends the research by mentioning the results of controlled laboratory studies, but Freedman, Fowles, and other researchers have criticized those studies as well. Fowles mentions one particular study in which "viewing *Sesame Street* or *Mr. Rogers' Neighborhood* produced a threefold increase in aggression among preschoolers who initially measured low in aggressiveness."[19] Overall, he claims, laboratory studies fail to show the effects the researchers claim with any consistency, and he raises serious questions about how we currently view media violence based on the current literature.

If Huesmann and other researchers who come to similar conclusions are correct, then there is a link between violence viewing and future behavior. If Fowles, Freedman, and others are correct, the established beliefs about media violence are at best inconclusive. Going even further, Fowles states that many studies show the opposite effects, indicating that people can use violent media to help release violent impulses "in a harmless way."[20]

What we don't know in the case of media violence seems to outweigh what we know with any certainty. In the end, I think it's fair to say that people's responses to violence in media are far more complex than sociological studies can fully uncover. The myriad factors pervasive in our culture, not to mention the constant changes in technology and society decade by decade, suggest that no one source of media influences people significantly, though it might have some effect. If television studies are less conclusive than we had thought they were, what about video games? Can a stronger case be made to support video game links to violence and crime, as some would suggest?

What Do Video Game Studies Tell Us?

Almost all of the research on video game violence so far has taken place in laboratory settings and has attempted to prove short-term correlations between violent game play and increased aggression. Craig Anderson, chair of the Department of Psychology at Iowa State University, is one of the few and most prominent researchers involved in such studies, and he regularly gives testimony before Congress and in major court cases. Like most video game researchers today, he relies on the long-term studies of television violence to validate the probable long-term effects of video game violence. However, he believes that video games, in contrast with television, are likely to produce stronger associations because they are interactive.

Anderson's assertion about the increased effects of interactivity is based on the idea that players play the part of and identify with the aggressor. Due to the interactive nature of video games, they actively participate in the acts of aggression. In addition, they "rehearse" the choices that repeatedly lead to aggression, and that very repetition creates a learning environment in which "their lessons will be taught repeatedly."[21]

As apparently clear and convincing as Anderson's conclusions seem, many equally competent researchers disagree with his studies and with his conclusions. Dmitri Williams, assistant professor at the University of Illinois at Urbana-Champaign in the Department of Speech Communication, disagrees that the results of television studies, even if valid, lead to the same conclusions when applied to video games. Researchers, he contends, need to know their medium. "Video games are fundamentally different from TV."[22]

Social factors are among the significant omissions in existing video game research. Williams views most video game playing as a social phenomenon, and testing in laboratory settings with solo players leaves out a big part of the picture. For instance, can peer pressure have positive or negative effects on players, causing them to act violently or antisocially? Peer pressure and social influences do affect people's behavior, but no data exist to show whether video gamers' reactions to peer pressure and other social influences result in any noticeably negative effects. Even if there are peer pressure effects, could they reinforce positive as well as negative behaviors? If negative, are they more or less severe than what we find in better-known social settings, such as schoolyards, families, street gangs, or college fraternities?

Also missing from the research, according to Williams, is the fact that video games today can be competitive or collaborative, or both at the same time. In a month-long study of video game players, Williams found no link between violent video game play and aggression. He thinks that more long-term study is needed, and he criticizes the methods of other researchers as being out of touch with the important factors that make video games unique. He believes more studies should be "carried out by people who understand games as well as scientific research methods."

Another important factor often overlooked in all the argument about video games and other media is the influence parents can have. Even with the TV research, Williams says that when kids watched violent TV with their parents, the effects were radically different. "Viewing 'negative' content with parental guidance," he suggests, "can have the opposite effects and can reduce the likelihood of long-term negative effects."

Why, then, are people so ready to jump on any research that suggests a correlation between video games and violence? Williams, Schechter, and others cite the history of media, where every new innovation was met with fear and resistance, from the birth of the modern novel to the early nickelodeons, newspapers, radio, TV, rock and roll, pinball, and so forth. Even such universally accepted non-media technologies as automobiles and telephones were seen as dangers to society when they were first introduced.

In summary, Williams suggests that we "fix the research before we begin fixing policy and messing with the First Amendment. Let's understand the medium."

Williams is only one of many researchers who disagree with current beliefs about video games. The arguments, for and against, have found their way into our court system, where laws attempting to regulate video game sales are tested in legal proceedings.

In 2002, a distinguished group of thirty-three researchers from universities all over the United States, as well as England and Australia, filed a friend-of-the-court brief to the United States Court of Appeals for the Eighth Circuit. The brief supported an appeal of the lower court decision that had, among other things, declared video games were not protected by the First Amendment. The same lower court decision had relied heavily on research by Anderson and his colleagues as primary proof of the link between violent behavior and video games.

Citing numerous articles and studies, the brief not only states that most studies failed to demonstrate a clear link between video game violence and violent behavior, but also that some studies were showing a positive release of emotion (catharsis) from such play. In addition, it criticizes the laboratory studies that rely on methods, such as word recognition tests and others, that produce positive results based on small pools of statistical data, out of context and without clear correlations with behaviors outside the laboratory.

In their brief to the Court of Appeals, these researchers also note studies of previous media, such as movies and comic books, which mistakenly associated media violence with real-world violence, including the Eron/Huesmann study of television violence. The thirty-seven-page brief cites studies and experiments that show either no direct correlation between video game violence and real-world violence, or even positive effects where the video game experience appeared to reduce violence. In this case—as in every other case where courts have looked at the research—the court found that there was no credible evidence of harm from violent content in video games.[23]

Contrasted with the Court of Appeals brief is the "Joint Statement on the Impact of Entertainment Violence on Children," presented in July 2000 at the Congressional Public Health Summit. It was endorsed by the American Academy of Pediatrics, American Academy of Child and Adolescent Psychiatry, American Psychological Association, American Medical Association, American Academy of Family Physicians, and American Psychiatric Association. The statement asserts, first, "Television, movies, music and interactive games are powerful learning tools, and highly influential media."[24] It then makes conclusions about what is being learned—in short, that viewing violence is likely to lead to violence as a way of settling conflicts. In addition, viewing violence in media can lead to "emotional desensitization" and reduce the likelihood of someone taking action on behalf of a victim of violence. The statement also concludes that entertainment violence leads people to see the world as a violent and "mean" place, increasing people's mistrust of others. Finally, it asserts that young people exposed to violent programming "have a higher tendency for violent and aggressive behavior later in life than children who are not so exposed."[25]

Although the Joint Statement makes very strong claims, it mentions no specific studies. In other writing and testimony by the principals in this statement, most of the research focuses on other media, not video games, and there seems to be an untested and unsupported conclusion that video games must be worse because they are interactive.

Respected researchers . . . respected psychologists . . . contradictory opinions—is there really a right answer? Henry Jenkins of MIT, one of the chief video game researchers in the country, offers a different perspective. He states that video game players clearly distinguish between video game playing and reality. "I don't believe that the media in and of itself will turn a kid into a psychokiller. I believe that media is most powerful in our lives when it reinforces our existing values and least powerful when it contradicts them."[26] Jenkins contends that, rather than becoming killers, video gamers are learning to be more critical and discerning thinkers.

Once again, in place of real and conclusive data, we have statistics and voices making authoritative but unproven statements. Perhaps more study would be worthwhile, but what do we study? If we seek only the negative connections, perhaps we can convince ourselves that they exist and find statistics to support that belief. Perhaps, if we can ever factor out the rest of the issues, we may one day find that clear connection. In the meantime, our own observation of a society that is clearly not overrun with emotionally desensitized zombies leaves us with a great opportunity. Instead of focusing on the negative—on the fears and the predictions—we can explore the medium of video games more carefully and find out how it differs from other entertainment media and how, in its differences, it also offers great new possibilities.

FANTASY LIVES

Statistical analysis and studies of aggression don't tell the whole story, in any case. What purpose does fantasy, including fantasy violence, serve? Clearly fantasy is prevalent throughout much of human history. Is it somehow necessary?

In his book *Killing Monsters*, Gerard Jones takes a look at the role of fantasy violence in the lives of children. Based on years of research and personal work with children, he concludes that fantasy violence is often not only beneficial but also necessary in a child's development. Children overly deprived of opportunities to express their deeper and darker fantasies often start to act out and show increased aggressiveness. Given an outlet for their fantasies, such as a toy sword or a video game, they calm down.

Not all children are blessed with healthy home lives or safe environments. For children growing up at risk, video games may offer a chance to find a level of control. Not surprisingly, they may gravitate toward violent games, but this does not necessarily mean they are reinforcing violent behavior. For instance, studies of soldiers returning from the Iraq war suggest that playing violent video games may actually help reduce the trauma associated with violence.[27] This discovery, though untested, suggests the possibility that some children growing up in violent worlds are actually unconsciously treating their own trauma through their choice of entertainment. To my knowledge, there is no area of research studying this possibility, but perhaps there should be.

Jones also talks about the rage that builds up in many children growing up as virtual prisoners (by their own description) of the school system, their parents' expectations and control, and what they perceive of as an uncaring society. For them, edgy entertainment actually expresses their pent-up rage and frustration. Jones writes, "When young people feel that the official world is hostile, indifferent, or irrelevant, the feelings of recognition and belonging that entertainment brings them can be transformative."[28] Jenkins also refers to what he calls a "fantasy of transgression"[29] that allows teenagers, in particular, to test the limits of their parents' culture. This ability to "transgress," along with the ability to take control in a video game, to master and excel—in essence, to beat the system—provides very powerful outlets for such youths.

While court judges are not video game experts, and what they say about video games should perhaps not be read as the ultimate authority, in one case a judge did deliver a very clear statement that I take to be instructive and thought-provoking. In 2002, Federal Court of Appeals Judge Richard Posner commented, "Violence has always been and remains a central interest of humankind and a recurrent, even an obsessive theme of culture both high and low. It engages the interest of children from an early age, as anyone familiar with the classic fairy tales collected by Grimm, Andersen, and Perrault are aware." Cautioning against undue restriction, Posner continued, "To shield children right up to the age of 18 from exposure to violent descriptions and images would not only be quixotic, but deforming; it would leave them unequipped to cope with the world as we know it."[30]

JUDGING THE EVIDENCE AND GOING FORWARD

So far, in all major court cases, the judges have weighed in against the critics, stating that the evidence is not convincing or conclusive. Despite an abundance of arguments on both sides of the scientific aisle, no conclusive results have been established.

Early studies predicted that exposure to media violence would lead to criminal activity. Some researchers have also suggested that the effect would be stronger with video games. However, national youth violence statistics fail to confirm any increase in youth violence that corresponds to the increasing graphic realism and violence of video games. In fact, violence statistics in the United States have fallen considerably during the years when video games have become more graphically violent and complex, and the gaming audience overall has been rising (see

Figure 1.1). While the real cause for the reduction in youth violent crime may have nothing at all to do with video games, the crime statistics, along with rising numbers of players, at the very least weaken the dire predictions of the most ardent critics and lend a little more credibility to those who question those predictions.

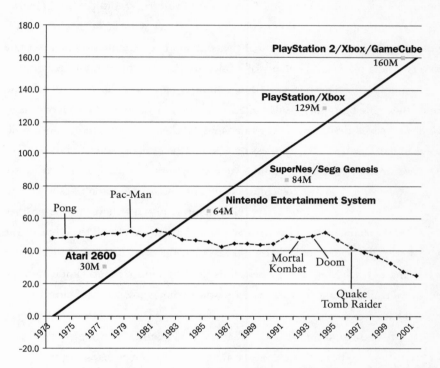

Figure 1.1 Youth violent crime in the video game era. Note that crime (dotted line) falls dramatically during the period in which the most realistically violent games were introduced and gamer populations increased, as measured by game console sales (straight line, in millions of units sold).[31]

Many people sincerely believe in the link between media violence and real-world violence. Have they found that link? Peter Vorderer is coeditor of *Playing Video Games*, a comprehensive book on video game violence research published in 2006. He told me in an interview, "I think there is enough evidence to state that playing violent video games can result in increased short-term aggression, but we know very little about mid- to long-term effects at this time. This is an important area of research, but there is no current evidence that suggests a direct link between violence in video games and how people will respond later in their lives."[32] Vorderer's statement falls in the middle—somewhere between the strongest critics and the strongest supporters of video games—but he fails to find convincing evidence of long-term negative effects.

Putting aside science and statistics, I believe that not all video game content is appropriate for all ages of players. Because the most controversial titles test the boundaries of social conventions, I recommend discretion and parental involvement with young players. I don't believe video games will turn them into killers and criminals, but I do think some of the content of some games is inappropriate for very young players, and plenty of games are perfectly fine for any age group.

While video games have not been definitively proven to lead to violence and crime, they have been universally hailed as learning environments. Anderson says, "Basically a well-designed video game is an excellent teaching tool, and a well-designed game will teach regardless of whether the designer intended to teach or the player intends to learn. I would love to see games that teach social skills useful for some subpopulation of children and adolescents who don't know how to treat others and how to interact."[33] Huesmann is also a believer in the positive potential of video games. "I think video games have the potential to be one of the most powerful teaching tools there could ever be," he says, "to teach skills that are important, to teach attitudes and behaviors that are important. You know they are very powerful teaching devices. The question comes down to, for any specific game, what is it teaching?"[34]

The fundamental question is, What are video games teaching? If they have not been shown to be teaching violence and mayhem, then perhaps they are teaching something else. As unsure as we are about the negative effects of video games, there is almost universal agreement that they are powerful learning tools, which is a primary focus of this book. On the other hand, while they are clearly teaching something, video games also come under fire for being too successful in this role and causing players to become addicts—which leads us to our next question.

CAN VIDEO GAMERS BECOME ADDICTS?

In 2002, the Associated Press reported the death of a young man in South Korea.[35] He had been playing computer games for eighty-six hours straight. That same year, a thirty-year-old man had seizures and died, and his death was thought to be related to his forty-eight-hour-a-week video game habit. In 2005, as reported in the *Washington Post*, ten deaths among young people in South Korea were linked in some way with excessive video game playing.[36] Both South Korea and China are now offering Internet addiction treatment to combat an epidemic of what appears to be addictive Internet and video game use, and another such center has opened in Amsterdam. Do these stark and disturbing facts represent a new and dangerous trend among video game players?

Fortunately, deaths attributed to video game playing are extremely rare, and cases like the ones mentioned represent very unusual cases of extreme behavior among literally millions of players. At the same time, although the more moderate habits of the majority of video gamers may be less deadly, they can pose real risks as well. Whereas death may not be a concern in most cases, loss of productivity, decreasing school performance, damaged family relationships, and declining physical health are, researchers suggest, among the prices some people pay by playing regularly.

One of the foremost authorities on video game addiction, Maressa Orzack, puts it simply. "It's about costs."[37] Like any activity, she says, some people may play video games in healthy ways and benefit from the experience. Others, however, may play excessively, to the detriment of their lives; in such case, game playing undeniably poses a problem.

People escape into reading, television, sex, Internet chatting, sports and exercise, shopping, gambling, and work. Such escapes can be temporary reactions to stressful conditions, or, according to Orzack, when they become constant or repetitive over time, they can be seen as a symptom. Like better-known problems such as eating disorders, compulsive shopping, gambling, and sexual obsessions, the long-term and detrimental effects of game playing can reflect deep problems, eroding the quality of the person's life until those problems are addressed and resolved.

Researchers are concerned that some people have become addicted to the Internet, to computers in general, and to video games. To Orzack, it's all part of the same problem. In place of the word *addiction*, which is typically associated with substance abuse and physical addictions, she prefers to call it "Internet usage disorder" or, more generically, a form of impulse control disorder. "These terms don't suggest that it is an addiction as such, but it's still something where people lose control," she told me. "Control is the biggest thing."[38] Like eating disorders or gambling problems, she suggests that therapy most often involves normalizing behavior to bring the person's life into balance.

Most people seem able to surf the Internet or play video games while maintaining productive lives and relationships. Why do some people seem to lose control while others do not? Nick Yee, a researcher at Stanford University, notes that therapists involved in online addiction research and treatment consistently find that clients being treated for Internet or video game playing disorders almost always also have depression or other mood disorders. Orzack agrees, stressing that this sort of response isn't isolated but often comes hand in hand with other symptoms, such as depression, attention deficit/hyperactivity disorder (ADHD), and obsessive-compulsive disorders.

Yee wonders, "How did depression get rebranded as a technological problem?" His recommendation is to treat people for depression or mood disorders and not for what he calls "another symptom."[39]

Yee contends that many people feel unhappy or uninspired in their lives, in school, at home, or at work. "Is it pathological to prefer being where you have social status and respect?" he asked an audience at the Palo Alto Research Center in 2006.[40] Video games level the playing field, and just about anybody can succeed if they want to, gaining respect, friendships, and status in a world, albeit a virtual one. For instance, a fifteen-year-old can compete successfully against a wealthy business executive or even a U.S. Army general. In fact, the fifteen-year-old would probably win if he or she is a practiced gamer.

Whatever the cause, however, any problem that seriously impacts people's lives must be taken seriously. Unfortunately, there isn't a lot of real data to show how many people are having problems or how severe those problems may be. Research is ongoing in the area of video game addiction specifically and Internet addiction generally, but so far no definitive statistics have emerged. Researchers are even still defining terms. Yee suggests, for instance, that the meaning of the word addiction often used in user surveys may be interpreted rather loosely, in a colloquial rather than a clinical sense. "How many golfers would fill out a survey saying they were addicted to golf?" he asks.[41]

Various Web sites (see Resources at the end of the book) offer useful links and checklists of symptoms to help determine whether someone is computer, Internet, or video game addicted, and various support groups are also available online. Meanwhile, Orzack offers some hope to people concerned with these issues. She suggests that people can deal with these problems with a little discipline and sometimes outside help. She adds that most of the people she sees in her therapy practice are brought in by someone else—typically a parent or spouse—because the gamer doesn't see any problem. However, once players are determined to make changes, they can do so.

As serious as video game addiction is, I caution parents not to overreact just because their children seem to be playing video games a lot. If the kids are doing their homework, getting a good night's sleep, and staying active, then there's little to worry about in terms of compulsive behavior. Even if they are having some problems managing their video game play, other factors are likely the cause. Before jumping quickly to the conclusion that video game playing is at fault, parents and spouses should always examine other aspects of the person's life. Did something traumatic happen recently? Have new stresses or pressure popped up in their lives? Is there tension arising from another area—fighting with friends or problems at work or school, for instance? Excessive video game playing might be a problem in itself, but it more often appears to be associated with other, more serious problems.

WHO IS AT RISK?

Is someone in your family particularly vulnerable to the video game lure? Although it may not be possible to predict with certainty, some characteristics do appear more commonly among those whose video game experience becomes obsessive.

Orzack typifies the clients she has seen in therapy for video game addiction as "very bright." "They are so bright," she adds, "that they are bored with school and what is presented, or they are disturbed at something that is going on in their lives. They are so bright that they neglect homework because it's not worth it."[42]

According to Yee, the game players most at risk are what he calls the "achievers" and the "escapists." Achievers, he says, respond to the way games stack overlaying goals and rewards, so that "even completing one task and receiving the reward does not remove the impulse to keep playing. There are always other rewards ahead."[43] For the escapists, personal empowerment is the key factor. "They are playing because the gaming environment empowers them in a way that real life does not."[44]

What is apparent is that individuals with certain tendencies may be more susceptible to the allure of video games. At the same time, these individuals, because of those same tendencies, might become involved in other types of activities that match their personalities—workaholics, shopaholics, sexaholics, and so forth. People, especially Yee's achievers and escapists, do respond well to the way games motivate players, because video games are designed, for both artistic and commercial reasons, to keep players involved. Imagine a game that quickly became boring. Who would want to spend their money on it?

Gaining control over any sort of impulse control disorder is difficult, whether it involves eating, gambling, shopping, or video gaming. Unlike overcoming drug addictions, however, quitting an addictive game experience does not have to be long and painful. Depending on the person, simply leaving the game for a while breaks the goal/reward cycle that Yee mentions. Once the player has "normalized," to use Orzack's term, he or she may even be able to return to the game with some self-imposed limits and better self-assessment, recognizing when the game gets too compelling or when the player is not taking care of himself or herself. In other cases, more consistent measures may be necessary, as not everyone will respond with the same amount of self-control.

In summary, video game addiction is really a form of impulse control disorder. Like compulsive eating, gambling, or shopping, video games can affect some players, particularly those who are already depressed or dealing with emotional issues, as well as very bright but disengaged individuals. In those cases where video game playing becomes a problem, outside intervention may be necessary because, according to Orzack, some players don't see a problem until it is presented to them in a therapeutic environment.

Ultimately, video games aren't like heroin or even cigarettes. The fact that a disorder can be associated with video games doesn't make them addicting. Even so, some people's lives can be adversely affected by their experience of video games, and for those people, the video game habit may be a symptom of other problems that need attention. For otherwise healthy people, video games can be entertaining and beneficial.

WHAT DO VIDEO GAMES SAY ABOUT MEN AND WOMEN?

Video games have often been criticized as being primarily male dominated. One statistic from 1991 claimed that men were depicted in video games thirteen times more often than women.[45] The audience for video games has been predominantly male as well, though more and more women are playing today, with some studies showing female players comprising nearly 40 percent of the overall market.[46]

In their depiction of women, who are often portrayed as either helpless victims or excessively curvaceous sex objects, video games have for the most part been justifiably criticized. However, where some critics also proclaim that video games are full of sex and even rape, such charges are untrue and misleading. Only one game released in the United States contained any rape, and it was a silly, marginal, and very rare game for the Nintendo Entertainment System called Custer's Revenge. Sexual acts in games, though somewhat increasingly common in recent years, are still mild, cartoonlike, and rare in video games compared with their preponderance in movies and television.

Some criticisms of gender issues in video games are more valid, however. Until the mid-1990s, women were generally victims who needed to be saved. In most American video games, the hero was generally an overmuscled aggressive he-man, although many very popular Japanese games tended to show more diverse body types among male characters and often had children as their protagonists.

In 1996, a particularly well-endowed protagonist hit the scene. Lara Croft, the main character of the Tomb Raider series, became a pop icon, a sex symbol over time (especially when played by Angelina Jolie in two movies), and a catalyst for changing views on the roles of women in games. Although she was definitely designed to appeal to male players, she was also a highly skilled, independent, strong-willed female character, and, more important, she was the character that the player controlled. For the first time, male gamers were controlling a female protagonist/heroine in a high-profile mainstream video game. The Tomb Raider series and Lara Croft's character are still popular today.

The prevalence of sexy women in video games is nothing surprising, and there are too many examples to list them here. In many ways, video games reflect our culture, and in sexual stereotypes, dominated by images of female pulchritude and unrealistic body image messages, video games, with their early appeal to male players, naturally followed suit. Although some games go out of their way to depict sexuality, the majority do not make it a theme. I would like to see games depict a more diverse environment that, among other things, treats women less consistently as sex objects and men less consistently as aggressive supermacho types.

WHAT'S THE PROBLEM WITH VIDEO GAME CRITICISM?

The rhetoric against games is often very strongly stated. People believe passionately that video games cause violence, antisocial behavior, crime, and addiction—among other things. The problem with some of these critics is that they often do not do their homework, relying instead on strong phrases and unsupported attacks. One Web site (www.mavav.org), which claims to be authoritative on the problems of video games, calls players of massively multiplayer online games (MMOs) "emotionally unhealthy and mentally unstable people" and "social outcasts." One politician claimed, "You score points for how many women you rape."[47] Such absurd and inaccurate statements cast doubt on other incendiary and absolute condemnations of video games and the people who play them.

The facts are inconclusive, and the experts clearly don't agree. Video games are not lily white. They are often intentionally controversial and jarring. They are also powerful. They attract millions of players all over the world. They represent an opportunity that we might miss if we focus only on what's wrong with them. As researcher James Ivory of Virginia Tech told me, "If you just look at the negative versus nothing at all, you don't get a very good picture. If you looked at food only in the context of negative outcomes, food would seem very dangerous."[48]

When people narrow their focus, they get a narrow view. If people open their minds, they may see a larger landscape. To see the whole picture, look for the positives and the negatives. They both exist.

Ultimately, the media we consume may be linked to deeper elements of human consciousness, and, if people like Harold Schechter and Gerard Jones are correct, violence and antisocial fantasy are not only inherent in our individual and collective psyches but quite possibly necessary. Socrates once said, "I only wish that ordinary people had an unlimited capacity for doing harm; then they might have an unlimited power for doing good." If video games somehow allow us that "unlimited capacity for doing harm" in fantasy, can they also provide us with "an unlimited power for doing good"? I think they can.

THE VIDEO GAME PLAYER'S PERSPECTIVE

Having been a video game player for nearly forty years, I'll let you in on a little secret: Most video game players don't see the violence the way outside observers do. They understand that violence is an element of play that serves specific purposes.

Games are about challenges. For avid gamers, having to pit their skills against one or a horde of virtual enemies is fun. It's why they buy the game. In many ways, it's like a NASCAR racer or a poker player who likes to test his or her skills against other competitors. In fact, it's like anybody who plays a competitive game, whether it is tennis or bridge or Monopoly.

As a player, I generally don't see the enemies in the games as people. I see them as challenges. In real-world warfare, the enemy is often depersonalized, no longer treated as human but rather as "the enemy." This desensitization to the "other" is one of the criticisms that have been leveled at video games; however, from the gamer's perspective, the correlation is missing. In the case of video game enemies, I am keenly aware that they are graphical representations of computer programs. People who worry about game players transferring actions from games to real life often miss the fact that, absent other sociological problems, game players know they are actually playing a computer program that generates graphical images resembling creatures and approximating (generally poorly) intelligent or purposeful actions.

The fact that enemy characters in video games sometimes look like human beings adds to the context of the action, making it more interesting and increasing the challenge. Even knowing that they are generated by a computer, I find it more satisfying to succeed against a dangerous opponent who can "kill" my character than against something that represents little or no challenge. I do not suffer any real harm when my character in the game is "killed," nor is there any harm done to other characters I "kill" in the game. More harm comes to the basket in basketball than to the characters in video games. Both represent the goals of the game, and if you think of the enemies you see depicted on a video screen as similar to the basket in basketball, you won't be too far wrong.

In the real world, I find the word *kill* a difficult, often disturbing, and very final concept. Like most video gamers, I fear death in real life and have no desire to see or participate in anybody's demise. In fact, I am far more squeamish than my ancestors who, in previous generations, viewed and participated in events that would morally outrage me or make me sick to my stomach.

As a gamer, however, I apply a completely different meaning to the word kill, based on the context of video games versus the real world. This context defines kill in colloquial terms, no more related to real-life violence than is the stockbroker who issues a "kill" order, the politician who "kills" a bill, the newspaper editor who "kills a story," or the stand-up comedian whose performance "killed" the audience.

How is it that we gamers don't see the violence the way nongamers see it? Part of the explanation can perhaps be found in Johan Huizinga's 1938 classic book *Homo Ludens*,[49] in which he describes the "Magic Circle" of play. In the Magic Circle, people clearly distinguish between play and reality, or nonplay. In play, inhibitions and rules are relaxed, and people perform acts that they would not perform in other moments of their lives. Game expert Henry Jenkins offers the example of apes, which clearly distinguish between play and nonplay. "In some circumstances, they seem to take pleasure from wrestling and tousling with each other. In others, they might rip each other apart in mortal combat."[50]

Taking the concept of the Magic Circle and applying it to digital technology, it's fair to say that there's a special Digital Magic Circle that didn't exist in 1938 when the term was first introduced. The basic concept is the same, however, and is perhaps even more powerful when we consider the fact that video games are so clearly and unequivocally not real in the physical sense of the word.

I want to mention one point with regard to violence and antisocial content: most people receive certain very strong moral and ethical messages from society and, in some cases, from personal experience. For instance, the essence of the Golden Rule is probably more powerful in society than any message contained within a video game.

We all know what it feels like to be hurt, physically or emotionally, and we all have some built-in empathy and moral code. Although outside influences can, and often do, override or corrupt this kind of inner knowledge, we still know right from wrong, helping from harming, and kindness from meanness. Like Henry Jenkins, I believe "media is most powerful in our lives when it reinforces our existing values and least powerful when it contradicts them." The messages of our humanity are stronger and clearer inside emotionally healthy people than the messages of video games, which rarely set out to promote a point of view or a morality (with some extreme fringe exceptions). In the commercial game world, the primary ideology is fun, freedom, and making choices, and if there is a moral message, with few exceptions it reinforces the notions that good triumphs over evil and that helping others is rewarding.

What about those games that appear to glorify lawlessness, random violence, and antisocial actions? I am personally uncomfortable with some of those games, which I think push the envelope to be sensationalistic, but I don't want this point to be taken out of context. I still think there's a good chance that such video games help people by allowing them to explore their Jungian "shadow selves" in a harmless environment. Over the coming years, we may see research that either reinforces or refutes that belief. In the meantime, I continue to believe in the freedom of expression that video games represent and in their ultimate positive potential—which is the subject of this book.

Video Game Addiction: A Gamer's View

Many game players are probably paying a price for their game-playing experience. They are certainly losing out on opportunities to do something other than play a game. Likewise, people all over the world are paying a price for watching television instead of reading a great novel or spending time volunteering at the local hospital. Even reading a great novel involves a loss of other options. Life is always about trade-offs, and playing a video game is another choice people make.

For me, as a gamer, playing a game represents many things at once: fun, intrigue, challenge, empowerment, escapism, social interaction, and, atypically, professional work. I have been accused many times of having the greatest of jobs: I get to play video games for a living. It's true that I enjoy playing games. It's also true that I played video games before I got paid to do so, and I would have played them if I never got paid, though possibly somewhat less than I have.

After all these years of playing video games, I still enjoy them and look forward to some of the most innovative among them. I admit that I have had to overcome a tendency to play too much. While I don't believe I am a video game addict because I maintain a healthy and balanced life and family, I have had to struggle at times against a tendency to play when there was something more important to do.

Among the people I have met while playing video games are practicing medical doctors, wealthy and successful business owners, quadriplegics for whom the game world is like a new lease on life, stay-at-home housewives with small children, university students, grade school children, dozens of video game designers, and many others from all walks of life. Most of them were intelligent, thoughtful, and generous. I have found the community of game players anything but the "mentally unstable" individuals some people would like you to think they are. Some of them are, in fact, among the most brilliant, creative, and humanitarian people I have known. It is my hope that as you continue to read this book, you will look past stereotypes and think in terms of new options.

In the end, controversial or not, what I think is most important is not whether a game contains violent or antisocial content, but whether playing that game has some tangible positive impact on the players. Perhaps not all games are suitable for all players. Perhaps some games we think are unsuitable actually fulfill a role, as Gerard Jones suggests. Video games offer much that is positive and empowering, and they can offer even more.

In this chapter, I have done my best to look at the most prevalent controversies surrounding video games. Not everybody will agree with my conclusion—namely, that much of what people have believed about video games is mythical or misinterpreted and that most criticisms are at best unproven. Even if you don't completely agree with my assessment of the controversies, I think the arguments only matter in the context that takes the negative view of video games. The positive context leaves little doubt that video games represent a new and powerful technology—a tool that can be wielded for entertainment and learning, both at the same time.

This book will describe some of the valuable contributions video games are already making to our education, our workplaces, our health, and our social awareness. I will look at how and why video games are so effective, and how they can realize their inherent potential for, in Socrates' words, "doing good."

Chapter 2

GAMERS AND GAME MAKERS

If life doesn't offer a game worth playing, then invent a new one.

—Anthony J. D'Angelo

As she attempted to adjust to the unfamiliar Land of Oz, Dorothy was told, "You aren't in Kansas anymore." Kansas was familiar and predictable, and its dangers were known and understood. By contrast, in the Land of Oz, everything was new, unpredictable, and, although it was colorful and wonderful, it was thoroughly unfamiliar.

The world of video games isn't in Kansas anymore, either. The assumptions we used to make about video games—who plays them, who makes them, and what they are all about—have been undergoing consistent change. Today the video game industry is not the stereotypical industry some people still assume it is. Gamer profiles are also quite different from what they once were.

This chapter is about gamers and game makers. Who is playing today? Who is making games today? What, if anything, stands in the way of game makers focusing on the positive impact of video games on players?

Let's look first at the "typical" video gamer today. Does such a person exist?

WHO PLAYS VIDEO GAMES?

Years ago, whenever I was asked to describe the typical video game player, the answer was easy and went something like this: "A thirteen- or fourteen-year-old boy." Simple. No confusion. That description of the "typical" video gamer has persisted and remains a common misconception about video games because, for one thing, boys grow up, and many of them have taken their enjoyment of video games with them.

31

While those boys in the first generation of video gamers were growing up, video games were changing, too. Over the years, video games have matured—becoming more complex, bigger, grander, and far more graphically realistic. At the same time, some video games have returned to earlier, simpler forms, appealing to a new and growing audience who want to play games more casually. Video games have evolved into virtual worlds that operate every hour of every day of the year and are inhabited by thousands of players. They also accompany people wherever they go—on cell phones and on other portable devices.

According to studies by the Pew Internet and American Life Project, anywhere from 31 to 39 percent of people who use the Internet have at one time played online games (see table 2.1).[1] The study showed that, although some demographic groups reported higher online game use than others, the lowest was 26 percent among respondents between fifty and sixty-four years old, while a surprising 30 percent of people sixty-five and older reported that they had played online games.[2] According to a March 2006 study by eMarketing, Inc., approximately forty million U.S. households have at least one video game console machine, and there are seventy million regular online game players.[3]

INTERNET USERS WHO PLAY GAMES ONLINE	
Men	36%
Women	37%
Whites	34%
Blacks	54%
Hispanics	42%
18-29	54%
30-49	33%
50-64	26%
65+	30%

Table 2.1: Percentage of Internet users who reported that they had ever played online games (Pew "Usage Over Time" spreadsheet – May/June 2005)

If so many people are playing video games of one kind or another, what are these players like? Are they all stereotypical zombies staring at the screen hour after hour? According to the Entertainment Software Association (ESA), the "average" gamer is quite different from the stereotypical button-pressing couch potato. Their surveys show that video game players may spend roughly an average of seven hours per week playing video games, but they spend three times that amount of time exercising or playing sports, volunteering in the community, participating in religious activities, pursuing creative endeavors and cultural activities, and reading. A surprising 94 percent of them follow current events, and 78 percent vote in most elections—far higher than the national average.[4]

The question of who plays video games is relevant today precisely because the answer is no longer simple. Because the video game industry and its customers have become so diversified, the range of video game possibilities has also expanded. Today, to describe a video game player, you need to include boys, girls, men, and women of all ages, socioeconomic groups, ethnicities, and backgrounds. You need to identify "hard-core" (or "power") players and casual players, social players, and even a large category called "dormant" players—avid video gamers who are unable to play often because of work, school, or family obligations. According to studies, dormant players are likely to return to video games when the circumstances of their lives allow them time to do so.[5]

CORE GAMERS

Core gamers are made up of two groups: hard-core gamers and social players. Hard-core or power gamers represent a relatively small but reasonably stable group of players who account for nearly a third of the revenues in the game industry. They tend to be younger, and overall they like action and variety. There is no single stereotype of the hard-core player, but many of them like head-to-head competitions against other players, deeper challenges, powerful imagery and graphics, exciting music, and an edgy quality to the fiction or setting of the game. Hard-core players may buy ten or more new titles a year.[6]

Whereas hard-core players seek challenges and excitement primarily, another recognizable group called social players seeks contact with other players. This does not necessarily mean they play different games but that their primary motivation for playing may be different. You'll often find hard-core players in the same games as social players, and, because such labels as "hard-core" and "social" are superficial, there is almost certainly a crossover where a player could be both hard-core and social. In part this overlap is because, even from their early arcade beginnings, video games have always featured a strong social element where players gathered together in person to play their favorite games in the arcades and at home. They also talked about games often at school, at work, and in other social settings—and still do.

Today, with advances in online technology and the increasing adoption of online games, players have found new ways to share their video game experiences. Many games function both as entertainment and as social systems where players come together individually as friends and collectively as definable groups within the game worlds. Large social networks are supported by both game and hardware manufacturers, such as Microsoft's Xbox Live, which links players through voice chat, information exchange, match-ups in multiplayer game sessions, and much more on Xbox systems. Meanwhile, many video gamers participate in Web-based forums, blogs, and fan sites, reading and writing (voraciously, in some cases) about their favorite and not-so-favorite games.

If video games are able to have a positive effect on players, I think the hard-core and social gamers are the most likely to benefit, even though they represent, by some estimates, only about a quarter of the total video game–playing population. They play more complex games for more hours at a time and more hours overall on a weekly or monthly basis. The complexity of the games they play offers more possibilities for incorporating positively oriented design strategies without negatively affecting the "fun factor" or "cool factor" of the video game itself. The hours spent, of course, mean that there is more opportunity for learning or positive inspiration. Social aspects of video games also open possibilities that use social engagement to teach and inspire.

CASUAL GAMERS

So-called casual game players represent a large and growing segment of the video gamer population. In September 2006, PopCap, the largest producer of casual games, released some surprising statistics. Based on a large-scale survey the company conducted among players of popular games such as Bejeweled, Bookworm, Chuzzle, and Zuma, only 19 percent of those surveyed said that entertainment was their primary reason for playing. Surprisingly, 88 percent said they experienced stress relief, while 74 percent claimed that mental exercise was a significant benefit. Distraction from pain was a benefit for 27 percent of the players, and 8 percent claimed that playing these video games actually relieved chronic pain and/or fatigue.[7]

The possibilities of casual games are only just beginning to be studied and considered, but many players are finding unintended benefits from these games. One example can be seen in the popular game from Nintendo called Brain Age, which combines brain exercises and mental tests in a game-like format on the Nintendo DS handheld gaming system. Brain Age has been surprisingly popular among more casual game players in Japan and the United States. Other popular casual games feature word puzzles that can increase vocabulary.

Although casual games tend to be far less complex than hard-core games for the mainstream audience, this large and growing audience might also benefit from more games with intentional positive impact. Also, casual games themselves have begun to increase in complexity as their audience becomes more sophisticated and developers seek new ways to differentiate their games. It's entirely likely that casual games will begin to take on some of the more complex elements of the mainstream game market.

MANY GAMERS; MANY GAMES

Customer diversity is echoed by an increasing diversity of video games. Early video games were all of the "arcade" variety, featuring a lot of action and a requirement for hand-eye coordination and pattern recognition skills. Over the years, new types of games have evolved, and many players prefer certain types of video games over others. Although some video gamers play just about every kind of game, players have begun to develop preferences for games of very specific and identifiable characteristics, and many video game makers specialize in games designed to cater to different players' preferences.

For game companies, customer diversity is significant, because they have to create games that will appeal to those specific audiences—a good news/bad news situation. On the one hand, it means that video games represent a great potential variety and range. They can be more diverse in content and presentation while appealing to an overall larger consumer base. On the other hand, it means that companies face additional challenges in determining who their audience actually is, what they want, and how many, of what kind of game, they can expect to sell.

THE VIDEO GAME INDUSTRY GROWS UP

Over the past decade or so, the industry of video games has begun to grow up, to take itself seriously as a business, and to expand into all kinds of niches in our lives. One way or another, video games can be available to us almost anywhere. They can be installed in cars (in the back seat, please), at airports and on airplanes, in hotels, and, of course, they can be played at home, at work, at school and even while sky-diving, if anyone wants to do that. Video games can accompany us wherever we go, on handheld consoles and on billions of cell phones worldwide.

In addition, video games today are more and more often turned into movies, where once it was only movies that became video games. Video games sometimes become aspects of the plot in movies and TV stories, subjects of documentaries, and, more and more commonly, advertising vehicles on the Web sites of major companies such as Coca-Cola, Nabisco, Nestlé, and Axe.

Advertising is everywhere today, but until recently, it was almost entirely absent from mainstream video games, a situation that is rapidly changing. The recognition of the power of video games to reach certain audiences through adver-tising is another strong indication of the increasing seriousness of the industry. In-game product placement is growing steadily, with companies paying to have their products featured in the game environment, just as they have done with Hollywood for years. Moreover, different in-game advertising experiments are being used to test the most effective methods of supporting games through adver-tising while offering the advertisers access to the growing video game population.

In part, the migration of advertising into the world of video games is logical, given the overall pervasiveness of advertising in just about all other media. However, it also can be seen as a response from the video game industry to rising costs and marketing challenges in an expanding market.

As creating successful video games becomes more complex and challenges grow, what happens to the games themselves? The makers of video games must constantly assess their markets and balance creativity and originality with risk, and sometimes they take a conservative and safer approach. For instance, accord-ing to a 2005 New York Times article, video game companies rely increasingly on sequels to successful franchises. For example, of twenty-six titles released in 2005 by Electronic Arts, twenty-five were sequels. "To be fair, sequels are a stock-in-trade of the industry; 9 of last year's 10 top-selling games were follow-ons."[8]

Some companies try to minimize risk by creating games with outrageous themes and graphics because players often are attracted to the most controversial products, especially if they are well designed and produced. Still other companies have an iden-tity that their fans recognize, and these game makers can remain true to their creative integrity regardless of what other companies and markets seem to dictate.

In contrast to those companies with very distinct identities, many game companies are often quite imitative. When one original video game becomes a big hit, many others will follow with similar themes or even very similar games. This sort of "follow the leader" principle sometimes works to establish whole new genres of games with a similar theme, concept, or play style. Other times it seems to contribute to industry stagnation until another original product comes to shake up the situation.

THE FINANCIAL REALITIES OF VIDEO GAMES

When the coin box for the first public test of the video game Pong became stuffed to overflowing within hours, the founders of Atari knew they were on to something. Ever since Pong was introduced in 1972, the coins have continued to flow, and, over the years, the video game industry has expanded, becoming more sophisticated and diverse, as well as more profitable.

What is clear is that millions of people are playing video games. Looking at sales numbers, it's equally clear that the video game industry is generating strong sales. In 2005, worldwide estimates of all forms of video game sales, according to eMarketer, Inc., were roughly $30 billion and growing. Predictions for worldwide video game revenues in 2010 range from about $41 billion to $51 billion.[9]

The current reality of the game business is that, while it can be highly profitable, it is also highly competitive. Making video games, once the domain of "two guys in a garage," now requires teams of more than a hundred specialized experts, such as artists, programmers, animators, designers, producers, and marketing experts. In short, it costs many millions of dollars to create a video game for today's markets, and the really high-quality games can cost in the tens of millions.

According to Kathy Schoback, a video game management veteran, the total cost of making a AAA title in 2005 was approximately $59 million, taking into account all expense categories (see table 2.2). Anticipated revenues for such titles were around $73 million, if all went well, with net profits around $13 to $14 million. What happens if the product sells below expectations? The losses can be staggering. If the company was relying on sales of a million units and sold only one hundred thousand, they would lose more than $24 million on that title alone. Lesser titles cost somewhat less to produce, but they still can add up to decent profits or damaging losses.[10]

To compound the risk, development cycles to create games are relatively long—anywhere from eighteen months to three years. The development cycle is all

APPROXIMATE VIDEO GAME REVENUES			
	AAA Title	**AAA Sequel**	**CurrentGen**
REVENUES			
Packaged goods sales console	$38,000,000	$26,600,000	$32,000,000
Packaged goods sales PC	$9,500,000	$6,650,000	$8,000,000
Packaged goods sales handheld	$16,000,000	$11,200,000	$12,000,000
Digital distribution revenue	$225,625	$157,938	$190,000
Licensing revenue	$750,000	$6,500,000	$0
International revenue all SKUs	$7,480,000	$5,236,000	$5,625,000
Greatest Hits revenue	$1,587,500	$1,111,250	$1,587,500
Wireless revenue	$0	$500,000	$0
Total Revenue	**$73,543,125**	**$57,955,188**	**$59,402,500**
EXPENSES			
Prototype	$1,000,000	$0	$1,000,000
Development console	$20,000,000	$14,000,000	$5,000,000
Development royalty console	$0	$0	$0
Development PC	$500,000	$500,000	$500,000
Development royalty PC	$2,000,000	$1,250,000	$0
Development handheld	$2,000,000	$1,400,000	$1,000,000
Development royalty handheld	$2,000,000	$1,400,000	$0
Marketing	$6,000,000	$4,200,000	$3,000,000
COGS/platform royalty console	$9,000,000	$6,300,000	$9,000,000
COGS PC	$375,000	$262,500	$375,000
COGS/platform royalty handheld	$4,500,000	$3,150,000	$4,500,000
Markdowns console	$3,800,000	$2,660,000	$3,200,000
Markdowns PC	$2,850,000	$1,995,000	$2,400,000
Markdowns handheld	$2,400,000	$1,680,000	$1,800,000
Variable cost (nonoverhead)	$3,175,000	$2,222,500	$2,600,000
Total Cost	**$59,600,000**	**$41,020,000**	**$34,375,000**
Net Profit	**$13,943,125**	**$16,935,188**	**$25,027,500**

Table 2.2: Chart of approximate revenues and expenses for current and next-generation AAA video games c. 2005 © 2005 Kathy Schoback[11]

on payroll and takes place in a competitive and constantly shifting environment. Technology is always improving, so that a game with three-year-old technology stands the risk of failing altogether, despite the time and money that went into it. Given that trends in game design are also quite changeable, one hit game that breaks new ground or introduces a new concept can affect the decisions of game customers as well as game designers who may be inspired to try new approaches in their games. Even more seriously from a budget perspective, changes in trends and popularity of various game genres or approaches affect the decisions of game executives who can—and do—regularly decide whether to support or kill any project at any point in its development.

Given the potential risks in video game marketing, the huge teams and the long production cycles, it is no wonder that game companies often take cautious and conservative approaches to their product choices. Companies often seek strong licenses, such as the Lord of the Rings or Harry Potter, or they attempt to create recognizable brands, such as Mario, Sonic the Hedgehog, the Legend of Zelda, Tomb Raider's Lara Croft, Warcraft or John Madden Football.

It's another good news/bad news scenario. On the one hand, there's definitely money being made, and video games have proven over the years to be highly profitable. On the other hand, the risks are also growing, and even the largest video game companies can't afford too many failures. Yet innovation and risk taking drove the industry into the position it is in today, and becoming overly conservative could lead to creative stagnation.

Video game executives and designers know all this, and they try to balance innovation with known formulas, risk against safety. At the same time, they know there are uncharted territories to explore and new customers to invite into the experience. While the most publicized video games often seem to be violent and antisocial, they are not the only games being produced, and even games with little obvious redeeming value other than entertainment may have hidden benefits.

In contrast to games with less obvious benefits, many games have transcended the stereotypes and offered players opportunities to learn and grow in various ways, to explore different values, or to experiment in virtual laboratories. In fact, video games have proven over the years their capacity for teaching and inspiring people in a variety of ways. What they have done so far is only the tip of the iceberg.

WHY AREN'T THERE MORE GOOD GAMES?

One of the least explored territories of video game development involves games that can promote positive personal and social change. Not every game has to live up to some standard of societal "goodness," but many types of commercial games do lend themselves to concepts I call "secondary effects" or "emergent learning." When game designers think one step further and consider how the story or structure of the game can promote some positive impact on the player, they can often make the game itself deeper, more meaningful, and more memorable. In later chapters, we'll explore some of the specific ways that video games can be used to improve people's skills, knowledge, and even self-awareness.

You may imagine that video game companies are all about thrills and controversy, and that the bottom line is all that matters. In some cases, this view might be correct, but not in all. As in any entertainment medium, there are as many perspectives as there are creators and consumers, and more often than you might suppose, the designers and producers of video games seriously consider the impact of their products.

Nearly every one of the top game designers I've spoken with expresses a desire to expand the relevance of video games in people's lives—not only as entertainment but as a deeper human experience. In an informal survey of some of those designers, I asked, "If you could create games that entertained and, at the same time, had some positive impact on players, would you do that?" Every one of them responded, "Of course. If I could see how to do that, I would." A few added, "We're already doing that."

This sort of perspective is hardly new in the video game field. For many years at the premier gathering of video game professionals—the Game Developers Conference—the keynote speaker was someone from outside the game industry whose speech was invariably designed to challenge and inspire game designers and producers to realize the great potential of games and to take seriously the impact they had on people who played their games. Even as recently as 2006, Will Wright, one of the most famous and influential game designers of all time, closed his keynote speech by saying, "Change your players at a deep level. We can influence their future careers. We shouldn't take this lightly. Don't squander this opportunity."[12] So why aren't *all* games expressly designed to be positive influences in their players' lives?

Designers' answers to that question range from "But we already do that" to "I don't know" or "We don't know how to do that within our budget and time constraints that already stress us." A few people answer, "It's risky."

A common conception is that game makers are insensitive to the impact they have on players. On the surface, it may seem that video games are getting more violent, more gory, and more antisocial. Certainly this is true of some games.

Many players like to play extreme characters in extreme situations—the bloodier, the better. This sort of escalation is consistent with other cultural trends in TV, movies, music videos, and comic books or graphic novels. There is a market for games that explore the darker sides of our nature, which, as mentioned in the previous chapter, is controversial but not necessarily bad. In any case, such games represent only the most publicized aspect of the video game industry. They are not the whole story.

Video game companies, like companies in other fields, have different identities and different ways of achieving their goals. Some certainly appear focused on testing the limits of society's boundaries, but even company executives, who are responsible for the long-range vision of the company and its success or failure, are often far more conscientious than you might suppose. I wasn't surprised when my informal poll of dozens of well-known game designers yielded positive responses to questions about games with a positive impact on players—that such games are not only possible but preferable. I was surprised, however, when I spoke with Louis Castle, vice president of creative development at Electronic Arts Los Angeles (EA), the largest video game company in the world.

I asked Castle the same question asked of the designers. I also asked him what would stand in the way of video game companies supporting games that had an ultimate positive impact on players.

"This is an important part of our process," he replied. "We ask designers, 'If this game ships, and it is as you imagine it will be, what will the impact of it be a year from now? Why is it important to the industry? What impact will it have on players?' Answers like 'It will have great graphics' don't cut it. We want to know how the game will make people feel more fulfilled, feel as if they've learned something. We want to make sure every product has you feeling enriched. That's really imperative for us."[13]

Castle was very emphatic in making this somewhat surprising statement. Essentially, he had confirmed that the biggest video game company in the world was on board with the subject of this book.

"We believe that if you leave people with some positive benefit," Castle continued, "they'll play longer, talk about it with their friends and feel better about the experience. When it comes to EA, it's really important that a product is not just a way to pass time, not just the game entertainment space. It moves our medium."

I next asked Castle about the barriers that game companies might face. Possible barriers might include the need to consider bottom-line sales first, the fact that video games are already very expensive to produce, and the complexity of adding more to the already-complicated design and development process. I also thought he'd tell me that video game designers aren't experts at providing positive impacts to players and therefore shouldn't be expected to do so. He might note, too, that there was little motivation to consider impacts on players other than that they thoroughly enjoy the game and want more.

Castle's response, again, was surprising. "I can see no barriers for games to be both entertaining and inspirational on multiple levels," he said. "We have the minds and hearts of millions of people in our hands, and we take that seriously. Consumers may not see what we're doing for a while. They will see it in the rearview mirror."

Now you know the well-kept secret: at least some people in the video game industry really are working for games that change our lives for the better.

Chapter 3

WHY WE PLAY

The supreme accomplishment is to blur the line between work and play.

—Arnold Toynbee

Few words in English have as many possible expressions and interpretations as play. You can play the stock market and be a "player." You can play a musical instrument, see a stage play, or watch the play of light across the bedroom. Your steering wheel can have "play" in it. You can play with words, play a part (play act), play the field, play the fool, play along, play out a situation, play up your strengths or play down your weaknesses, play your cards right, play with fire, play dumb, play dead. You can play nice or play for keeps. And you can play football, baseball, Scrabble, tag, cards—and video games.

Despite its diversity, the meaning of the word *play* is generally recognized by its context. For the purposes of this book, we'll define *play* as something we do for fun, with a playful attitude, and most often for recreation and entertainment.

Does that imply that there is a clear, black-and-white separation between work and play? Is play, then, only the most frivolous of pursuits?

Attitudes about play vary from one culture to another. In some, play is seen as an integral part of life, and a playful attitude is generally rewarded. In other cultures, play is the opposite of work and therefore regarded as nonproductive and mostly the province of children too young to be serious about life.

Although it often seems that American values tend toward the latter view, even in contemporary U.S. society, many famous and successful people have affirmed that work and fun do not necessarily need to be separate. "Money was never a big motivation for me, except as a way to keep score. The real excitement was playing the game." So said Donald Trump. Similarly, Thomas Edison stated, "I never did a day's work in my life. It was all fun." And, according to economic historian Arnold Toynbee, "The supreme accomplishment is to blur the line between work and play."

Understanding the nature of play in human life, generally, offers meaningful insights into the nature of video game play, specifically. In this chapter, we will explore some of the fundamental principles that describe the various aspects of play and how it functions in our lives. This discussion, in turn, will help us understand why video games are so popular.

EVOLUTIONARY FACTORS

Play is one of the oldest activities of civilized people. In early civilizations, playful activities fulfilled very serious educational roles, primary examples of which were storytelling and skills practice.

STORYTELLING

Storytelling is an ancient art of entertainment and education. It was used for thousands of years to teach both history and moral values, to help explain the natural forces of the world, and to venerate gods and heroes. Stories helped bring people together in common beliefs and may have been the first ways that laws and legal codes were passed to people. In some cultures, the storytellers were highly revered and essential to the continuity of the tribe or specific civilization.

Anne Pellowski, an expert on the history of storytelling and author of several books, including *The World of Storytelling*, states that evidence of storytelling dates back thousands of years—to the early picture cloths of India and the Westcar Papyrus, which describes how the pharaoh Cheops (2551–2528 B.C.) tells a story to his son and how that story is also a lesson. "This is one of the earliest descriptions of a storytelling event in which you hear the story and the context in which it was told. The same is true of the Panchatantra, a very famous Hindu text which explains that its stories are meant to be told to teach good Hindu moral values through entertainment."[1]

Pellowski adds that when anthropologists refer to early storytelling, they aren't referring only to the oral tradition—someone specifically telling a story to a group. They also refer to stories told through pictures, song, and dance, among other creative methods. In the Pacific islands, for example, a circular string was used in storytelling, and among the Inuit tribes, children learned "story knifing" using a ceremonial knife—the first toy they were given in childhood—to inscribe stories in the snow. Among Australian aboriginal tribes, women and girls tell stories by drawing in the sand, and their role is considered very sacred.

In these various ways, storytelling used an entertaining medium to teach and inspire, to preserve history, and to unify a cultural group. Seen from that perspective, the art of storytelling has often involved what today would be called a multimedia experience, with song, dance, and other methods combined with the story. In some African areas, there are even interactive stories, called "dilemma stories," which can have three or four different endings. At the end of a dilemma story, according to Pellowski, "The storyteller would ask the audience, 'Who is right in the story?' or 'Who is the main hero?' The audience then goes back and forth and mutually agrees on which ending they like best."

Storytelling is frequently described as an art, perhaps because the storyteller—speaker, dancer, singer, painter—is skilled at presenting the story in an entertaining way. And when written versions of stories appeared, this entertainment quality remained. Thus we have *Gilgamesh*, *Beowulf*, and *The Story of Sigurd* (Siegfried) from the Norse traditions; *The Tain* from the Irish; and *The Song of Roland* from the French. Ancient stories of Greece inspired the *Iliad* and the *Odyssey*, and many other stories have been recorded from the pantheon of Greek, Roman, and Norse gods. *Aesop's Fables*, the *Arabian Nights*, and Sufi tales from the Middle East; the *Ramayana* and *Bagavad Gita* from India; hundreds of Chinese parables, including those of Confucius and Zuang Zi; even stories and parables from both the Old and New Testaments of the Bible—all of these and thousands more represent stories from almost every culture that has used writing as a method of preserving history, myth, and a particular world perspective.

Modern methods and technology have forever changed the art of storytelling, which today is represented in a variety of ways, such as novels and short stories, stage plays, movies and television programs, public speakers of various kinds (including stand-up comedians), and, of course, video games.

Of all these modern storytelling methods, video games have the unique distinction of allowing the audience also to be directly engaged in the story—something like an actor who plays a role in a stage play or movie. But unlike the actor, whose course is fixed by the script, the game player decides how the story will unfold through his or her choices and actions, somewhat reminiscent of the African dilemma stories, but representing choice to an even greater degree.

In video games, when players both act the roles in the story and determine the outcome by their choices and actions, the story is at the same time working on them—changing their experience. If video games are a new form of an ancient art, they also provide new opportunities for making the stories even deeper and more meaningful.

SKILLS PRACTICE

Many people see play as preparation for life through the practice of useful skills. In aboriginal cultures, boys' games often involved mock hunting and fighting—useful skills for boys who in manhood would hunt and fight in hand-to-hand combat. Modern boys also play a lot of make-believe fighting and "gun" games, which in the Wild West era was certainly relevant practice, and, sadly, in the twenty-first century may still be a form of preparation for real-life events.

Researchers who study the nature of play have produced some remarkably detailed theories about why we seem to enjoy the repetitive practice of skills, which, at least in childhood, we call "play." These theories often delve into brain chemistry to explain the mechanisms that support our enjoyment of playful activities. In short, chemicals are released when our attention is engaged, other chemicals when we are confronted by novel situations, and still more chemicals when we feel rewarded. All of these chemicals may, in fact, add up to an explanation of why people play, but what is the origin of this chemical soup—why does it function so well in our brains?

Once again, part of the answer may well be evolutionary. We are curious beings. We seek both mental and physical stimulation. Whether we are ruled by brain chemicals or other forces, we are constantly seeking . . . something. And in that seeking, we often turn to play, because play provides stimulation, engaging our attention, offering novel situations, and rewarding us with joy, laughter, and feelings of success.

For millennia, people have played games of hide-and-seek, scavenger games, games of mock battle, and even games that require the high level of discernment necessary to spot differences among items or within environments. All of these "games" were also useful practice for a hunter/gatherer lifestyle—the only type of life available to preagricultural societies. In addition, we are drawn, as a species, to adopt animals as pets. In evolutionary terms, this is represented by people who used animals for protection, fighting or hunting, as well as herdsmen and cultivators of animals. Surprisingly, this same instinct appears often in video games, most obviously in the form of "virtual pets" in games but also, arguably, in role-playing games where the object of the game is to "raise" a character. In fact, animals in video games are used in many of the same ways they have been used historically—as companions, hunters, and protectors most of all. Some games, however, allow players to become herders or even breeders of animals—again reflecting our evolutionary history.

Certainly games directly related to war and human conflict have existed for thousands of years. Some of these games simply involved skills practice such as a child's practice at doing stunts on horseback, firing toy bows, or even throwing rocks. Team games also date back to early civilizations and were often used to practice war-related skills in mock conflicts with nondeadly goals. Today's team sports such as soccer and basketball are remarkably similar to games played by ancient warriors. Other war games are more strategic, ranging from games like chess and Go (and their ancestors) to today's modern military war games, which entail repetitive practice of skills and strategic maneuvers.

Video games, too, play at war. In doing so, they seem to serve the human fascination with conflict, taking sides and prevailing over an enemy. Some are essentially action oriented, while others are more strongly focused on strategy, but all video war games involve strategy and tactics to greater or lesser degrees. Contemporary war games are common, such as the very popular Call to Duty series. Other war games are more or less accurately based on history, while still others postulate fantasy worlds of the past, the future, or alternate dimensions.

All games involve learning, practicing skills, and overcoming challenges. Games based on war and conflict are no different, although one obvious question to ask is, What are players learning? At their best, video games may teach the realities of war, both political and human, but even where no such lessons are offered, video games require problem solving and good strategic thinking. Moreover, like conventional games of chess and Go, many video war games often present players with difficult challenges that require more brains than brawn to solve.

Video games often seem to mirror the skills we have valued throughout recorded human history, but with the advantage of unlimited contexts, safe experimental environments, and repetitive practice in an entertaining medium. In later chapters, we will explore more about skills practice and video games, including how video gamers may be practicing not only ancient skills but those skills needed in the modern world.

EVOLUTIONARY FACTORS IN VIDEO GAMES

Both storytelling and skills practice are fundamental aspects of video game design. Although the styles and purposes of both storytelling and skills practice have changed considerably over the millennia, these evolutionary factors are as relevant to modern video game stories and situations as ancient games were to our ancestors.

Some video game stories can be seen as metaphors. For instance, many fantasy games are set in days of magic and swords—the so-called swords-and-sorcery models. And although most of these games have borrowed heavily from J. R. R. Tolkien's *Lord of the Rings*, Tolkien in turn was heavily influenced by ancient stories and myths. In this sense, such swords-and-sorcery video games are a part of a long legacy of heroes and monsters, good and evil, falls from grace and redemption, conflict and resolution.

Other games relate stories in fantastical futures, in alien worlds, and even in cartoon-like environments where the rules often defy known principles of physics. Games may also place us in modern settings, where the relevance of the game experience is even more directly tied to current culture, attitudes, and even economic realities.

Video games do not merely relate stories and metaphors, however. Because they are interactive, they involve players in activities that reflect skills practice as well. Many games involve activities reminiscent of hunting and gathering, fighting, strategic decision making, resource management, and other skills.

Even as these games carry forward traditions hundreds or even thousands of years old, they may also be relevant to human life in any era. The struggle of good versus evil, and the need to take action, to plan and prepare, to gather resources and investigate facts, to make critical decisions, and to respond in the moment to changing conditions—all relate equally to the world of video games and the real world. In these areas and more, playing video games echoes our human roots and past skills, needs and methods, sometimes more obviously than the more common activities of shopping in malls and supermarkets, working in offices, and passively watching television.

BEHAVIORAL, PSYCHOLOGICAL, AND PHYSICAL FACTORS

Do evolutionary factors alone explain why video games are increasingly so popular? They help to explain human tendencies toward play to some degree, but in the modern world, other factors contribute to the widespread desire to play as well.

MOTIVATION

Why do we do what we do? What drives us? In order to explain the "why" of our lives, researchers have come up with various theories of motivation, which are often summarized as the biological, emotional, cognitive, or social forces that activate and direct behavior.

Those factors cover a lot of ground. For instance, biological motivations include eating, sleeping, sex and procreation, as well as self-preservation. Emotional motivations are more complex, but you can't help but notice them if you look. Have you ever noticed how people in a social group tend to dress similarly? Or how people may go to great lengths to find relief from stressful situations? They are motivated to feel a particular emotion or to avoid one. Some people excel at tasks because they are motivated to learn for learning's sake and feel the pride and sense of accomplishment from doing so. Others work to avoid the humiliation or embarrassment of performing badly. In sum, people can be motivated to move toward or away from specific emotions, which ultimately lead to satisfaction as they define it.

Motivation may also be considered in terms of action, persistence, and intensity. *Action* determines the activities that people choose—what they decide to do out of all the choices they might have. *Persistence* is a measure of how consistently they will work on some goal, even when obstacles and challenges block the way. And *intensity* describes the focus they will bring to their actions.

If motivation is what is behind our actions—the force that "activates and directs behavior," then it is powerful indeed. If you can successfully address what motivates people, you can get them to do just about anything.

Most theories of motivation don't explain why people will seek activities where there is no apparent motivation to do so. For instance, why do we play when it addresses no obvious practical or survival need? One theory, called *intrinsic motivation*, became popular in the 1980s. In a 1987 paper, "Intrinsic Motivation and Instructional Effectiveness in Computer-Based Education,"[2] M. R. Lepper and T. W. Malone proposed the following motivational factors: challenge, curiosity, control, fantasy, competition, cooperation, and recognition—all elements completely familiar to any video game player and obviously associated with the phenomenon of video games.

Of these seven factors, control is also one of the most powerful and unique aspects of video games. Some games satisfy our needs to control our surroundings and to feel secure by providing a safe environment—a world where we can test our limits, challenge ourselves, and even fail, without dire real-world consequences. For many people, immersion in a fantasy environment feels safer than the world outside. In such instances, people may temporarily lose themselves in fantasy, whether through books, movies, or games, in order to avoid an unpleasant or threatening real world.

FLOW

In *Flow: The Psychology of Optimal Experience*,[3] author Mihaly Csikszentmihalyi suggests another motivator—a psychological factor that powerfully beckons us toward a state he calls "flow." And while previous authors have suggested that mammals, with their relatively complex brains, require something called "optimal arousal states" to combat boredom and lethargy, Csikszentmihalyi believes that the flow state is in many ways the most desired human state of consciousness. He contends that people naturally seek an optimal experience state and that this is one of the oldest truths of human nature. Even twenty-three hundred years ago, he writes, Aristotle identified the primary goal of all men and women to be happiness, and, he contends, the situation has not changed.[4]

Csikszentmihalyi describes this optimal experience state, or flow, as equivalent to what people experience in, for example, the all-consuming creation of music and art, the "sweet spot" of a perfectly hit tennis ball, the ultra-focused concentration of a deep game of chess, or the suspension from a rock face with every bit of will and strength devoted to making it to the next hand or foot placement. Flow is those moments when we are happiest, most absorbed, and most timeless.

This timeless quality is frequently associated with activities that completely absorb the mind. It is that "zone" we enter into when we start a creative project, say, in the early evening and are surprised to see the sun coming up suddenly— times when we are so absorbed in what we are doing that we don't even notice that a whole night has passed by. Painters, writers, musicians, people engaged in sports, and video gamers all may experience this time-shifting effect from time to time.

Many game designers have read Csikszentmihalyi's work, finding that it not only is relevant to their work but also echoes something that both game professionals and game players know instinctively—that games can and do provide that peak, timeless, and intensely immersive experience that Csikszentmihalyi is describing.

GOALS, CHALLENGES, AND REWARDS: MOTIVATION IN VIDEO GAMES

If motivation is the force behind our actions, then video games have found a powerful formula for motivating people. The basic elements of this formula are goals, challenges, and rewards. People like to solve puzzles, and our curiosity drives much of what we do as human beings. We want to know what we don't know, discover what we haven't seen, and find out what happens next. Games are constructed so that players are always seeking answers to puzzles or solutions to situations. Video games are about unfolding stories, exploring territories, and solving mysteries. Players are continually pitting themselves against adversaries, human or virtual, and they are seeking to accomplish goals, often many interrelated goals simultaneously.

In fact, game players are never without goals. Games provide goals at all stages, ranging from immediate goals such as finding a safe place to hide or vanquishing an enemy who stands in the way; medium goals, such as finding a lost puppy and returning it to its master or successfully besieging a castle to acquire new territory and weaken an enemy; and long-range goals, such as saving the planet or rescuing a princess or defeating the arch-villain. These goals often exist simultaneously in the video game framework, and players are constantly tracking them and seeking resolution.

At the same time that players are pursuing goals at all stages of a game, they are also rewarded by frequent successes. Immediate goals offer immediate rewards, and they are often practically constant throughout a game. In fact, a common enticement is to "drop" random rewards of very high value in common situations within the game. The expectation of such random exceptional rewards is in some ways similar to the hope of hitting the jackpot on a slot machine—statistically unlikely, but probable with a lot of repetition. Other goals are rewarded less frequently, but often the rewards from longer-range goals are also more substantial and worth the required effort. And, of course, attaining most goals requires some effort, such that the reward is a combination of the tangible gains the player receives and the satisfaction that comes with successfully meeting a challenge, overcoming an obstacle, or solving a puzzle.

The motivational mix of goals, challenges, and rewards combines with the freedom players have to choose their strategies. This element of choice means that every player plays his or her own game, uniquely different from any other player's game. In fact, when gamers play a video game a second time, it is likely that they will make different choices and try different approaches. In part, they will be trying to do it "better," because many video game players don't simply want to achieve goals but want to achieve them in the most efficient, the most dramatic, the most elegant, the most exciting, or the most challenging way. In part, their games will differ also because players are always experimenting. Experimentation and curiosity go hand in hand in video games, as in life.

I am reminded of a story about Mozart. When he was very young, a great pianist visited Mozart's family. It grew late and Mozart was sent to bed. The pianist played downstairs but stopped playing the song before sounding the final chord. Later, when everybody was asleep, young Mozart, unable to sleep this whole time, crept downstairs and played the final, resolving chord. Satisfied, he returned to bed and slept.

Video games are like that unfinished piano composition. Players have a somewhat compulsive need to resolve the unresolved. Where there are goals to be achieved and puzzles to be solved, video game players, like young Mozart, can rarely walk away when resolution still beckons.

Acknowledging this human propensity to seek and resolve challenges, video game designers are masters of motivation. Using complex multilayered goal-and-reward structures, video games effectively immerse players in a world of experience where they are constantly motivated to accomplish goals and are rewarded frequently by their successes. The ability to provide constant motivation, with almost no interruptions, is simultaneously one of the secrets of video games' success and one of the keys to unlocking their greatest power and potential.

THE ROLE OF BIOCHEMISTRY

If we can explain motivation in terms of our seeking specific challenges, experiences, goals, and rewards, we can also describe it in terms of the kinds of messages we get through our biochemistry—particularly through the chemicals that are released in our brains. Could biochemistry help explain why millions of people like to play video games?

When our attention is engaged, as it typically is when concentrating on a video game, the cholinergic system is stimulated—in particular, the neurotransmitter acetylcholine, which causes excitation in the brain and stimulates muscle contraction. Acetylcholine balance is critical to our overall functioning and also helps facilitate learning.[5] Acetylcholine is so important that, in more extreme examples, deficiencies of the neurotransmitter are associated with Alzheimer's disease, while biochemical agents such as the nerve toxin Sarin, and even the venom of the black widow spider, do their work by inhibiting catalysts that naturally suppress acetylcholine.[6]

When people encounter novel situations, again as they often do in video games, their brain releases norepinephrine (also known as noradrenaline) and serotonin, both of which, among several other effects, help regulate our emotional responses to situations.[7] Both norepinephrine and serotonin are widely used in the treatment of depression through drugs such as Prozac, Zoloft, and other "reuptake blocking agents," and even in some treatments for attention deficit/hyperactivity disorders (ADD/ADHD). In simple terms, altering biochemistry in these ways works because both norepinephrine and serotonin contribute to feelings of well-being. And, if these "feel good" chemicals are released during real-life exposure to variety, novelty, and surprises, we might assume that they're also released in the brains of video game players as they, too, experience variety, novelty, and surprises—albeit in the zone of fantasy.

Finally, another neurotransmitter is released when we feel rewarded, as we often do when playing video games. Dopamine is a naturally occurring chemical that provides several functions. It is critical to our motor systems, and severe shortage of dopamine can lead to Parkinson's disease.[8] Dopamine is also involved in regulating the secretion of prolactin, which stimulates the production of milk in a mother's breasts. It has also been associated with a sense of satisfaction after sexual intercourse and with many effects of recreational drugs. Perhaps the most well-known characterization of dopamine is the "pleasure principle" that highlights its association with pleasurable sensations in the brain and reinforcement of motivation. Linked to the pleasure/reward center of our nervous system, dopamine is another "feel good" neurochemical, and research in the past few years has shown that video game players have higher levels of dopamine in their brains after a gameplay session.[9] Finally, the same chemicals described briefly here are often associated with deeper learning as well as a sense of well-being. As we discuss the power and potential of video games, keep in mind how these effects can converge to create a powerful experience and fertile ground for immersive learning environments.

CHALLENGE AND MASTERY

In work and in play, we are often confronted by challenging situations. Some get us down. Some provoke fear. Some excite us. Whatever our emotions in the moment, whenever we meet a challenge head-on and succeed or master the situation, we feel a sense of well-being, pride, sometimes relief, and always accomplishment.

In contrast to our successful moments, when we are confronted by real-life challenges, we cannot always master them. Consequently, we may feel defeated, depressed, and discouraged. The results may matter a great deal to us, even involving life-and-death matters. Imagine someone like Tom Hanks's character in the movie *Cast Away*. He's alone on an island, unprepared for survival in a primitive environment. His very life hangs on his ability to deal with the challenges he faces. The stakes couldn't be higher. In the movie, Hanks's character meets the challenges and experiences great exhilaration as a result. He grows as a person and becomes more confident and more in touch with what is really important in his life. Another person might fail to survive, no matter how hard he tries, and ultimately succumb to hunger, thirst, disease, or injury. Real-life challenges are neither fair nor predictable, and the consequences matter.

In video games, challenges can also present life-and-death consequences, but the consequences only matter in the realm of fantasy. Yet, because our imaginations are rich and powerful, we can transfer ourselves into the video game character, experience the intensity of the challenge, and achieve the sense of mastery and the exhilaration of success. And even if we fail, we live on to try again. In virtual worlds we get to meet adversity again and again and, through practice, become masters of our fate. Because of the very experimental and nonthreatening nature of video games, we are motivated toward success, rewarded frequently on the way, and allowed to achieve mastery.

PERSONAL EMPOWERMENT

While mastery is an important motivator for game players, personal empowerment may be just as significant for many people. *Empowerment* is the ability to feel a sense of control in their world. Many people in modern society feel powerless. They may feel powerless financially, politically, or even socially. In extreme examples, they may have debilitating diseases, they may live in highly dangerous and threatening environments, or they may be exceptionally shy and awkward socially.

In video games, people play characters who are almost always endowed with the abilities needed to master every challenge. Games are set up so that people can ultimately succeed, although they may occasionally meet challenges that are harder than others. While they may fail on occasion, that failure is usually temporary, the consequences are rarely severe, and players know that if they practice, they can eventually succeed. Because video games are designed to enhance motivation, because they are seen as play and not work, players will persevere, always believing that they can succeed with practice and that no matter how hard they are really working to achieve that success, they are at "play," not "work." Video games, through their structures of goals and rewards, and their careful control of difficulty, enhance players' belief that success is possible. In the end, players can be superheroes in games in ways that nobody feels in the real world.

For some players, video games provide the most empowering experience in their lives. You might think that is a sad commentary on their lives, judging that empowerment in games is not a great substitute for empowerment in "real" life, yet in some cases the empowerment they experience in video games can help people feel more at ease in other areas of life, increasing their self-esteem and confidence that they can, in fact, succeed. Ultimately, perhaps, success in something is better than success in nothing at all.

FANTASY

Often a metaphor for real life, fantasy combines many of the factors we've discussed so far that help explain why we play. It can function as a safe world in which to explore our values, test our limits, and enjoy ourselves at the same time. Good fantasy always relates to basic human values, needs, and emotions. It may seem removed from reality, an escape from harsher truths, but fantasy can also provide a medium for exploration and a bridge for making order out of chaos or sense out of the sometimes confusing scramble of life's lessons and challenges.

All video games are fantasy. Even when they are "reality-based" simulations of real-world events or processes, they are not reality. In other words, a story can more or less accurately model the world we know today and still be fantasy. While many video games are far removed from current events and immerse players in stories of ancient history or myth, they can also depict modern life and situations, including some of the grittier and more disturbing aspects of modern life such as war, inner-city violence, organized crime, and even scenarios with extreme political ramifications.

People willingly enter fantasy worlds for entertainment. They aren't necessarily seeking great enlightening truths. Some fantasies depict issues in very black-and-white terms, while others explore gray areas—complex and conflicted heroes, for instance, and even villains who aren't all bad. In all fiction, the "suspension of disbelief" allows people to enter into worlds that are often quite unlike those they know. This is true of video games as well.

In video game worlds, players can try on different hats, play characters very different from themselves, and have daring adventures not available in the typical modern, more or less safe life. However, even within this context, in video games we can also encounter puzzles, conundrums, moral dilemmas, and situations in which truth is not measured in crystal-clear terms. In short, fantasy-based video games are where we can revisit the ancient role of storytelling as teacher, moral guide, and entertainer, all rolled up into one.

Moreover, these fantasies dare us to look at the darker sides of our natures, which many psychologists consider important to our overall mental health. As Carl Jung once wrote, "One does not become enlightened by imagining figures of light, but by making the darkness conscious."[10] As worlds of fantasy, video games are a safe haven to do just that.

STRESS RELIEF

No one would argue against the notion that play relieves stress; however, what really relieves stress is the attitude associated with play. People who approach their work with a playful attitude report a joy in what they do, even the flow experience described earlier, whereas people who approach work with a very serious attitude often complain of stress.

Recent research on how we experience stress suggests that from infancy on, we learn to adjust to changing circumstances by making subtle changes in brain chemicals and hormone secretions. We constantly seek stability, or *homeostasis*, in technical terms. When these adjustments get out of balance, we experience stress. According to author Bruce McEwen in *The End of Stress as We Know It*,[11] we can never eliminate all stress from our lives, but we can reduce it through our life choices, such as eating sensibly, exercising regularly, getting enough sleep and having a break from work.

There are many causes of stress—including random events, lifestyles, diet, drugs, family conflicts, politics, work, and our general environment—and similarly many common antidotes for it centered on relaxation and fun. The idea that games can contribute to stress reduction is well established. A search on Google for "stress reduction games" produced nearly ten million hits. Companies that market so-called casual games for a wide market get letters almost constantly reporting how their games have helped people reduce the stress in their lives. Immersive activities that allow our minds to focus away from the causes of stress can help us.

Stress relief makes a valuable contribution to our lives, not only to improve our health but to enhance our learning as well. Again, brain chemicals come into play here, but fundamentally some researchers believe it is a question of emotions. According to Margaret Martinez of the Learning Orientation and Intentional Learning Team, for example, "Stress is a by-product of emotions. People in stress are less able to deal with new information as both their learning capacity and memory are affected. Think of it as a bucket where they can put information. People in better emotional states can fill that bucket better than those in stress. Well-designed games create a positive environment that actually eliminates stress and enhances cognitive and social abilities."[12]

As with any theory, however, there is a matter of perspective to consider. In some ways, play does not necessarily eliminate stress but changes its impact. Think of a sports fan who gets very excited when his team is winning or when it is losing. The fan is experiencing stress, even though he may be having a great time with his friends and other rabid fans. Likewise, when people are playing games, they inevitably experience stress because all games involve stress via their innate goals and the challenges to meeting those goals.

We might conclude, then, that not all stress is all bad. Sometimes it can lead to great innovation and learning. In the real world, many great discoveries, such as the invention of the sewing machine or the discovery of the benzene ring, were accomplished in very stressful circumstances. Technological innovation often comes as a result of stressful societal situations, such as war, but the idea of how stress can act as a motivator for learning goes back much further than these more modern examples. Take, for instance, the ancient Chinese story "Zen and the Art of Burglary."

The correlations between video games and stress may be complex. On the one hand, because game playing is voluntary and the game world is safe, we can suspend our natural, and stress-producing, "fight or flight" response temporarily. This lets us "fill our bucket" more completely. In this way we relieve stress when playing because we know we are safe. In that receptive state, we also can learn more effectively because the threats we are assessing are not real and we know it. On the other hand, through the inherent competition and challenge of games, we create stress—voluntary stress—and that stress also may function to help us learn. This type of stress may be more associated with motivation than with unpleasant or unhealthy responses, and because we enter into it willingly, perhaps it even helps us establish more healthy responses to stress outside the games we play.

SOCIAL CONTACT

Play has always been social. From the earliest days of storytelling to the most primitive forms of skills practice, people historically gathered together to have fun. And while many people enjoy solitary pursuits such as playing alone or reading a book, the social aspects of play are well established in modern times as well. We gather together to watch or to participate in sports events, to play board games and card games, to entertain each other at meals—in short, to share our recreational activities with others.

Video games are immensely social in the same ways—and in different ways, too. Players often gather to play competitively or cooperatively at friends' homes. They also do something that was previously impossible: they play games online with thousands of other players in the same virtual world. Additionally, many players talk about and write about games incessantly. There are whole communities of game players who discuss their favorite games, trash some, love others, agree, and disagree. In this sense, video games become the focal point for a special interest social network.

Zen and the Art of Burglary

One day, Goso Hoen said:

"When I am asked to explain what Zen is, I say that it is like learning the art of burglary.

"The son of a burglar saw his father grow old and thought: 'When he can't practice his profession anymore who will take care of this family if not me? I have to learn this craft.'

"He shared this thoughts with his father and he agreed.

"On one night, he took his son with him to a large house. They broke through the fence and got into the house where the father opened a big chest and asked his son to step into it and hand out the clothes. But as soon as the son was inside the chest his father closed the chest and locked it.

"The father sneaked back into the courtyard and knocked at the door, so that the entire family awakened while he got away through the hole in the fence. The inhabitants jumped out of their beds in excitement and ignited lights but didn't find anyone inside the house. The son, locked inside the chest, was deeply shocked about his father's cruelty when he had an excellent idea. He made a noise that sounded like the gnawing of a rat. The people told the housemaid to take a candle and look into the chest. As she pulled back the bolt, the young burglar jumped out of the chest, pushed the girl aside and escaped.

"The people started to chase him. On the street he saw a well, so he took a big stone and threw it into the well. The people crowded around the well to see how the burglar drowned in the dark hole. But in the meantime he had safely reached his father's house.

"Enraged, he told his father how closely he had escaped. His father said: 'Please don't be mad at me, son. Tell me how you escaped.' When his son had finished telling him the whole adventure, the father said: 'Well, now you know all there is to know about this craft.'" [13]

Because play in general, and video games specifically, are inherently social, they lend themselves to many types of social systems, such as one-on-one competition, small and medium groups in competition or cooperation, and massive groups in competitive or cooperative interactions. Some of these social groups are temporary, lasting only long enough to accomplish some short-term task. Other groups may become semipermanent, with memberships, rules, and a definite social order.

Because of the infinite flexibility of game technology, social interaction in games can take place on battlefields, in neighborhoods, in cities, in outer space, haunted houses, political centers, business offices, schools, and just about anywhere you can think of, each with unique possibilities for learning and socially relevant skills practice.

The specific and unique ways that video games contribute to social systems—and how those social systems are affecting the way we play, learn, and gather together—are changing constantly. The importance of social factors in video games is so important that I will return to it again in different contexts throughout this book.

So, Why Do We Play?

As this chapter has shown, we play for a variety of reasons. We play to learn and practice skills, to achieve beneficial mental states, to feel empowered and rewarded by successes, to explore fantasies, to experiment with forbidden activities, to relax, and to socialize. One of the most powerful aspects of games is their ability to motivate us to immerse ourselves in worlds where our minds are wide open and ready to learn and persist in that learning.

If we take anything from this exploration of play, it is that we may work just as hard—or harder—when we play as when we work, but we do it because we want to, because we are highly motivated to have fun and to experience those positive brain states that we get from having fun. Thus, motivation is the fulcrum on which we can place the lever that will move players toward learning and other beneficial effects. Using the video game player's motivation to explore, to meet challenges, and to succeed, we can do just about anything.

Chapter 4

YOUR BRAIN ON GAMES

Games force you to decide, to choose, to prioritize. All the intellectual benefits of gaming derive from this fundamental virtue, because learning how to think is ultimately about learning to make the right decisions: weighing evidence, analyzing situations, consulting your long-term goals, and then deciding.

—Steven Johnson[1]

Working in and around video games for many years, I often heard people talk about what you could learn from playing them. I knew I was learning something every time I played a new game, but I also learn something new every time I do anything I haven't done before. Like most video gamers, I didn't really stop to think about it. I played for enjoyment and not specifically to learn a skill or a subject or anything I thought was relevant to my life outside games.

Starting this book project, I had some questions about learning. For instance, what is learning? Is it memorizing facts? Is it acquiring and perfecting the skills necessary to accomplish specific tasks? Is it a process of force-feeding information into our brains, or is it something more complex?

No single theory has been universally accepted to explain learning. Modern theories involve principles drawn from many disciplines, and each discipline attempts to explain the process of learning in its own terms, leading to more than a little disagreement. Neurologists study brain development, chemicals, and hormones and how they affect learning and memory. Educators and educational researchers study practical techniques for maximizing the learning potential of students. Psychologists are now studying the role of emotion in learning. In these disciplines and others, the question is often repeated: What is effective learning?

The *Concise Oxford Dictionary* says learning is "gaining knowledge or skill."[2]

A typical psychological definition is "a relatively permanent change in behavior that is attributable to practice and experience, inferred from improvement in performance."[3] From a neuroscientific position, "Learning is the process by which we acquire knowledge about the world, while memory is the process by which that knowledge is encoded, stored, and later retrieved."[4] A cognitive psychologist would say that learning is the process of integrating new information with existing knowledge.

Marc Prensky, author of *Don't Bother Me, Mom—I'm Learning!* offers a useful definition: "Human learning is the set of processes people employ, both consciously and unconsciously, to effect changes to their knowledge, capacities and/or beliefs."[5] Prensky suggests that his definition takes into account that learning is not a single process but the result of several processes that may or may not be interrelated. Also, he points out that it is the person learning who does the work of acquiring knowledge and skills, not the person teaching (or anyone else). Finally, he suggests that learning is more than simple facts (knowledge) and capacities (the ability to do things), but also beliefs, which, he says, are "theories, understanding of how and why things work or happen."[6]

Whatever the definition, it's clear that people tend to have differing views on what learning is. Memorizing facts (rote learning) is not necessarily learning the skills necessary to put information into practice. For instance, we can learn from a book or lecture that an internal combustion engine uses a spark to ignite gasoline that has been pressurized by a piston, which is driven back down into a cylinder, and the force of the piston is thus translated into the movement of a crankshaft, which ultimately provides power to the wheels. We could answer various questions correctly on a test. But it's likely that we could not build an internal combustion engine or even fix one if it broke.

On the other hand, someone might work in an auto repair shop and learn all the practical steps involved in fixing automobile engines, but, at least in theory, not know the names of the parts or the scientific explanations of how they function.

In both cases, learning has taken place. In both cases, the learning might be useful under specific circumstances. In the case of the auto mechanic, the learning is highly practical. In the case of the student, the learning is mostly theoretical. Of course, a third scenario is also possible, in which the auto mechanic also learns the science behind the internal combustion engine and the names of all the parts, or the student enrolls in an auto mechanics class that involves hands-on work with engines. In either case, both the theory and the practice converge, and one might say that the learning is complete. Or is it?

Much of what this chapter explores about learning and games is established and accepted by experts, but some of it is entirely theoretical and has yet to be fully tested. Still, it is my firm belief that video games are all about learning, and it is primarily a matter of design decisions that determine their impact on players. Whether we pay attention to this aspect of video games or not, game players are in a learning environment. The question, then, is, What are they learning now? What will they be learning in the future?

EVOLUTIONARY LEARNING

Ultimately, learning in complex life forms is about survival. Creatures who don't learn and adapt ultimately don't survive. For instance, everybody knows that fire burns and burning yourself is dangerous to your health. You probably learned that lesson by touching something hot and feeling pain. If you didn't ultimately learn that lesson, you might have ended up incinerating yourself.

If it is true that learning is about survival, then we human beings are learning machines. We have not only survived—we have thrived, becoming the dominant life form on the planet. It's safe to say that people have always learned, and those who survived and thrived probably learned best.

The nature of teaching and expectations of learning have changed as society and technology have changed. At the time of the American Revolution, the functional literacy required of an average person was the ability to sign one's name, or at least an X, on deeds and other legal documents. Aside from the aristocracy, reading, writing, and math were neither taught nor required. Other skills, such as hunting, fishing, building, farming, tending animals, and fighting, were probably far more important to most people.

The focus on education as we know it today developed in steps during the nineteenth and twentieth centuries. Little by little, people were expected to process and understand vastly more knowledge in an increasingly complex world. Today, people are challenged to understand the history or background of a field and its current knowledge base, interpreting and applying vast amounts of information.

Modern education must be oriented to help students develop intellectual tools and learning strategies that facilitate acquiring and applying knowledge; asking meaningful questions; and thinking productively about history, science, and technology, social events and other human phenomena, mathematics, and the arts—not to mention themselves!

Given how far we have come in education, it is not surprising to consider that we also have far to go—or at least that future learning horizons may contain new and thus far undreamed-of opportunities and challenges. Our understanding of learning and education has changed in a variety of ways. Once it was considered radical to teach women in classes with men, for example, and impossible to teach children with disabilities. We are now doing both—and more.

Games and video game technology can present us with new ways to learn and possibly even better ways than we have tried before. Video games might enhance our educational systems by providing information and experiences that we do not teach in schools or in work-related training, for various reasons. Video games may even become more embedded in school curricula. As we move forward in the twenty-first century, video games may well become more and more recognized for their power and potential to teach and inspire.

PROBLEM SOLVING

One of the difficulties that researchers have identified occurs when a subject is taught only in a very narrow context. Pioneering work by the Cognition and Technology Group at Vanderbilt University in the 1990s suggested that ideal learning would be "situated" in real-world problems and presented in story, or problem, formats.[7]

In fact, various approaches to instruction use problem formats instead of simple "tell-memorize-test" types of teaching. The Vanderbilt solution is called *anchored instruction*; slightly different approaches are called *case-based* and *problem-based learning*. The goal of each is to stimulate learning in the form of problems that inspire greater understanding in students while also exposing them to different approaches to the problem. Ultimately, through these techniques, students learn the abstract underlying principles of a subject and how to apply them in a variety of situations.

This is a highly simplified description of these learning approaches, but perhaps it's enough information to make the point that video games are essentially "situated" learning environments. James Paul Gee, a linguistics professor at the University of Wisconsin and author of the widely respected book *What Video Games Can Teach Us about Learning and Literacy*, states, "Since video games are simulations of experience, they can put language into the context of dialogue, experience, images, and actions. They allow language to be situated."[8]

Video games can involve players in "simulations of experience." Thus, part of their potential as teaching environments is that they involve players in a variety of experiential problem-based challenges, not so different from what the learning experts propose as ideal learning environments.

Even more interesting is that, while some games involve players in very specific experiences with built-in challenges, other types of video games offer environments with less explicit goals and challenges. In those more open-ended environments, players actually create their own problems and find their own solutions. This, too, is a feature of learning systems such as Vanderbilt's anchored instruction model.

TRANSFER

Knowledge in the modern sense depends on the ability to apply what is known to specific situations and to transfer it to other contexts. Thus, the knowledge we gain from basic mathematics easily transfers to mundane operations like making change or balancing a checkbook, but surprisingly, some people can go through basic math in school and not know how to do either of those things. They may have learned their times tables, but they have not been able to transfer that knowledge and apply it in other situations. Even more interesting is the phenomenon of people who can perform tasks such as calculating the best prices of supermarket items or performing sales-related calculations but cannot answer typical school math questions, even though they are using the same knowledge.

Transfer in this context refers to taking what you learn and being able to apply it in different situations and in different parts of your life. Significantly, what you learn in school should transfer to your life outside school, and if it is to benefit you in the long run, it should certainly transfer to your work life.

Some of what we know about transfer may be summarized as follows:

- All new learning involves transfer based on previous learning, which has important implications for the design of instruction that helps students learn.
- Knowledge that is overly contextualized can reduce transfer; abstract representations of knowledge can help promote transfer.
- Transfer is best viewed as an active, dynamic process rather than a passive end product of a particular set of learning experiences.

One way to deal with narrowly contextual learning is to broaden its scope, which can be accomplished by offering examples of the same learning information in different contexts or to challenge students to show flexibility by changing parts of the problem and asking, "What if?" Another way is to present a set of related problems. For example, instead of simply calculating the time for a single boat trip, students are asked to imagine they run a boat excursion company and manage a whole system of excursions in which flexibility and smarter models must be used.

Some video games fall into a very narrow context, and when they do, whatever knowledge they impart may not transfer into a player's life outside the game. Other games, however, present experiences that do transfer exceptionally well. In simulations that model different systems, a great deal of useful information is imparted. The example of running the boat tour company is a natural game concept, for instance, that is almost identical to a commercial game called Railroad Tycoon (and many other games like it).

Another factor to consider is that game players are voluntarily immersed in the game experience, as described in Chapter 3. For that reason, they may spend hours with the game, and all that time they are exposed to whatever the game can teach, practicing the skills it offers again and again in different situations. This practice and variety broadens their ability to use those skills in other contexts—that is, to transfer their learning.

Some critics of video games refer to this very phenomenon of transfer as dangerous, claiming that many video games teach players to kill. Chapter 1 offered an alternative video gamer's view, where I argued that there is a clear distinction between fantasy and reality, and that people's basic moral and ethical underpinnings are stronger than media. If someone is mentally disturbed or unbalanced, it is possible that violent video game playing, for instance, might serve to reinforce existing thinking errors, but in the majority of players, the taboos against violence will be stronger than the fantasy experience. If this were not the case, we could expect all soldiers who are taught to kill, especially those who have actually killed in real-world battle, to engage in murder on a regular basis. Such a scenario does not occur, either.

PATTERNS AND ORGANIZATIONAL THINKING

How do experts do what they do so much better than other people? Part of the secret is that they have developed, over many years of practice and study, methods for organizing information into meaningful structures and important concepts. In essence, they have automated certain procedures. For instance, for a physicist, knowledge of Newton's laws of motion is essential, but not just the ability to recite them. Experts recognize where these laws are applied and can transfer their understanding to other situations. They are able to see connections and functions as whole mental structures—what academics call "chunks"—and examine a subject more deeply as a result.

This ability to see structures and connections is a type of *pattern recognition*, and it surfaces in a wide variety of disciplines. For example, a chess master who has put in as many as a hundred thousand hours in practice can see whole sets of chess pieces in configurations that quickly can lead to more sophisticated strategies and clear understanding of which approaches will have greater chances of success than others. Expert musicians can recognize whole passages of music notation at a glance. A trained physician can take in a variety of clues from the human body to form a diagnosis based on a large array of organized conceptual structures related to medicine and disease.

Video games may help teach players how to recognize patterns in many ways. For instance, players recognize patterns of movement in other characters, patterns related to story structures, and patterns related to complex strategies. Games reinforce such pattern recognition and the ability to organize thinking partially through the game player's motivation to achieve goals and partially through reward structures that help reinforce that sort of thinking. In addition, most good video games present problem-solving scenarios, which contribute to a greater level of understanding and improved ability to understand the patterns learned in the game to other situations. How much such abilities transfer to life outside games is unknown, but I believe some such transfer does occur. With outside guidance from teachers or with more conscious attention to transfer as a goal of video game design, this effect can be significantly increased.

FLUENCY

It takes brain power to think about things, and our brains can only handle and process so much information consciously at a time. Therefore, the more fluently we know a subject—meaning the less thought we have to apply to accomplishing a task—the more processing power we have left over for other tasks or for a deeper level of thought about the task at hand. Experts, people who have learned a subject thoroughly, can chunk information, as we saw before, but they also have the advantage of fluency. They simply do what they do with a minimum of mental effort and can often delve deeper into a subject or thought because parts of it are processed nearly automatically.

Fluency comes with practice and with clear models that allow a person to grasp a subject or situation immediately. For example, when people first learn to drive a car, they must concentrate on all the information they are getting and the many tasks they must perform in order to drive without incident. Their attention is fully engaged in steering; shifting (if necessary); watching the road for other cars, pedestrians, and other dangers; and learning to "feel" the car as it moves and as they adjust speed and direction. There's an almost overwhelming amount of information flooding into consciousness.

After a remarkably short time, these same new drivers are having conversations, listening to their favorite music, talking on cell phones, thinking about what they'll have for dinner or some project they're excited about—in fact, just about anything except driving. All that stimulus and all those skills have become automatic, freeing their brains to work on or enjoy other ideas.

Again and again, it is clear that effective learning involves doing. Someone might tell you everything you needed to know about driving a car, or you might read it in a book, but the superficial knowing that comes from outside sources cannot create the kind of fluency with driving that actually sitting behind the wheel, firing up the ignition, and taking the vehicle for a ride does. Nothing replaces doing, although other sources of knowledge can help us grasp situations faster or more deeply.

Video games are all about doing. Even if not in the physical world, in games you take action and directly accomplish tasks. There are limits, of course, but driving a car in a game situation gives you more experiential information than reading about it in a book. I imagine it would be interesting to compare how quickly new drivers who have played in computer driving games learn compared with those who have never driven a simulation. Clearly, in pilot training, simulations are valuable. Even commercial off-the-shelf programs like Microsoft Flight Simulator have been used for partial flight credit in pilot training, and big aircraft simulators are used by commercial airlines and military schools to teach pilots and provide them with practice in a variety of situations. Simulations are even being used to help teach surgeons and medical practitioners.

In terms of fluency and automatic responses to situations, it would seem that practice and experience in a variety of situations help hone a person's thinking and create recognizable patterns. In the end, practice and experience are necessary for someone to learn anything deeply. Games can provide the motivation to play combined with the practice and variety to achieve greater levels of fluency with the ideas and skills they present.

SELF-ASSESSMENT

Academic circles refer to *metacognition*, but in simpler terms, this concept means "self-assessment." It refers to the ability of people in learning environments to predict how they will perform in various tasks based on their present level of mastery or understanding. It also refers to a person's ability to assess his or her progress and reflect on what needs improvement. This sort of self-assessment seems to be associated with how well students can transfer what they learn to other situations and events.

In game terms, self-assessment is a constant. Game designers expect players to be continuously assessing their own current abilities, predicting their likely successes, and reassessing results as they move through a game. In fact, game playing is all about metacognition as learning theorists think of it, and although probably few game designers and even fewer game players know the term, they understand the principle instinctively.

Why is this sort of self-assessment so common in video games, but not always so common in other learning environments? Perhaps, in part, it is because video games are structured to present challenges incrementally, so that they will become gradually harder or more complex. Players learn how to play games very little by listening and almost exclusively by doing. They must develop strong skills at prediction and assessment to succeed.

ADAPTIVE EXPERTISE

Another term used in modern learning theory is *adaptive expertise*, which refers in many ways to an expert's style of learning and application. For instance, some people are good at what they do, but they do it "by the book." They don't stray from the rules. And, although they can be considered experts, they are limited by the system they have learned. Some theorists call these people "artisans."

Artisans seek only to accomplish a task as given. If artisan architects are asked to design a house, they will do so according to the exact specifications of the client. They view new situations as opportunities to use their existing expert skills to perform efficiently.

In contrast is another group, called "virtuosos," who approach new situations and problems as opportunities to explore and expand their abilities. They more often come up with novel solutions and also are more likely to find unexpected connections in new situations. They approach situations with more flexibility and, perhaps most important, continue to learn throughout their lives by stretching their knowledge. Virtuosos are also more likely to be happy in their work, which they view as a constant opportunity for improvement and discovery.

In good video games, players are encouraged to think creatively and to find novel solutions to problems. A game that is completely "by the book" would be boring. Game players seek, and expect, surprises, unexpected challenges, and situations that require ingenuity, skills, and/or cleverness to resolve. Game players are often encouraged to think "outside the box" and to seek more than one solution to any given problem. It is common in game scenarios to offer obvious solutions that are far less successful, in the long run, than the less obvious strategies. Game players are implicitly trained, therefore, by experience, to seek creative solutions—exactly what the virtuoso expert does. In this way, video games encourage adaptive expertise, at least in the realm of game playing. Since video games can deal with almost infinitely diverse subject matter, it is entirely possible that game playing can be linked with adaptive expertise in a variety of real-world skills.

TIME AND PRACTICE

Real understanding and expertise in any subject is a matter of time spent learning and practicing the skills inherent to that subject. This is a pretty obvious statement—as obvious as "Practice makes perfect." Consistent practice, however, is less likely without motivation. As noted in the previous chapter, with motivation we will spend a lot of time doing something, whereas without motivation we will be far less likely to dedicate the same amount of time.

Motivation can come from many sources, including need, fear, and even outside force, but one of the most powerful and effective (and reliable) sources of motivation is pleasure. If we are having fun, we will do something for hours at a time and hardly notice the time passing. Time really does fly when you're having fun. And, as stated earlier, this is one of the ultimate secrets of video games: they motivate, and they do so very well.

Given how well video games can motivate players, it stands to reason that they can provide hours of practice in whatever skills they may be modeling and teaching, as a function of the game's design and the designer's intentions. In how they encourage time spent practicing, video games excel. Of course, it may be possible that players will spend hours learning a lot about nothing very important. But it's also possible that players can spend many hours of enjoyment and at the same time be learning and practicing skills that will help them in their lives. That's what this book is about—power and potential.

(RE)PLAY IT AGAIN, SAM

One unique quality of games further enhances how they function as learning environments. Where repetition can deepen learning, experimentation—learning from both failure and success—can promote much deeper understanding, especially if the player stops to consider the underlying causes at work. When talking about "real life," how often do we get to repeat an action to get a better result, without risking sometimes serious consequences? Even though risk and reward are a part of life, and even failure is a great teacher, the results of failure in real life can be extreme. Recovery from failures in significant areas of real life can be difficult and can take years of hard work, at best.

Games, on the other hand, have an amazing feature that many of us who play video games wish we had in the real world. It is called the "saved game." The saved game lets us try things—even very risky gambits—and, though we may fail, we learn. And we load the saved game and try again. With each attempt we learn more. In video games, we know there is always a solution, so even if we fail again and again, we try again by taking a completely different approach.

Even when we succeed, we may try other paths. Because good games are about choice, the saved game lets us explore more of the choices our game "life" has to offer. In games, there doesn't have to be a "road less traveled" because we can, at least in theory, travel all roads. Video gamers will often try several approaches to a problem, even if their first one worked, because they want to succeed with more elegance or efficiency.

In video games, style counts. For instance, imagine that a valuable jewel was hidden within an almost equally valuable vase. The easy method of obtaining the jewel would be to break the vase, and many players would start there. What if the vase has value, too? Many players will stop and think: how can I get both the jewel and the vase? Players are always trying to figure out how to have their cake and eat it, too, and in video games, that is sometimes possible.

This ability to "redo" allows game players to learn not only by repetition but by experimentation as well. Remarkably, game players rarely succumb to failure. They generally know they can try again and do keep trying, learning, and, ultimately succeeding.

Social Impacts on Learning

People have an effect on other people, and nowhere is this more apparent than in learning. Social systems can accelerate learning through collaboration. They can also restrict new and innovative approaches through the adoption of social norms that tend to ostracize original thinkers and mavericks.

Many successful teachers engage their classes in discussions about what they are learning. Some even have smaller groups of students work independently and then come back to share what they have gained with the whole group. Cooperative learning often deepens and accelerates the process.

It also appears that people are more highly motivated when their work will be shared with others, so that, for instance, assignments that are meant to be shared with the class or even with outside audiences seem to result in highly motivated students. Moreover, if students believe what they are doing is useful to others, they are also highly motivated. In both of these cases, people clearly want to reach out to others, to communicate, and even to have a positive impact on the world around them.

In cases of collaborative learning, students are engaged in a shared experience that can allow them to communicate ideas, thoughts, and feelings to each other, each benefiting from the contributions of others. Even those who are clearly mistaken can help the group understand a subject better, and in environments that encourage openness and risk taking, students can learn more deeply by exploring all paths of knowledge, even those that lead to dead ends. In doing so they learn what works, certainly; but, more important, by exploring what doesn't work, they can learn why things work the way they do.

Video games have many social effects. They have become a subculture among young and not-so-young people. Within that subculture is a language and understanding that, like other subcultures, encourages a shared identity among video game players as well as opening avenues for dialogue and discussion based on mutual interests.

Video games are more than a subculture, however. Game players discuss the nuances of games, the tricks and techniques, strategies and tactics, the various merits and shortcomings of their favorite and less liked games. They are critics, strategists, researchers, and analysts. They are critical thinkers without even knowing the term. This sharing of ideas is all outside the actual game itself.

Inside games, more and more often players cooperate and compete directly in multiplayer environments, some of which are strictly competitive, yet gamers enjoy the competition and are highly motivated to succeed. Cooperative games are increasingly common, and with massive multiplayer worlds (which can have thousands of players simultaneously sharing experiences), the possibilities for cooperative play have been multiplying year after year.

The social impact of these games is surprisingly complex, and residents of "virtual worlds" are engaged in an extensive number of activities simultaneously. According to Constance Steinkuehler of the University of Wisconsin, one of the leading scholars of massive multiplayer online game worlds, "Successful MMOGameplay is cognitively demanding, requiring exploration of complex, multi-dimensional problem spaces, empirical model building, the negotiation of meaning and values within the relevant gaming community, and the coordination of people, (virtual) tools and artifacts, and multiple forms of text—all within persistent virtual worlds with emergent sociological cultural characteristics of their own."[9]

Within the context of "social gaming," players are engaged in complex interactions that go far beyond simple competition and cooperation and begin to function as autonomous societies with economies, rules, and social mores of their own. Not only are players in these worlds constantly learning simply by their participation, but the potential for accelerated and more specific learning opportunities is immense.

PERSONALITY PROJECTION

People identify with characters depicted in just about any story. Even in the ancient days of oral storytelling, listeners of stirring tales probably imagined themselves, if only briefly, in the roles of the gods and heroes of the stories.

According to storytelling historian Anne Pellowski, "You see it over and over with the telling of the *Ramayana* in India. Every boy is Rama, and every girl is Sita. There is definitely identification going on, and it has probably gone on since ancient times."[10]

Such identification is clearly present today in popular forms of entertainment such as novels, movies, TV, and video games. In some way, we come to identify with the hero, the heroine, even the villain. Each person, through the power of imagination, transfers some of his or her attention and personal identity, however temporarily, to the characters in a story.

In video games, this identification goes much further than in other media. Because players are actively engaged in the actions and choices that the game character makes, they are at the same time making those choices as players in the real world and as characters in a fictional world. Consider, for instance, if you played a complex hero like Frodo in *The Lord of the Rings*. Frodo was, essentially, a pacifist. He would not allow harm to come to Golem, no matter what horrible acts the creature did. How many of us, playing Frodo in a game, would choose the exact same course? When we read the book or see the movie, we cannot change Frodo's actions or responses. We can only feel some connection with him and his quest to enter the realm of evil and destroy the One Ring.

In a game setting, it is technically possible for Frodo (or Sam) to kill Golem or to take a different route into Mordor. The choice would ultimately be based on the player's choices, but it would be affected by the goals of the story and, to some extent, by the personality of the Frodo character. Because it is a game, the outcome of the player's choices might differ significantly from the outcome of the book.

As this example shows, identification in video games is both more intense than in other media and slightly more complex. Characters in games may have different needs and goals than people playing them, just as the characters in all stories have different needs and goals from those of their audiences. In video games, because the player is, in fact, controlling the main character of the story, a complex identity triad results: the player, the player's character, and the player's projection on the player's character. This third category is described by James Paul Gee as the "projective identity"[11]—the intersection of the player's goals and interests with the virtual character's identity.

Given that a person playing a video game is determining the character's actions, the player's goals and even ethical and moral beliefs and values can often affect how the character in the game acts and grows. Even if the character in the game has specific abilities, such as the ability to steal items from other characters, the player still decides whether to guide the character to steal or not. If the player's morality is strongly against stealing, then it's possible that he or she will not guide the character in the game to steal. Even if the player does choose to guide the character in the game to steal, a good game will include possible consequences that might range from apprehension and imprisonment to death (of the character) or remorse (again in the character, but probably having an effect on the player). The player's character might even regret doing immoral actions and want to atone for these actions in the game. It would then be up to the player to help find a way for the character to accomplish these new goals.

This scenario assumes that stealing and other antisocial acts are necessarily bad in a game context and should be punished or otherwise provided with consequences that reinforce society's moral and ethical values. However, the opposite may also be true. Acting through the characters, players can decide to do things that they would never do in the real world. In this way, they role-play an antisocial behavior—try it on for size where it will not do any real harm. In fact, this sort of role playing can be beneficial. According to Gerard Jones, "We all are curious about what it would be like to be something other than what we are and it is a relief to go to a play where there are no real world consequences. One of the functions of fantasy in play is to get to do what we might not want to do in real life. We experience relief from the bounds of society and get to play a different kind of creature for a while."[12]

According to Gee, identities are important to deep learning. As he says in his book, if you are going to learn physics, you need, at least for a while, to adopt the identity of a physicist—to act and think according to the rules of physics. Approaching a problem of physics as, say, a soccer player would not result in deep learning of physics. You might think, "I'm a soccer player. Why would I be interested in physics?" or "I'm a soccer player, and everyone knows that jocks don't get science."

Imagine that you are that soccer player. Putting other identities aside and pretending or imagining how a physicist would approach a problem allows you to use the tools and language of physics, almost as if you had adopted a virtual identity. On the other hand, approaching physics both as a soccer player and as a physicist might allow you to apply the lessons of physics to your game of soccer, understanding better, for instance, the flight and trajectory of the ball or the subtleties of the ball's motion and velocity when kicked.

The concept of the virtual identity ties directly into video games, because in games players are given an identity over which they superimpose their own values, goals, and intentions. How such projective identities can be used to provide opportunities for learning positive impact is a challenge that game designers can tackle.

SECONDARY EFFECTS AND REWARDS

Secondary effects are impacts that we obtain from our activities that aren't the primary intended effects. You might think of these as "collateral" or "emergent" effects. In ideal circumstances, these collateral effects are positive, what I will call secondary rewards. However, we can also have negative secondary effects, such as physical addiction to morphine after it has been used legitimately to control pain.

As an example of a secondary reward, consider that people who watch the TV show *Jeopardy!* are, for the most part, not seeking to become more educated. They are being entertained. A possible secondary reward for people who watch *Jeopardy!* is that they actually learn facts that in all likelihood they would never have learned otherwise. Whether these facts are useful in their lives is often debatable, but I imagine that only a few *Jeopardy!* fans watch the show primarily to learn trivia.

In the first *Karate Kid* movie, Pat Morita's character, Mr. Miyagi, instructs his young student, Daniel, in martial arts by having him do a variety of chores, such as painting his house and waxing his car. The chores were repetitive and boring, but through them Daniel was, according to the movie, learning and practicing martial arts movements without knowing it. This is another clear example of a secondary reward where the teacher engaged the student in activities that did not obviously relate to what he wanted to learn, but as he discovered, he was learning all along.

The difference between Mr. Miyagi's approach and what happens in video games is that Daniel was resistant to doing the chores he was given. In contrast, video game players are enthusiastic about engaging in game activities. Gamers are not reluctant or resistant to the game's engagement.

In video games, secondary rewards can take many forms, including improved eye-hand coordination, factual information about history or science, or even stronger problem-solving abilities. This phenomenon, which we could also call "collateral learning," may be one of the most important mechanisms by which commercial video games can have positive influences on the people who play them. Of course, the phenomenon of secondary effects could conceivably have other unintended effects. Issues of potentially negative secondary effects, such as violent behavior or desensitization toward violence, were discussed in Chapter 1.

Another secondary effect of games and media in general has more to do with our worldview. For instance, kids who grew up in the 1950s were exposed to a lot of television shows in which the good guys literally wore white hats and the bad guys wore black hats. Good and evil was truly black and white. In other shows, parents were all wise and understanding. In all of these shows, there was some kind of conflict or situation, and in every episode that situation was resolved. A happy epilogue assured us that everything was all right again: The bad guys were vanquished. The family or social emergencies were all fixed. The world was good.

Simplistic messages were prevalent in the early days of television, and the attitudes that they instilled in a generation of baby boomers are still being felt. *There is a distinct and obvious difference between the good and the bad. The good will always triumph in the end. Life is good because good always prevails.* Such messages are not realistic, as we know today, but for kids growing up with *The Lone Ranger* and *Father Knows Best*, these were important influences.

Kids growing up with video games today are getting different, much more complex messages. Some of them are dark and, on the surface, antisocial. Some are almost identical to those old 1950s messages. Once again, even in modern games, there is context, and in the majority of games, the player-hero is engaged in a justifiable struggle against clearly evil enemies. The same morality exists, but it is somewhat more sophisticated. Some games do blur the lines by suggesting that the good side may not be all good, and the bad side may not be all bad. Some even take the player a certain distance into the game and then reverse the player's beliefs, such as in the game Deus Ex, in which the agency that the player starts out serving turns out to be the enemy.

Video games today are not so very different in content from other modern media. The information we get today is far more complex than it was fifty years ago. The subtleties and nuances of modern culture, combined with technologies that put information at almost anyone's fingertips and link us together in ever-wider social networks, have changed society completely. All modern forms of entertainment reflect their cultures, and video games are no different. Where there may be secondary effects that we don't prefer from playing video games and consuming other media, it's also clear that video games can offer opportunities for positive collateral learning.

Chapter 5

THE MAGIC EDGE AND TMSI

Education is not the filling of a pail, but the lighting of a fire.

−William Butler Yeats

The previous chapters have discussed game controversies, the game industry, society, the history and meaning of game evolution, and why we play as well as how we, as human beings, learn. All of the preceding chapters have led to this one, in which I propose the Next Step for video games. Simply put, *the Next Step is that games will become an intentional medium of positive change in individuals and society*. This will not be the only step games and gamers will take along their own evolutionary pathway, but, to me, it is the most important step. Why?

As we have seen in previous chapters, games are highly successful commercially, and they also fill roles in our lives by providing entertainment. Games do not stop with entertainment alone; they provide experiences that no other entertainment medium provides. They motivate players, provide a sense of accomplishment and mastery, empowerment, and choice making. In remarkable ways, they match learning processes, not only biochemically and neurologically, but in terms of effective and well-established learning principles and structures. According to some researchers, video games are among the best learning environments ever invented.

Many researchers contend that games already have very positive and demonstrable effects on the people who play them. I have touched on some of these positive effects in previous chapters on play and learning. In this chapter, I will introduce two key concepts, one that helps explain why video games are so effective and the other that describes the basic ways in which they can have positive impact on players. I call these two concepts the Magic Edge and TMSI (teach, model, simulate, and inspire).

WHAT IS THE MAGIC EDGE?

The Magic Edge is what empowers video games, allowing them to be immensely successful entertainment media and, simultaneously, highly effective learning environments. The Magic Edge is unique to video games.

What I call the Magic Edge is not one single property of games but a combination of properties that, taken together, provide the unique quality that separates video games from other media and learning environments. Think of it as chemistry. Each of the properties I will describe—motivation, immersion, identification, interactivity, and choice—taken alone has certain meanings and implications, just like, for instance, hydrogen and oxygen each have their unique individual chemical properties. When you combine hydrogen and oxygen under certain conditions, you get another substance—water—with qualities quite different from either hydrogen or oxygen. When you combine motivation, immersion, identification, interactivity, and choice in the specific medium of video games, you get the Magic Edge, which I consider to be an identifiable quality unique to video games among popular media.

MOTIVATION

Chapter 3 considered motivation at some length and from different perspectives. Motivation is one of the primary elements of human consciousness, and it is from this primary function that much of the power and potential of video games arises.

Along with various theories of motivation, I discussed specifically how games provide motivation in players, through multi-tiered goal structures, challenges and puzzles, and a variety of types of rewards. I have broken this down to a very simple definition: Motivation is an inner drive to action. Video games provide that drive to action by offering challenges to overcome, puzzles to solve, feelings of mastery, tangible rewards, novelty, and surprises. All this and more take place in a contextual world consisting of situations, stories, and characters, with room to explore, to solve mysteries, or to conquer.

Video games sometimes provide players with social acceptance or personal self-esteem. In some cases, playing video games might offer an enjoyable diversion from life's ordinary stresses or, in extreme cases, relief from a dreary existence or the pain of disease or a dysfunctional family environment. At the least, video games, like good books, allow us figuratively to turn the page on a great adventure, but in this case it is our own very personal adventure in which we are both the actors and, in a sense, the creators. In all these ways, games provide motivation by providing opportunities to obtain what we want, thereby driving us to action.

Not only do video games provide motivation in terms of goals and rewards, but they work with something called *expectancy value theory*, which states that not only are we motivated by something that has value to us, but we also have the expectation of being able to achieve it. Video games are structured to allow players to succeed, and they enter the video game experience believing that success is possible. Thus, video games fit the expectancy value theory quite well.

In short, motivation is at the core of the power and potential of video games because, through the motivation provided by multilevel goals, challenges, and rewards, along with the expectation that success is possible, players simply want to keep playing. They play because they are having fun—an enjoyable experience—even if they are working hard at it.

In his book *Everything Bad Is Good for You*, Steven Johnson relates a story about showing SimCity to his seven-year-old nephew. He suggests something of the power of motivation and learning in video games when he says, "My nephew would be asleep in five seconds if you popped him down in an urban studies classroom, but somehow an hour of playing SimCity taught him that high tax rates in industrial areas can stifle development."[1] When people of any age are motivated and having fun, they will be more likely to continue what they are doing—even if it involves learning complex ideas.

IMMERSION

Many forms of entertainment are immersive, meaning that we forget ourselves and get very involved in the experience. This is true of movies, books, and even work-related activities. And, while it is true that immersion is not unique to video games, in combination with the other elements of the Magic Edge, it adds an important element to the mix.

When we are immersed in an activity, we are concentrated, focused, and engaged. We may even achieve that timeless and ultimately satisfying *flow* state described in Chapter 3. When we are immersed and highly motivated by an activity, we could continue to engage in it for hours.

Can immersion be a bad thing? In extreme cases, people can become so immersed in what they are doing that they lose sight of other aspects of their lives. Most people, however, are capable of enjoying the experience of immersion in tasty, refreshing doses, and they continue to manage the responsibilities of their lives. In such a context, immersion is not only good but desirable.

IDENTIFICATION

In Chapter 4, I spoke about identification and personality projection as elements of learning environments. Identification with characters in a story or game is also one of the most powerful elements of immersion. It places us mentally into an outside projection of our imaginations, an imaginative world that we are allowed to experience from another person's point of view.

In movies, novels, and other entertainment media, we often identify with the protagonist. This sort of identification is one reason that we respond so emotionally to stories and adventures involving people who are often very different from ourselves. We say we can "relate" to their experience, however different it is from ours.

In video games, identification is at the same time more complex and, potentially, more powerful. Not only do we have the ability to perceive the characters' world from their perspective, we also guide our "player" characters through that world and through the decisions they make, the actions they take. As we do so, we also bring our own personal goals and perspectives to the situation.

Because we are both ourselves playing the game and, in a sense, the character with whom we are identifying, we can learn a lot more about ourselves. For instance, we can explore different interactions and responses in a variety of situations, perhaps alternating between our personal motivations and those of the character, or making creative combinations between the two. We can go all-out with the virtual character's reality or temper it with our own goals, sentiments, or values. We are, at the same time, the actor, the director, and the writer of our own adventure, and within this complex structure, we have opportunities to experiment—to try any and all approaches to a variety of situations, assess the results, and try again.

INTERACTIVITY

The difference between entertainment and play is that entertainment tends to be more passive than play. In the case of so-called passive entertainment, the information is going in one direction only. The audience/observer is not changing the entertainment, even if the entertainment is changing the audience. In video game play, information goes back and forth, with the player acting and the game responding in a cycle of actions and responses. This is what interactivity is all about—a two-way street.

To understand the difference between passive entertainment and interactive entertainment, it's helpful to realize that even "passive" entertainment is not passive. There is a lot going on. When viewing or reading, we identify with characters in movies, TV, and books. When listening to music, our bodies move, we respond emotionally, and even our heart rate may change. Even when we are viewing a fine painting, we are probably changed and actively affected. Neurological changes occur, based on the kind of experience we are having. Most of these responses are unconscious. We do not exert influence over the book, movie, music, or painting. They exert influence over us.

Many people are satisfied to say that games are interactive and that interactivity sets them apart from other media. In a simplistic sense, this may be true. When you are comparing video games with television, movies, and literature, for instance, this distinction is obvious, but when looking at video games in the context of all other possible activities, it's clear that video games are not unique in being interactive. Parlor games, kids' fantasy games, and all competitive sports are interactive. Video games are distinguished in part by the range and quality of interactivity, along with their ability to provide players with constant, up-to-the-split-second choices.

One way to define interactivity in a learning context is to see it as a *process that systematically involves learners as active participants in their own learning.* Let's look a bit closer at the significant elements of this definition:

- *Interactivity as a process*: It is neither static nor passive. It is an ongoing event.
- *Systematically involves learners*: *Systematically* implies that learners function within a system. A system, in turn, implies rules and structures, much like video games. And *involves* could be an admittedly weaker but analogous way of saying "motivated," which is precisely what video games do.
- *Active participants in their own learning*: Clearly these elements of action and participation are essential components of video game playing as well.

Because video games are all about learning on at least one level, this definition of *interactivity* could easily be changed to *Interactivity is a game in which players are motivated through rule systems and incremental goals, challenges, and rewards to participate in an entertaining process that involves learning.*

Interactivity in video games involves a high degree of give and take. What the player does often has a significant effect on what happens next. Depending on the game, players may be able to change the course of history—within the game, of course—or determine by their actions wholesale changes in the plot or outcome of the game's reality. Equally important is how the game can change the player. Each decision or action taken by the player can have a small or a profound effect on the game, but each change that takes place within the game also affects the player's next option. In this sense, games are a learning environment in which players are constantly presented with opportunities to take action and observe the results, then take new action based on assessment of those results. This kind of involvement is true of many games, not just video games, but the almost unlimited range of options in many video games sets them apart from other games, which operate in a narrower field of possibilities.

CHOICE

Without choices, there would be no Magic Edge. Choice is really what makes games work. Without choices, all those goals and rewards would have little meaning, and challenges would mean even less if there were only one way to do something. In fact, many video game designers define video games as a "series of meaningful choices."[2] In other words, games provide players with choices, but not just any choices—meaningful ones, choices resulting in consequences, which, for good or ill, affect the player's experience and the game itself.

Other types of games also offer choices. The game of Monopoly is full of choices—do you build houses or hotels, buy up the premium properties or the railroads, invest your money or hoard it? However, Monopoly can never change its rules in midstream or allow players to go off the board. Users make decisions while playing the game, and these decisions do affect other players, but they do not cause essential changes to the Monopoly world, other than to own and develop properties on the board.

Video games also allow choices, as do board games, but video games frequently take place in responsive "living" worlds, and they always take place in worlds that can be altered on the fly, almost without limit. Even if, in structure, video games are similar to other games, their versatility and range of choices and consequences far exceeds any nondigital entertainment medium. Of course, much of the flexibility of video games is up to the designers themselves, and designers always impose restraints on a game in order to provide a more or less stable learning environment. If players aren't able to learn the rules and strategies needed to play successfully, then the game will fail. Like other good learning environments, games are set up to challenge players but also to ensure that they can succeed with some effort.

In video games, two-way interactivity allows players to create and alter the game experience, assess the results of their actions, and respond directly to changing situations. Video games thus encourage active and adaptive learning while engaging the player/learner in an entertaining and engaging experience.

UNLOCKING THE POSITIVE POTENTIAL OF THE MAGIC EDGE

Not one of the five factors of the Magic Edge—motivation, immersion, identification, interactivity and choice—is found only in video games and nowhere else. Every one of them can be found in many areas of our lives, both in entertainment media and in other activities. All five may be present to some degree in various activities, such as in collaborative work environments, team sports, and social interactions of various kinds. But certainly in no other entertainment medium are all five found as reliably and as consistently as in video games. These five qualities, so perfectly combined, create the Magic Edge that can open the doors to learning and positive change.

I call it the Magic Edge because it seems to work like magic. Clearly the Magic Edge has allowed video games to evolve from humble dots on a screen to a multibillion-dollar industry with many millions of players worldwide—and the numbers are still growing.

Game makers understand the Magic Edge, even if they don't define it as I do, but knowing their advantages does not guarantee that they will always make the best use of them. Even most video game critics agree that they can and do provide positive impacts and help teach useful skills. On the other hand, I think it's fair to say that much of the positive impact from video games occurs unintentionally because of the very nature of games. Only a handful of video game designers have intentionally worked to provide such impact as part of the game structure.

I hope to inspire some change in that thinking. I hope to see more video games in which the designers consider not only their gamer fans and the profitability of the game, but also its potential impact on players. The *intentional* use of the Magic Edge can lead to even greater and more varied results than we see now.

The next question to ask, then, is how do you do it? How do you create games that have a positive impact on players? And the answer is first to explore what aspects of games can be used toward these ends. The answer, in short, is TMSI.

TMSI

As mentioned earlier, TMSI stands for teach, model, simulate, and inspire. This is where the power and potential of video games resides, because video games can do all of these things, not just one or two. The ultimate variety of approaches possible in video games is almost limitless, and any perceived limits are rapidly shot down each year as innovative designers and players find new ways to expand the limits of the game play experience.

TEACH (INFORM)

People have recognized the potential of video games to teach for decades, almost from the very beginning of the video game era, and games of various kinds have been used successfully in schools and in other settings as teaching aids in a variety of subjects. Parents often use video games to entertain and simultaneously teach their children.

Teaching implies that specific knowledge or skills are imparted to the game player—such as learning a new language or gaining skills in math, science, or business. This learning is an active handover from the game experience to the player through direct transmission of information and through practice, assessment, and consideration. Complete learning may be outside the realm of commercial video games alone and would require good instructional methods, but some learning is possible even with off-the-shelf games.

Most players do not use manuals or strategy guides to learn how to play a game, though they may refer to other resources in order to perfect their understanding or learn a game's secrets. To begin playing a new game, most gamers simply load it and play it. If players couldn't learn how to play the games essentially through the act of playing, many games would fail because players would give up.

Video games naturally teach, and players naturally learn. Game designers instinctively know how to create teaching systems, because they know how to guide players through a process of guided or trial-and-error learning—or both. They know how to add new "lessons" incrementally so that players continue to learn as they play, and they know how to make these "lessons" fun.

This same learning environment can be applied also to teaching information and skills not directly related to game play or the game's central story. Although some video games already do so, overall the idea of teaching outside the game's own context is not a fundamental aspect of video game design. It happens occasionally by accident, where many games inadvertently teach problem-solving skills, even touching on history or science through the context of the game. It happens also intentionally and by design, as in the case of famous games like SimCity and Civilization, which include clear and definable opportunities to learn about city planning in the former case, and about history, innovation, and even diplomacy in the latter.

What may be missing in video games is the transference of skills from game to novel situations in life. Real learning requires reflection on what has been learned and the ability to apply it outside the learning context—in this case, the video game. In formal education, this is particularly necessary, but even in considering off-the-shelf commercial games as learning environments, the best results will come when gamers are not only learning but thinking about what they are learning. It remains to be seen how well such reflective thinking can be implemented in video games, but I think it can be encouraged.

MODEL (SHOW)

What I call teaching involves presentation of information and practice using it, preferably in different situations and contexts using a problem-based approach. On the other hand, sometimes information is not really expressed directly, such as by naming the Pythagorean theorem or listing the phylum of every living thing. Sometimes information is presented by example. "Actions speak louder than words," the saying goes, and modeling an idea, a behavior, or a concept often speaks louder than just saying it or trying to teach it explicitly.

When adults want to show children how to behave, they may lecture children or tell them what behavior they want, but hopefully they will also behave in that same way. For instance, if an adult tells a child not to use swear words but regularly swears himself, the child gets a mixed message. When the adult models the behavior he is describing to the child, it is bound to be more effective. In fact, children often learn as much or more from how people actually behave than from what they say. "Practice what you preach" is another phrase that describes modeling.

In the digital world, the word *model* has different meanings. When you create a digital image, such as the digital image of a character, it is referred to as a "character model." When a programmer creates a complex program that represents a system, such as a program that controls weather events occurring within a game, this might be thought of as a "weather model." The Department of Defense defines a model as "a physical, mathematical, or otherwise logical representation of a system, entity, phenomenon, or process."[3]

In a sociological sense, to model means to represent a behavior or social system. For example, you can model good or bad behavior. You could model effective or ineffective communication between a parent and a child or a husband and a wife. You could model negotiation techniques, public speaking, or even how to "dress for success." (Think about how fashion models demonstrate—model—how clothing might look in idealized situations.) In this context, modeling is demonstrating or presenting examples.

Video games can present examples of human behavior. They do so now, but with advances in technology, they will be able to do so more and more accurately. What is remarkable about video games is that not only can they model various complex human behaviors, but they can also allow players to interact within those models, learn what works and what doesn't, and improve certain skills—not by explicitly teaching a subject, but by presenting examples. Players can observe and act within these models and notice the consequences, trying different approaches and noticing the consequences again. In this way, they can learn what works and what doesn't based on the results they get.

Critics of video games may point out that in many ways video games model some of the worst aspects of society—war, murder, sexual exploitation, and stereotyping of many definable societal groups, for instance. Even if these criticisms are true in some cases, the converse can also be true: video games can similarly model all kinds of attitudes and values that are honored by society.

Moreover, those games that are criticized as modeling negative attitudes and values often do so with consequences within the game environment that point out their possible flaws. In other words, those negative values that might get modeled in games are, at least in some games, punished within the game environment.

Video game designers can decide how to use modeling techniques and in what context. However they are being used today, they can be used for better purposes tomorrow.

SIMULATE (THE LABORATORY)

In the previous section, I mentioned computerized models of simulated systems, such as a program that controls weather in a virtual world or game. Such a weather model might be very simplistic and merely provide the illusion of changing weather in a virtual environment. Or it might be very complex and accurate, based on the wide variety of factors that actually cause real-world weather to change.

Such complex models are called simulations, and they are often used in games, both for commercial release and also within business and medical environments and in the military. In fact, the so-called war games conducted by the military are examples of simulations of war. Flight simulators are used to help train pilots without actually taking them off the ground. Surgical simulations help teach doctors how to deal with different surgical situations, without ever cutting into a real body. Simulations are used to predict weather, to predict economic factors, and even to predict responses to disaster situations. In a sense, simulations are largely mathematical constructs that calculate different outcomes based on different inputs.

As dry as that definition may sound, simulations can be highly enjoyable, offering great visual imagery and allowing participants to experiment with different situations to see what would likely occur. Simulations are great "what if" machines. Try something—anything—and see what happens. Because it's a simulation, it's safe to experiment.

Unlike most video games, simulations often lack specific goals or outcomes. They simply create a responsive model of a world or situation, tools for manipulating the parameters of that world or situation, and an invitation to experiment. As such, the goals contained within a video game simulation are generally the goals the participants set for themselves, unless they are set by an instructor in an educational context.

Suppose you were put in charge of the world's energy output. You could decide how much energy needed to be produced and how to go about supplying it. You could change the balance of oil, gas, coal, solar, wind, hydro, biofuels, and other energy sources the world would use. You could change the amount of carbon dioxide released by factories and cars and other sources throughout the world. You could also decide how much forest was cut down and how much was left alone. Perhaps you could decide on other important factors, such as farm subsidies, pesticide use, and emission standards for industry. Perhaps you could also control how much money was devoted to exploration in search of new sources of fossil fuels and how much was devoted to new energy technology research or public education about energy.

In contrast, let's suppose you didn't have unlimited resources, and every decision you made had an effect. Also, you couldn't determine the weather or the composition of the atmosphere directly. Neither could you control the way people reacted to events. Your control is limited to certain factors.

Now suppose you begin with a world more or less like the one we have today. You begin to make changes, small or large. Why do you make those decisions? Are you trying to make a healthier and more stable world? Are you trying to make the world more productive? Are you looking ten years into the future? Fifty years? Or only to next year? Perhaps you want to see the worst-case scenario and make decisions based on what you think will bring that on. You are setting your own goals, and the simulation will respond to your actions.

What happens when you change one or more parameters of the simulation? Perhaps some good comes from your changes, but other effects aren't so desirable. You can keep trying to make things work out, or, if you've clearly gone in a direction you don't like, you can start over and try an altogether different approach. You might even find one simple change that balances the mess you've made.

You can be very scientific and only change one parameter at a time. You might conduct the world as if it were your own personal environmental and social orchestra, making changes by instinct or by scientific understanding or by personal beliefs.

The power of a simulation is the power to experiment and learn by observation and by direct feedback. Everything you do within a simulation will affect the outcome. You create your own goals and then attempt to accomplish them. The more accurate the simulation, the more relevant the learning.

Through simulations, you can learn finances, good business practices, global economics, what affects weather systems, how the world evolved, how cities work, global or domestic politics, techniques of driving and flying—and a whole lot more. Simulations can also be used therapeutically, and trials are already being conducted to use simulations in therapeutic situations for posttraumatic stress disorder, other psychological maladies, and physical diseases.

Simulations can be the basis for a whole game, such as the famous SimCity or other "sim" games. Simulations can also occur as parts of a larger game that have more traditional game elements. For instance, in some games you may be involved in an adventure that includes hunting and fishing and possibly fighting with enemies and defending cities. There's a definite game, and the goals are pretty obvious. You want to win, thrive, and survive while coexisting with or defeating and possibly conquering enemies. The game could essentially be territorial, or it could be a more individual adventure with the player as the hero.

In such goal-oriented games, there can also be simulations of ecology, so that as you hunt deer for food, the predators become hungry and start attacking your townspeople. Weather might change if you deforest large areas to build your cities. Land may become barren if you farm it but don't replenish the soil. These effects result directly from the actions and choices you make in a game, but they are all governed by simulation elements within the game program. In this way, they can also be used to help you as a player recognize the consequences of actions in a dynamic system. And, given that it is a game, you can try different approaches and see what kinds of effects you get by doing so. This sort of testing environment can lead to a deeper understanding of *how* things work, compared with telling someone simply "This is how it works." (Note that all of the ecological effects mentioned earlier have been featured already in various video games.)

Even though not all simulations are fun (and some are quite dull, in fact), video game designers are all about creating enjoyable experiences. They always make sure that game-related simulations are like a great big sandbox filled with interesting activities. Players enter the sandbox and start playing, making up their own games with the tools and toys they are given, and they will play for hours. Depending on the simulation, they will learn something, whether it is how cities work or the relationship between resources and production, how to run a space exploration program, or how populations might respond to different systems of government.

INSPIRE (INFLUENCE AND MOTIVATE)

What inspires you? Is it a great political speech? An act of heroism? Someone with integrity? A thousand-year-old tree? A great professional athlete? A well-written story or a powerful painting? Lyrics from a pop song or the guy at Benihana's who can flip a shrimp across the table directly onto your plate?

Certainly we are inspired in many ways, but probably few people would say, "I was inspired by video games" in the same way they might say, "I was inspired by Michael Jordan" (or Martin Luther King, Jr., or the first moon landing). Too bad. In fact, I believe that video games can be inspirational, in large and in small ways.

Video games can inspire by the stories they tell, by the situations they model, by the characters they bring to life, and by the consequences of players' actions. They can inspire by the heroism of the characters, by their sacrifices, by the horrors they can depict, or even by the simple act of placing minority characters in positive roles. Video games can also inspire by presenting new information that players want to explore further, such as history or math or science or even social environments.

In combination with teaching, modeling, and simulating, video games can provide positive and inspiring learning environments. All that is needed to increase the inspirational qualities of video games is vision—and the inspiration to provide these experiences.

THE NEXT STEP

What I call the Next Step is really very simple. It is not a whole new technology or a hypermodern new gaming system. It is not even a shift in morality among game companies. It is, however, a new paradigm at a very basic level. Stated in the simplest terms, *the Next Step is a perspective that inspires game designs and concepts with positive impact models.*

It's not necessary for every game to have positive impact on players. It's not necessary for every designer to become an altruist or a social worker. It is possible, however, for game designers to ask themselves how their games will impact players, not only in the obvious ways but in the TMSI ways described here. Can they teach, model, simulate, and/or inspire players with something that, at the end of the day, makes a positive impact on players' lives, in addition to the obvious entertainment they receive?

The question any interested designers might ask is, "What more can I do to deepen the human impact of this game?" Seen another way, they might strive for the subtle power of a long legacy of art and culture, of which they might be the latest culmination. Can video games be the next great art form? Will they come to rival, in their own terms and using their own methods, the great art that has inspired humanity for centuries? Could some video games be considered among the great artistic accomplishments of history—Shakespeare's plays, Picasso's *Guernica*, Swift's *Gulliver's Travels*, Beethoven's Ninth, Michelangelo's *Pietà*, the ceiling of the Sistine Chapel, Arthur Miller's *Death of a Salesman*, Margaret Mitchell's *Gone with the Wind*, or any of the works of inspiration and genius that have affected generations of people?

To suggest that video games could possibly live up to humanity's greatest legacies may be asking a lot. In doing so, I'm suggesting not that game designers must succeed but that, if they are open to the idea, they might consider using the tools of the Magic Edge and TMSI to strive for such greatness. In doing so, who knows what they might accomplish?

Finally, I think it bears repeating: video games are definitely not a replacement for life, nor are they a replacement for teachers and a good education system. Video games are a leisure activity, separate from work, school, family responsibilities, society, and basic survival. Play in the real world can be very satisfying, whether it is a pick-up game of basketball on the local court, a golf or tennis session, or a weekly poker night out with the "boys" (or the "girls"). Some of these nonvideo games are probably more beneficial overall than others, healthier for the body, the brain or the psyche. Games can also have a destructive side—such as gambling and losing your money, overextending yourself and getting injured, becoming obsessed with play at the cost of other aspects of life, and so on. Playing in any context involves balance and self-awareness.

Video games, similarly, should not be a way of life that eliminates physical action, productive accomplishments, and in-person learning and socialization. Yet, video games can be not only a really entertaining activity but they can also effect positive change and benefit to players and to society at large. The Next Step is designing games with those purposes in mind—the topic of the next chapter.

Chapter 6

BETTER GAMES, BY DESIGN

Design is not just what it looks like and feels like. Design is how it works.

−Steve Jobs

From their earliest days to the present, video games have influenced players. They can't help it. They are, by their nature, learning environments. It is the part of the interactive process that entails players influencing the game as the game is also influencing them. Through the power of the Magic Edge and TMSI, video games provide an experiential environment in which players are learning and using different types of thinking while developing new skills, new imagery, and new ideas.

Video games are a combination of technologies that include digital graphic design and animation, programming, artificial intelligence, and game design. It is the game design element that takes prominence in this book, because, like programming and digital animation, game design at its core is a technology, and as such, it can be used to accomplish a variety of purposes—entertainment being only the most obvious.

This chapter introduces some specific ways that video games can accomplish various TMSI goals, whether in games with specific educational intention or in games primarily concerned with entertainment (see Chapter 8 for video games that use the technology of games to accomplish specific educational purposes). It goes one step further than the previous chapter by introducing several specific elements of game design in which the TMSI approach can surface—namely, context, inclusion, role modeling, and story elements. Each of these components can be used to convey meaningful information and experience to the person playing. Anyone seeking to understand how video games work and how to identify what is happening within the game will benefit from understanding these basic design principles.

CONTEXT

One of the easiest ways to make an activity vital and relevant is to place it in a vital and relevant context that motivates a person or provides specific meaning to the activity. The key question "Why should I do this?" can be answered in a nearly endless variety of ways within video games: "Because I am a bloodthirsty beast who wants to kill every living thing I see." "Because I have been falsely accused of a crime and I seek justice." "Because I must rescue someone who has been kidnapped." "Because the enemy will destroy the world and kill millions of innocent people if I don't stop them." "Because I am guiding my civilization to success through innovation and good diplomatic decision making."

Context is often used in video games to provide motivation and, in some cases, justification. If the character you play is motivated entirely by selfishness and greed, you will most likely play a game from that perspective. If the character you play is motivated by a sense of right and wrong or if you operate from a moral high ground, you will most likely play from that perspective. This is not to say that games are necessarily better if the player is given some high-minded context. Sometimes being given much more ambiguous contexts can create much better games. Other times, reversing the context is very effective.

On the other side of the coin, if you're playing a hit man in a game, then your role involves killing people. That's the bottom line. Perhaps the victims are bad people and deserve to be killed, or you are working for the "good" side. This is weak justification, perhaps, but we have all seen the same scenario played out in movies where we rooted for the good guys—even killers—to defeat the bad guys. The ever-popular James Bond series comes to mind, for one, but even less morally justifiable characters appear often in novels and movies as heroes and antiheroes. Consider the popularity of the characters in a movie like *Pulp Fiction*, clearly bad guys but made in the movie to be amusing and, in a sick way, sympathetic. An even better example might be *The Silence of the Lambs*, in which the cannibalistic killer Hannibal Lecter stole the show with his wit, cleverness, and charm as played by Anthony Hopkins. Lecter was working with FBI agent Clarice Starling (played by Jodie Foster) to help track down another serial killer. Repellent as this man might be, by setting him in the context of "helping" the good guys, making him so charming and seductive, and playing him against Foster's character, he became an intriguing, highly popular character. Showtime's series *Dexter* is similar in that it features a serial killer (presumably reformed) working for the good guys, and of course HBO's *The Sopranos* is a wildly popular romp into the lives of Mafia bosses. Some readers might find these examples distasteful, but both *Pulp Fiction* and *Silence of the Lambs* were highly successful and point to the fact that it isn't always the knight in shining armor who can capture our attention, not to mention our loyalty.

In video games, such less savory protagonists are also fairly common. These characters may have personal motivations and stories that justify the player's involvement and identification with them even though they may violate the mores and behaviors of society at large. They make good video game characters for a variety of reasons: They may have powers that ordinary people do not have, and superhuman powers are always fun in games. They may allow players to transgress and explore darker aspects of their natures and, significantly, to play the roles of characters vastly unlike themselves. Yet, in almost all cases, the player is also playing within a specific context that makes sense for that character. Context is where the *meaning* of the action changes. For instance, a vampire who kills simply out of malice is different from one who kills in a quest to cure himself or herself or to accomplish some selfless goal.

In the end, context is just a tool, but it is one that can change mindless responses to meaningful ones. Context can be used to provide player motivation and deepen players' involvement, challenge beliefs and morals, justify otherwise questionable actions (or at least suggest justification), and make situations clearer and more understandable—or ambiguous and intriguing. Through the simple act of considering context in games, a designer can dramatically shape the message and impact of the game. Because context makes such a difference, it is one of the most powerful tools of video game design and storytelling in general.

INCLUSION

Inclusion is more subtle than context as a tool. Inclusion is literally what you include, but by extrapolation, that also means what you leave out. The nature of inclusion often comes into play in communications between people, such as where a lie can simply be an omission of important facts, or where a successful negotiation can occur by the inclusion of some significant part of an offer.

In video game terms, *inclusion* refers to the choices that game designers make about what they put in a game and what they leave out. Imagine a situation in a game where the player confronts a man in a house. The man is perhaps aggressive or, at any rate, not friendly to the player. If the player fights with the man, possibly kills him, or if the player steals something from the man, there is a context of the player against the man. Probably the player will feel some emotional response—regret or remorse or, often, pride and satisfaction at winning. Chances are they won't feel too bad about their actions in this context. After all, the man was aggressive to begin with. (Remember, this is a video game. If players can enter a region or location, they assume there is something to be gained there, and the designers intended them to check it out. Breaking and entering in video games is generally different from its counterpart in the real world.)

Now change the scene slightly. Include a wife and child in the house. The same man may be acting the same way, and the player still has the same choices. But will the player make the same decisions given the presence of the wife and child? Fewer players will rob or kill the man with the family present. Including the family changes the context, and changing the context affects the player's decisions.

In the same situation, imagine instead of a wife and child included in the scenario, a demon that seems to have the man under its control. Would the player still kill the man or, realizing that it isn't the man who is responsible for the aggression, try to eliminate the demon instead, thereby freeing the man from enslavement? Inclusion again changes the context and changes the player's decisions and experience.

You may ask, "Don't these examples invalidate the concept you mentioned in the first chapter, that players don't see game characters as real?" Yes and no. Where the "people" in a game are used as obstacles, such as enemy soldiers, they are clearly vehicles to advance the action and challenges to the player's goals. The majority of video game violence is of this sort. In some settings, however, characters can have more individuality and personality. They are not merely props. In such contexts, players can feel emotions about those characters as they would in a story or fairy tale, and games that allow violence toward these characters can, by context, either reinforce moral values or violate them. In either case, the player is the one deciding and also feeling the emotions involved. The lessons learned, if any, are based on the player's own morality mixed with their in-game character's motivations. There could be negative results from encouraging antisocial behavior; at the same time, there could be cathartic results from exploring our darker natures, as suggested in books such as Bruno Bettelheim's *Uses of Enchantment* and Gerard

Jones's *Killing Monsters*.[1] So far, no definitive research proves one theory or the other, and I suspect there's some truth in both, depending on circumstances.

While inclusion in game design affects the "meaning" of the situation, it can also affect the choices available to the player. For instance, suppose the player is in a dangerous situation: someone is coming to try to kill him or her. Including a gun or other weapon in the player's environment presents an obvious solution, but what about including a telephone instead of a weapon? What if there's a phone book or possibly a pizza parlor menu on a desk nearby? Notice that the player might still use the telephone as a weapon, but other options also may present themselves, such as calling for help or ordering a pizza delivery to act as a diversion so that the player can escape. Maybe the player can call the killer and negotiate; maybe they even discover that they are on the same side and form an alliance against some other danger.

Take another, perhaps more subtle example. Suppose the player is walking through a village or on a city street. There's probably a certain amount of traffic, plus shops and merchants and people passing by, hard at work, walking purposefully to unknown destinations, or loitering. Many video games feature certain shops that the player can enter and certain, generally predictable, types of characters with whom the player can interact. Suppose, contrary to the usual stereotypes, the player happens on a confrontation between a man and his wife—an altercation in which the two seem to be unable to communicate effectively. At this point, we have a situation not atypical of real life but certainly not typical of video games, and different enough to catch the player's attention.

Going further with this example, suppose the player can actually attempt to mediate the couple's argument and help them resolve their issue. In this case, the player might learn something about how to communicate and how to mediate a dispute—good skills to have in real life. The player might also learn to recognize ineffective patterns of communication by observing the dysfunctional couple.

To make the mediation scenario more interesting, successfully helping the couple might result in a meaningful reward to the player. Some types of games do present apparently random events that lead to positive benefits for players who deal with them effectively. These events are often unrelated to the players' main goals and are therefore completely optional.

Another scenario of battling spouses, though less interactive, would be to have a third character (computer controlled) come up to the couple and allow the player to observe how he or she mediates successfully. This would be a case of modeling medi-ation and good communication. The first example would be actually teaching through skills practice, goals, and rewards. The second example, though more passive, would present a learning opportunity for the player. Perhaps later in the game, the player would have another opportunity to step into a dispute, perhaps one even more significant to the storyline, and this time it would be the player's job to mediate and resolve the dispute. What they were able to learn by observing the mediation model would then come in handy and would become practical, experiential knowledge.

All of these examples rely on designers recognizing that they could include, or not include, specific elements in the game and, by choosing to include more interesting options, they present new opportunities that can dramatically affect the player's experience.

ROLE MODELING

Three types of role modeling can occur in games:

- Modeling roles
- Depicting roles
- Specific role playing

Each of these types of role modeling can change the impact of the game on the player.

MODELING ROLES: BEHAVIOR, SKILLS, OR KNOWLEDGE

The section on inclusion presented an example in which a nonplayer character entered a scene and helped a couple resolve an argument. In that example, the mediator character was modeling a role for the player. Another example might occur when a player observes a nonplayer character doing some martial arts moves or successfully navigating a difficult and challenging sequence of actions. The player may learn some new techniques or tactics through observation.

Modeling behavior or skills by observation isn't too common in video games, but it isn't totally unheard of. A few video games have allowed players to learn from what they observed in the game, and certainly players are always learning through observation, though not always in the role-playing sense. In multiplayer games, for instance, players often observe and learn from the successful strategies and techniques of their teammates or their adversaries.

We have previously discussed how characters might model useful skills, such as in the mediation example. Similarly, characters in video games might model good business practices, such as effective management, or even kindness, generosity, courage, and integrity. How the characters act in video games can send a message, and ultimately that message is entirely under the control of the people who create the games, the characters, and the situations.

DEPICTING ROLES (CHARACTER DEPICTION)

Another type of role modeling involves how we depict characters in games. For instance, in an extreme example, if all the villains were white skinned and all the heroes were black skinned, obviously we would be getting a message about good and bad associated with skin color.

Although video games are not generally so literally black and white, they often create and continue to reinforce stereotypes in games. In many American and European games, the hero is typically white and muscle-bound. In Japanese role-playing games, the heroes are often children, most often male, though sometimes female. You rarely see a player as a soldier who is tall and thin or short and stocky, even though most real-life soldiers, even very famous ones, were anything but athletic superheroes.

As discussed in Chapter 1, women in video games are often depicted as victims or as sex objects. While women's roles in video games may have expanded to include more heroic female characters, there's a lot of room for improvement in how women are depicted in video games if our goal is to promote equality and respect.

In a society of appearances, it may be difficult to create heroes who do not conform to standards of attractiveness. We choose our movie stars, at least in part, because they are handsome or beautiful. Video games are designed to appeal to the same people that movies, television shows, and advertising are aimed at, and they reflect the same values and public interests. On the other hand, a few video games have been able to create main characters who defied these conventions. One excellent example is Abe from Abe's Oddysee and Abe's Exoddus. Abe was, by any standards of beauty I can imagine, an ugly character. In fact, when I first saw him, I thought he was downright repellent. Yet, because of the games' excellent game design, graphics, and story, I soon found Abe to be a sympathetic and appealing hero, not only because he defies stereotypes of appearance but also because he is nonviolent and has no ability to fight at all, contrary to many accepted video game conventions.

Villains in video games (as in movies) also tend to be stereotyped physically as well as ethnically. Few video game villains are subtle or ambiguous. Video games often want to be sure the player is strongly motivated to defeat the enemy, and so enemies are generally mindlessly or diabolically evil. Occasionally, such stereotypes are avoided, such as in Halo 2, where the player first controls a human hero, then, as the game progresses, he or she controls the alien hero, experiencing both points of view in an interstellar war. The humans and the aliens, players discover, are equally vicious, each convinced of the rightness of their individual and species' course of action.

Role depiction in games does not concern only the character the player controls, as in the case of Lara Croft, whom the player controls and who represents a primarily positive female role. Other characters advise and befriend a player's character or play otherwise positive roles. Still others are antagonistic to the player or even quite evil. How are these additional characters depicted? Here's an opportunity for video games to break stereotypes and put people from different cultures, ethnic groups, and any other subgroup in positive roles where they have largely not been placed before, and to consider how these different groups have been depicted previously in games.

SPECIFIC ROLE PLAYING

The third type of role modeling entails actual role playing. In nearly all video games, players in some ways project into the personality of the character they play (see Chapter 4)—for example, when the player, through his or her character, is given a specific role to assume in the game. Of course, players have a primary role throughout the game. They are the hero of the story, though "hero" in video game terms can take on several different connotations. In any case, it is the player, through the character he or she plays, who makes choices and ultimately drives the game forward.

The player may also be given other roles that are separate from or in addition to the main role. Let's return to our earlier example of a man and wife arguing, with the player stepping in to act as a mediator. In this sense, the player has stepped into the role of mediator through his or her character.

In another case, the player might have the opportunity to help a failing business by taking over its finances or operations. This might be a necessary aspect of succeeding in the game, or it might be what is called a *side quest*, a nonessential activity that players can electively pursue. Side quests generally result in some game-related reward, but sometimes the fun and experience of the side quest is worth more than any tangible gain the player gets. In these examples, the player is, for a time, role-playing a conflict resolution mediator or a businessperson practicing the skills of running a business. In a strictly educational context (i.e., a classroom), many people might consider such activities "boring," but within a game context, those same activities could provide interesting, intriguing challenges and even be fun. Because of the Magic Edge described in Chapter 5, game players don't think about the value of role plays in educational terms. They're simply part of the game.

Role-playing a business owner is a great example of how video game role-playing can go beyond the video game association with violence and antisocial themes. In the previous example, the player might encounter an incidental opportunity to role-play a business manager while playing a game whose ultimate goals and activities are not about running a business. However, several successful games focus entirely on running a business and place players in the business owner role. Many of these games contain the word tycoon in their title, such as Railroad Tycoon, Rollercoaster Tycoon, Zoo Tycoon, and even Pizza Tycoon. In The Movies, players get to be film industry executives guiding a studio from its inception in the early twentieth century to modern times, if they can keep it afloat. Even the fun casual game Diner Dash offers some simplistic lessons on running (literally and figuratively) a business.

When the player is allowed to role-play a specific character in a story, it enables positive identification and understanding. Consider if the player could role-play more than one character in the same situation. I call this the "Rashomon effect," after Akira Kurosawa's 1950 epic movie, which depicts a controversial rape and murder incident from each participant's point of view. This landmark film was one of the first to explore the fact that reality can be very subjective and truth often hard to identify. In video games, players can actually "be" the different roles and "act" from the perspectives of different characters in the same situation—for instance, in a crime drama or in a domestic violence scenario, as I will discuss later on.

STORY ELEMENTS

Not all video games have stories. Puzzle games, such as the very popular Bejeweled, have no plot. A nondigital game like Monopoly or a card game like bridge has no real story, though there is an experience that creates, for each player, an unfolding story in real time.

Some video games offer only the most basic story to motivate the player. For instance, the story of the landmark game Doom was essentially: "You are a space marine in an abandoned facility swarming with vicious alien creatures. Your task is to clean up and sterilize the station. Good luck." Doom's story is typical of many shoot-'em-up games, where all you need is a context but little in the way of plot. The action determines the game play. Such minimalist story contexts work fine for video games because, in essence, the player creates the story by experiencing it. In the player's mind, each encounter is a new chapter in the ongoing story, and nuances of character, role reversals, red herrings, or mysterious events may happen organically as part of the game play, not necessarily because designers wrote them in. The story of Doom is, for each player individually, an unfolding story of one player's heroism and skill in defeating numerous enemies.

Despite the fact that a game like Doom sounds rather uninspiring as the platform for great fiction, consider that its synopsis is not too different from a synopsis of the movie *Alien*. What made *Alien* and its sequel great movies?

In *Alien*, the simple premise is aided considerably not only by its intense atmosphere and powerful HR Giger-inspired graphics, but by the inclusion of strong characters, plot twists, drama, danger, and excitement. Without the characters—say, with Ripley alone in the story—the movie could have been a thriller with some appeal, but it certainly wouldn't have been nearly as powerful as it turned out. Characters drove the story and provided a larger context for the plot and for Ripley's character and conflicts.

Characters, conflicts, plot twists, mysteries—these are all story elements that can make any story better. They work also in some video games, and using them creatively can offer opportunities for those games to be far more powerful and to have more impact on players. With the power of story elements, all kinds of issues, skills, points of view, scientific facts, historical perspectives, and much more, can be included through character interaction and through plot elements.

Video games are different from other media when it comes to stories, however. Because video games are interactive experiences that, to be any good, must provide players with meaningful choices, their stories are most effective when they are the least predetermined or linear. That is, video games are best when they offer range and opportunities for different types of interactions and results. Many movie actors doing voices for video games have been shocked to find that the scripts are generally at least four times as long as typical movie scripts. The game scripts must take into account the myriad choices that players can make.

Some video game designers argue that the only good game stories are "emergent" stories, meaning a story that develops as a consequence of what the player does in the game world, as in the previous example of Doom, and not something the designer has predetermined. For instance, if you take a kindergarten class and hand out Native American garb and Pilgrim outfits and tell the kids exactly what to do in a reenactment of the meeting of John Smith and Pocahontas or the Thanksgiving story that they learned in school, you will likely get an adorable but fairly predictable, uninspired performance. Hand those same kids the same props and tell them to make up their own story, and who knows what will happen? Probably the outcome will be less predictable and considerably more lively. Do the same thing in a video game where their imaginations are not limited by physical reality, and you could expect even more unpredictable and creative results.

In another example, suppose two football teams were given an exact script of what plays they would use throughout the game. They could not deviate from the script, although there would be provisions for different situations. Suppose every game played by every football team followed that same script. Somehow I doubt that football would be nearly as exciting or unpredictable (or popular) as it is today. It is the creative adaptation to the circumstances of the game—to the ebb and flow, the score, the field position, the wind direction, and much more—that makes each football game a unique event, where "on any given Sunday," as they say, any team can defeat any other.

Like the kindergarten play and the football teams, video games can provide the props, the characters, and the settings for players and allow them, through their choices and interactions, to make the game's story come to life. In this setting, the emergent story will be directly related to what the player chooses to do, and it will be different when the player makes different choices. This is an example of very good game design because not only is the player the primary actor in the game, but the game can be played over and over again with different results. Every free-form kindergarten play will be different. Every game between two football teams will be unique. And every time through a video game will, likewise, provide a different experience.

Some games combine emergent stories with more traditional story elements by including *quests* or *missions*—specific tasks the player must take to reveal a previously hidden area of the game or new play options, and to receive certain rewards, such as money, items, skills, awards and recognition, or even the ability to advance further in the game. Even quests and missions may offer different outcomes based not on merely completing a quest or mission but on how the players complete it. For instance, what choices did they make, what specific actions did they take, and what actually happened? Did someone die? Did they complete the quest without being discovered by the enemy? Did they leave witnesses? Did they obtain or destroy an item or machine or something that might later be significant? What if they failed? Does the story progress in a different but no less interesting way?

Game stories can involve many complex plots, variations and interrelated consequences, which is both a part of the challenge of creating good games and one of the ways that games can offer such rich experiences for players. By clever and intentional use of these story elements and techniques, designers have the option to create games with solid entertainment value and many kinds of positive secondary effects.

Let's return to our argumentative couple from previous examples. Suppose the player is successful and helps them resolve their conflict. What kind of reward or show of gratitude might the couple offer? Perhaps they have nothing to offer but a thank you. To make the game more interesting, perhaps they could offer something more tangible from the gamer's perspective, such as secret information the player can use to explore new areas of the game that would otherwise have been ignored. They might give him a mysterious artifact that itself leads to great adventures, discoveries, powers, and rewards. Or they might invite the player to their home, where they turn out to be vampires that the player now has to defeat or escape.

Suppose, on the other hand, that the player fails to help the couple and, in fact, manages to turn them both against him or her. What consequences might result from this outcome? Perhaps they would fight. Maybe only the player's reputation would be damaged, as the couple spread the news of how this busybody interfered in their private affairs. Perhaps in their anger, they would blurt out something that has meaning to the player and leads to some important discovery—a discovery that would not have been revealed if the player had succeeded with the couple.

One event in the game can lead to all kinds of story possibilities, yet the player might have walked by the arguing couple and done nothing, in which case another story would have unfolded. No other entertainment medium can offer such a broad range of choices from a simple event, because in other media, the story must be predetermined. In video games, the story emerges from the players' choices and actions, success and failure, and, in some cases, the specific abilities that they have developed for their virtual characters.

Much like in real life, the choices players make can determine the story they live. And the choices that designers make can determine what players can take away from the game experience. Using story elements breaks open the box of possibilities and allows video games to involve players in almost any kind of situation or activity.

SITUATIONAL LEARNING AND SKILLS PRACTICE

Video games are all about situations. Some game situations are abstract. For instance, a puzzle game might provide a certain number of letters from which to form words or offer objects of specific colors or shapes to match in order to score points. In contrast, many games provide situations that have real-world parallels, and these types of situations lend themselves quite well to what I call *situational learning*, although a similar academic concept is called *situated learning*.[2]

Whenever someone is practicing and attempting to master skills, learning is taking place. What I propose is that video games can present situations in which specific skills useful in real life are learned and practiced, making situational learning and skills practice another powerful tool for learning and positive secondary impact on players.

How might this work?

Suppose a player is involved in a life-or-death adventure, as often occurs in video games, and to survive the player must find a way to activate a particular machine. Perhaps the machine is needed to analyze a piece of evidence or to activate a defense system that will activate the defenses required to survive an imminent invasion. Whatever the machine is used for, it needs electricity, and the power is down. Now the player must find a way to get the power working again.

This kind of puzzle is not unusual in some sorts of video games, but the solutions are often very simplistic and don't require the player to learn anything about electrical circuits or wiring. Suppose, instead of an easy solution, the game required the player to find tools that could trace where the current is broken, then open the wall where the break has occurred and splice the wire. Suppose the player does that without first turning off the main breaker. Electrocution. First lesson: don't repair wiring when it is "hot." Now the player may use the great "saved game" redo option and try again. This time the player has learned about electricity and turns off the breaker before attempting the splice. Everything goes well, except that when the power is turned on again, the player's crude splice causes a short circuit and blows everything out. Back to the breaker, where, finding some electrical tape, the player secures the splice so that it can't cause another short circuit. Possibly this scenario could also have resulted in some damage to machinery from the short circuit, but we'll give the player a break and assume that power is restored and the operation is a success.

In this simple scenario, which many game players would be willing to explore, the player has learned what tools to use to identify a break in an electrical line, how to open a wall to expose the wire (presumably in a way that doesn't do too much damage), how to turn off a breaker before repairing the line, how to splice a broken wire, and how to wrap it so it is safe. Depending on how the scenario is developed, the player might have to repair the wall as well. If this situation is based on accurate information, players will have learned something that could actually come in handy. At minimum, I'll bet they won't try to play with electrical wires without turning off the breaker in the real world, because they actually died trying it, however virtually. Such "deaths" do make an impression. Players don't like it when their characters die, so they tend to remember the conditions that lead to such events—a necessary skill when playing video games if you have any hope of winning.

Countless other situational learning opportunities arise in games. The example I gave previously about mediating a family argument is one. Creating a job interview or negotiation scene in a game is entirely plausible, and this context could be used to help people learn more about how to interview for a job or how to negotiate effectively. If the situation is accurately depicted, players will be able to take away something that could help them in real life. And the beauty of it is that players will do it for fun, not thinking "I'm learning skills here" but "If I succeed in this scenario, I will get a reward or will get closer to achieving my goals in this game."

Scientific and Historical Accuracy

In the examples offered for situational learning and skills practice, I argued that the actual details of the situation must be accurate and based on real-world criteria to be useful beyond the game. Otherwise, they are just puzzles to solve without any relevance outside the entertainment value they offer.

Not everything in a game has to be scientifically or historically accurate, but in certain types of games, such accuracy leads to much better game play and more useful results outside the game. In Larry Holland's World War II simulations (Battlehawks: 1942, Battle of Britain, and Secret Weapons of the Luftwaffe), Holland did considerable research and depicted a very carefully detailed experience for players that, as accurately as possible, reflected what it was like to fly a Spitfire or a Messerschmitt during the Battle of Britain, a P-38 or a Zero in the Pacific war, or even a B-17 or the German experimental jet Me 262 over Germany. Moreover, he offered considerable historical detail in the manuals accompanying the three games, such that players of these combat flight games got a real sense of history from playing them. In order to assure that his games were accurate, Holland not only did his own research but also worked with military historians.

Historical accuracy is becoming more and more common in war games, such as the Medal of Honor series, which are based on real events, and also in historically based strategy games, such as the Age of Empires games, which combine entertainment and some real information about specific cultures or historical periods. Unless a game is entirely based on a fictional world or one that we cannot know accurately, the more accurate the information, the better.

Scientific accuracy is a great way to teach players about physics, chemistry, biology, and a variety of other subjects as they surface within game scenarios. In fact, physics is being represented more and more accurately all the time in video games, thanks to improved game technology. When cars crash or a bat hits a baseball, a spaceship hits a gravity well or a bullet hits a wall, game makers can now very accurately model what would happen based on principles of physics such as mass, velocity, angles of impact, friction, and so forth. The challenge is to use this ability to enhance learning that players will be able to apply outside the game environment. For example, if the factors of tire traction are accurately depicted in driving games, players can learn about driving cars with different types of tires on different road surfaces or about the effect of traction on the driving characteristics of different cars. Although we all live with real-world physics all the time, in video games we have opportunities to experiment and learn from actions and situations that we would not likely encounter in ordinary life—or even to experiment with situations that we might encounter and discover what might happen if we take different approaches.

A higher degree of accuracy means a higher degree of correlation between the gamer's experience and his or her understanding of the real world. It also suggests the possibility of situational learning and skills practice that, when accurate scientifically and procedurally, can actually teach players within the game-playing context.

SOCIAL MODELING AND ARTIFICIAL INTELLIGENCE

Like accuracy in science and history, accuracy in social models is also important, though perhaps more complex to achieve. The more realistically game characters can respond to the world around them, to other characters, and, in particular, to player interactions, the more possibilities there are for helping people learn social skills such as good family dynamics, effective communication, and successful negotiation and mediation. Even such difficult issues as domestic violence and abuse could be modeled within video games to help people learn more about their causes and how to respond to such situations.

Social skills are frequently modeled in games. For instance, a gamer could play an employee seeking a raise, a boss who wants to motivate his workers or who has to break bad news to them and win them to his side, even a child who needs to deal with a bully at school. One common scenario in multiplayer games is how to share the rewards (loot) obtained from group activities. Often players must practice negotiation skills simply within the context of such discussions.

Modeling social interchanges in video games is not easy. People are far more complicated than machines, and so far the state of artificial intelligence falls short of modeling realistic human behavior. The alternative is to program all the exact responses of the artificial character. Although reasonably effective in a simplistic model, this approach is necessarily limited by the programmer's knowledge of human behavior, time to program every complex possibility, and money to develop the game design until it is reliable and effective. This method of creating artificial personalities is a little like trying to create a functioning human brain by physically piecing together the individual cells.

In time, human artificial intelligence will get more and more accurate. Meanwhile, experts in communications fields can work with game designers and programmers to provide accurate models for social interchanges, or the designers themselves can research and learn about specific communications subjects. Video game designers have proven in many of their games that they have the ability to research and incorporate new information to their craft. Given that, I believe all that is needed is, first, the realization that social skills can be modeled, taught, and practiced in video games and, then, the motivation to make it so.

SOCIAL CONTACT

According to Electronic Arts founder Trip Hawkins, "All media is more about contact than content. I think you can make the case that we don't read books, for instance, to become enlightened, knowledgeable, or wise but to have more to talk with other people about. In the end, it's all about contact."[3]

From the beginning, many video games have been inherently social. Can you imagine a game of Pong (or tennis) without another player? I've tried to work both Pong paddles, successfully, but it's boring. Without someone else, Pong is not much of a game. With another player, on the other hand, it's still a hoot, even after thirty-five years.

Online gaming revolutionized the game industry by opening up the possibilities of social gaming that had never before existed. Sure, people have always gathered around at someone's house to play cards or charades or any number of social games, but it was pretty much a requirement that everyone involved lived nearby. What online games have done is to eliminate the geographic barriers and throw the doors wide open.

It took a few years for the necessary technology to get in place, but today, in most parts of the United States and Europe and all over the Far East, people regularly play games with other players who may live miles or continents away from each other. They may play in small-scale games with as few as four and as many as twenty players at a time, or they may play with thousands of other players in the same virtual world.

In addition to opening geographic boundaries, social game play knocks down less tangible boundaries as well. Online games can place people—a few, dozens, even thousands, as noted—from very different areas, with very different world-

views, and even living in very different conditions together in a common experience. While they are having the shared video game experience, players often begin
to exercise that wonderful human quality—curiosity. Through curiosity they learn
about other people—people who would never have been able to drop by for some
social gaming in days gone by. The potential for sharing ideas and perspectives
among diverse populations is one of the great unintended benefits of video games.

Video games bring people together by putting them in the same game world
and facilitating their communications through chat or voice interfaces. People
meet, play with or against each other, or simply hang out in a virtual space where
they talk and socialize. Many game players form real bonds with other players and
often communicate outside the games. Players can talk through typing or using
voice technologies, exploring not only the game world but all subjects under the
sun. (One unexpected result—another secondary learning effect—of such interaction is that many young people playing social video games become exceptionally
adept typists who can even carry on typed conversations while simultaneously
engaged in battling monsters or running through a complex landscape.) Players
often become real-world friends—or more: marriages have become more and
more common as a result of in-game interactions.

People who meet first in video games and later get married sometimes report
that they would not have been interested in their current partner if they had met
them in other circumstances. In the game, they learned what kind of person they
were interacting with. Were they trustworthy, kind, generous, or clever? What
were their values and beliefs? Clothed in the virtual bodies of heroes and heroines,
people sometimes can get to know the essence of someone in ways that they might
have missed in the flesh. They might be exploring deadly territories together,
watching each other's back, seeking adventure, reward, and conflict; but at the
same time, they may be learning who they really are. Such deeper relationships
take time and don't happen in every encounter. However, they do point out that
the depth of social interaction in video games can be very powerful indeed.

All multiplayer worlds offer players the opportunity to play competitively or
cooperatively with other people, and most also allow and encourage players to create relatively stable groups, often called *guilds*. Social structures give rise to many
fascinating phenomena, with leaders, hierarchical structures, rules and regulations,
and active Web sites containing everything from rumors and gossip to game strategies and stories of the members' exploits. The organizational challenges of these

guilds, which can have hundreds of members, can become full-time jobs, and the social interactions of "belonging" and "membership" offer opportunities to learn—through practice, observation, and experience—useful real-world social skills such as communication, leadership, advocacy, cooperation, and teamwork.

Game players love to express their ideas and opinions about games. They love to share strategies, brag about their accomplishments, and compare notes. They love to play with and against each other. Thus, games can foster greater connections among game players, connections that can take place at home, when a bunch of players get together to play in someone's living room, or online in a variety of ways.

Game discussions often go beyond superficial likes and dislikes, and many sociologists who have studied games call such interactions "meta-games," suggesting that there are really two games going on at once. One is within the game's fictional world and context while the other involves players' relationships, their discussions and examination of rules and rule breaking, and their sometimes detailed discussions of fairness, loyalty, competition, and other relevant social issues. Players engage in trash talking and verbal challenges, but also in supportive comments and what would, on the sports field, be called "good sportsmanship."

The importance of social structures is well understood by the video game industry, which includes many well-designed tools to allow people to interact as well as to host many online fan sites and forums. Even more significant are approaches by giant game companies like Microsoft, whose Xbox Live and Live Anywhere services link players together in different ways, allowing them to find other players with similar interests, assess their strengths in various games, invite them to play in specific games, and become buddies. Players on Xbox Live can also trade items with other players and form association groups such as guilds and clubs through the Live interface.

Nintendo also recognizes the value of social contact and creates games like Pokémon and Animal Crossing, which allow players to connect their systems, either through physical connections or, more commonly now, wirelessly, and share games and items.

No game can match the complexity of the human mind, and players love to challenge themselves by competing with other players. They also love to play with other people cooperatively, and the range of possible activities with real people is much greater than it is with artificial characters. Real players can offer unusual and unexpected ideas and creative approaches in game contexts. Players carry out mission objectives far better than computer-controlled characters (most of the time), but even failures can be fun. I've been involved in some outright disasters with other characters and ended up laughing for several minutes because it's all so funny. Nothing like that happens when the characters aren't real people.

Socialization within games can be complex and surprising. Players create new social structures that have little to do with the structures they encounter in the real world. Inside the game, a twelve-year-old player can be the equal of a player thirty years old, based on skill and intelligence. The game equalizes people based on age, gender, race, religion, or politics. Surprisingly, players do not care much for braggarts and bullies, and most will jump to defend weaker players and respond with generosity toward new players who honestly ask for guidance. Even within games that feature violence and competition, in my experience most players display generosity and a deep-rooted sense of justice and fairness more often than not.

Video games can always expand in the areas of social interaction. Using multiplayer technologies, video games can offer different types of games that currently don't exist but that challenge not only our eye-hand coordination and strategic decision making, but also our communication abilities and our civic awareness, or even our prejudices and preconceptions. The range of possibilities within the multiplayer game space is still wide open, and it is one of the key factors that future designers will be using to provide fun and positive effects on players.

EMPOWERING/ENABLING PLAYER CREATIVITY

Players are often provided with the opportunity to create and contribute to their games in very personal ways. From the earliest design-your-own-levels programs like Lode Runner and the Pinball Construction Set to today's mod editors, user creativity has always been part of games and continues to be an increasingly important aspect.

Mod editors are programs included with a game that allow players to use some of the game designers' tools to create sophisticated and sometimes completely different versions of the games—called *mods*—which then can be shared with others. Because creating mods requires a lot of hard work and skills, players can learn programming, art, animation, and story/game design as well as project planning and organization skills.

Video simulation games like SimCity actually only become games when players assign their own meaning to the open structure offered to them by creating their own definitions of success and failure. For the most part, it is their own personal goals that make the product a game and not merely a simulation. Putting it another way, it is the imagination and creativity of the player that makes the game fun by giving it meaning.

Video games offer players creative alternatives in many ways. Many video games offer players sometimes very detailed options for their character's looks, gender, clothing, and other items to further distinguish it from others. Character customization is increasingly common in video games and increasingly expected by players.

Role-playing games that use skill systems and character statistics offer players considerable range in how their characters develop. For instance, will they be very strong and slow, but very smart, or will they be not so strong, but very fast and not so smart—or any other combination of strong, fast, smart, agile, charismatic, lucky, and so forth? There are generally trade-offs in such games, but within the limits the game imposes, players can choose the kinds of characters they play and, as a consequence, feel more ownership of these characters.

To me, creativity is a positive benefit of playing such games all by itself. Encouraging people to express themselves and to be creative opens their minds and allows them to think more critically while providing a sense of achievement and accomplishment.

OUTSIDE THE GAME: ADDED VALUE

The experience video gamers have is not limited to what happens inside the game itself. A whole range of involvement extends beyond the game, including, as mentioned earlier, players interacting socially, discussing details of games, learning to create their own games, studying the complex structures of the games, and even participating in the building of new modern myths. Many of these outside activities also provide opportunities for learning and positive effects that occur naturally as a result of the players' involvement.

MODS: LEARNING TO PROGRAM, PLAN, AND CREATE

As noted previously, today's video games often come with special programs called mod editors, which are in some cases very close to the same tools that the original designers used to make the game itself. Players can use these editors to create mods—games of their own or "levels" of the game the editor supports. These editors range in complexity and depth, but some have the capability of creating games that would eclipse almost any game from the early 1990s, at least in technical and graphical terms. The game play is still up to the designer.

Most mod editors are not simple to use, though they try to make the process of creation easy. Despite that, creating a game or level with an in-game editor requires a variety of skills, including good planning, programming and art skills (in many cases), computer-related skills, storytelling, continuity tracking, and project management, to name a few. Anyone who can successfully make a good mod of a game has practiced skills that are useful in other aspects of his or her life and has demonstrated considerable abilities for envisioning a project and carrying it out.

Admittedly, not all players' mods are created equal. Some are far better than others, but when they are good, they are very, very good—so good, in fact, that they can become huge commercial successes on their own. So good that many game companies actually hire players who have created good mods based almost solely on that accomplishment. In time, I wouldn't be surprised if other businesses don't begin to recognize the abilities of "modders" and begin to seek them out as, in the early days of computer programming, IBM hired musicians because they saw a correlation between music ability and programming. The correlations between modding and creative project planning and management, not to mention self-motivation and persistence, are obvious.

RESEARCH AND WRITING

Game playing may also encourage research and writing, at least in some players, counterintuitive as it seems. First, many players read a lot about the games they play. They learn to search the Internet for information about the games they want to play, as well as cheat codes, FAQs, and strategy tips about games. They buy strategy guides and read them cover to cover, absorbing the most complex statistical data and making sense of some very complex relationships. They learn to read maps and often to create their own.

How much does all this writing and research impact game players beyond game playing? It's not clear that they will actually research other subjects voluntarily, but they may gain skills that come in handy when they do need to find something on the Internet or do school- or work-related research. Because research is a skill that can be learned, video games might contribute in a small way to developing that skill.

Game players also write a lot. They type to each other in online games, and some of them get to be outstanding typists. They also write comments about games and FAQs and detailed strategy guides. None of this writing is required by the games themselves, other than perhaps communication with other players in some online games, but many players do read and write more because of video games than they might have done otherwise, even to the point of offering very thoughtful analytical commentary on the games they play.

I don't want to give the wrong impression. Video games do not replace literature or important textbooks. Reading and writing are skills that may be somewhat enhanced by video game–related experiences, but in terms of literacy as it is taught in schools, grammatical usage, and even spelling, video games are not a panacea or even a close substitute for books and teaching. Though video games should never replace the study of literature, reading, and writing, because they are voluntary and because players may spend a lot of time in games, at least some players may be getting positive literacy and research skills as part of their experience.

MODERN MYTHS AND ARCHETYPES

Every generation and culture creates its mythology, role models, and cultural archetypes. In ancient times, the stories that explained nature and life were based most often on the gods, such as in ancient India, Greece, South America, and many other places and cultures around the world. Later, the monotheistic religions—Judaism, Christianity, and Islam—also created archetypes, stories, and cultural histories.

In addition to religion, social and political ideals have influenced people throughout the ages, such as the democratic ideals of Greece, the empire of Rome, and the sweeping conquests of Alexander the Great and Genghis Khan. Philosophers have had a lasting effect on many different cultures—from Plato and Aristotle, to Maimonides and Lao-tzu, Descartes, and Voltaire, Locke and Hume, to name but a few—as has entertainment (see, e.g., the discussion of storytelling in Chapter 3).

Modern technology has changed how we are influenced. More and more, the influences of East and West have mingled, and our cultural philosophies are influenced by contemporary sources of fiction and entertainment. As the newest kid on the block, video games also have appealed to a generation of players who grew up with them, and they continue to attract new generations growing up today.

Within the world of video games, new cultural icons and archetypes are forming. Mario is the new Mickey Mouse. Pac-Man is arguably the new "smiley face." Lara Croft is arguably the video game world's first sex symbol. Abe (from Abe's Oddysee) is a nonviolent hero fighting oppression and greed. Sonic the Hedgehog frees animals entrapped in robotic shells, rather than killing his enemies. The language and imagery of video games, for better or worse, have become part of the language and imagery of millions of players around the world, and so they can exert considerable influence by becoming the cultural foundations for current and future generations.

Because we are even now creating the imagery and the archetypes that will one day be remembered (or forgotten), it is difficult to know what lasting effect the video game phenomenon will have. Much video game content is clearly based on other forms of entertainment, history, and myth. Many of the characters and ideas featured in video games are simply old ideas recast in a new medium. Whenever a hero protects the innocent against an evil power, that hero is following a long tradition found in stories throughout human history. Video games often feature themes not unlike those of Tolkien's *Lord of the Rings*, in which only the efforts of a heroic character or group can stop an impending doom. Characters in video games often have much in common with fictitious characters such as Zorro or Robin Hood. Others may be more like Napoleon, Beowulf, or Ulysses.

Can video games provide something new and establish some human ideal or thought that hasn't been seen previously? Probably not. What video games can do is provide the new fairy tales, the new morality plays, and new opportunities for current generations to explore themselves—both the "good" and the "bad"—and remember the lessons of humanity. Through new characters and new stories, and through the medium of interactivity, they can experience their modern myths in ways that were not available to our ancestors, often having the opportunity to try more than one side in a situation and, perhaps, understand the motivations and drives of both the hero and the antihero.

Video games today allow players to embark on many interactive "heroic journeys," and perhaps ultimately they will begin, more and more, to model Joseph Campbell's vision of the hero as a complex seeker of truth and self-knowledge, and more and more players will embark, each in his or her own way, on such journeys.[4] Only time will tell if such a future comes to pass and what the real impact of video games will be, but that impact will depend in large part on how video games evolve and how present and future game designers approach their craft.

Chapter 7

PLAYING TO THE FUTURE

Games require players to construct hypotheses, solve problems, develop strategies, learn the rules of the in-game world through trial and error. Gamers must also be able to juggle several different tasks, evaluate risks and make quick decisions. . . . Playing games is, thus, an ideal form of preparation for the workplace of the 21st century, as some forward-thinking firms are already starting to realise.

—*The Economist*, August 4, 2005

A thorough review of the history of video games (which I have done in *High Score: The Illustrated History of Electronic Games*),[1] reveals that video games have contained a lot of very positive information and ideas. When I analyzed games from a historical perspective, I found more than fifty different experiential and inspirational aspects of video games, which included experience with very practical skills in areas like finances, basic economics, running a business, interior design, landscaping, city planning, and investment. I noted several social skills like leadership, cooperative work/play, and relationship building, as well as responsibility to others. Concepts like fairness and justice, patience and restraint are common in many games, as is the idea that actions have consequences. To a lesser degree, history, geography, and other traditional educational subjects were taught, though more experientially than factually. Finally, conceptual skills like pattern recognition, 3D navigation, programming skills, mapping and visualization, creativity, and personal accomplishment can be enhanced by playing video games.

Not all games teach or model the same concepts and skills, and certainly some games teach very little, while others may teach more. Although I think it is important to recognize that commercial video games can have positive effects,

I am more inspired by the idea of expanding that list. Rather than be self-congratulatory, video game producers can use their skills to go further and to provide even greater benefit to people playing their games.

Moreover, I see no limits to what video games can teach, model, simulate, and inspire. For example, the Partnership for 21st Century Skills[2]—which comprises representatives from many organizations, such as Microsoft, Time Warner, and the Ford Motor Company Fund, as well as the American Federation of Teachers, the American Association of School Librarians, and the Corporation for Public Broadcasting—has identified twenty critical skills in four categories that this group thinks will be needed by the professionals and leaders of twenty-first-century business:

21st Century Content
- Global awareness
- Financial, economic, business and entrepreneurial literacy
- Civic literacy
- Health and wellness awareness

Learning and Thinking Skills
- Critical thinking and problem solving skills
- Communication skills
- Creativity and innovation skills
- Collaboration skills
- Information and media literacy skills
- Contextual learning skills

ITC Literacy
- Skills in information and communications technology

Life Skills
- Leadership
- Ethics
- Accountability
- Adaptability
- Personal productivity
- Personal responsibility
- People skills
- Self-direction
- Social responsibility

Although the main emphasis of the Partnership for 21st Century Skills is to advocate for changes in the education system to meet the needs of corporate America, remarkably, every single one of these skills can actually be taught, in one way or another, through games.

If you think I'm kidding, here's some food for thought from John Beck, coauthor of *Got Game? How the New Generation of Video Gamers Is Reshaping Business Forever*: "From the results of our survey of 2,500 businesspeople all over the country, one of the most important variables was, Did you grow up playing video games? Across the board, having grown up playing video games makes you have the attitudes and behaviors that are more like what they teach at Harvard Business School than not having grown up playing video games." Moreover, he says that gamers in business are more sociable and more loyal. They like to win, but they also have the ability to think more strategically and "go meta" to gain perspective on situations. "Because of all these factors, gamers are better prepared to deal with the challenges of the future than any other workforce before them."[3]

Beck's comments may seem surprising, but everything he says is consistent with the kinds of repetitive learning and experience gamers gain while playing. If Beck and others are correct about the current generation of video gamers, then video games are already having a powerful positive impact. How much more might they do with a little focus on the skills people need in society as well as business?

For the rest of this chapter, I look at ways to expand the positive impact of video games in several areas, including school subjects, simulations, social issues, personal issues and growth, business-related skills, and a few others.

This chapter represents only a cursory look at what could be a very detailed design approach, full of specific scenarios and structural game elements far beyond the scope of this book. What I hope you will take away from this chapter is an expanded vision of commercially available video games and their potential.

SCHOOL SUBJECTS

In the commercial game world, where players are simply playing for fun, there is not much opportunity to tailor learning to curriculum goals, to assess the results, or even to teach whole subjects in comprehensive ways. That doesn't mean that commercial video games can't help people learn educational subjects, however, where they can immerse players in various ways and even inspire curiosity so that some players will want to study a subject more deeply after exposure within a game. In these ways, commercial games can become assistants or boosters to school learning in conjunction with teachers, schools, and well-designed curricula.

Through the collaboration of a teacher, whether at school or in the home, video games can be even more powerful. The teacher helps bring lessons learned in the video game to consciousness, pointing them out or challenging students to think more deeply about what they have observed, practiced, or learned. This combination of teacher and video game offers a promising area of exploration in education, but is also worth considering in the home where involved parents can significantly enhance the practical learning potential of video games (see Chapter 9).

MATHEMATICS

Many video games already involve numbers and basic math operations, ranging from simple transactions with merchants and other players to complex formulas used to predict how characters will perform in various game situations. Most players aren't exposed to anything more complex than basic practical math in games, but for some the opportunity exists to delve into ratios, basic algebra, and even some geometry.

Teaching math, of course, requires more than buying and selling, bidding at auctions, or even intuitively understanding complex calculations. Embedding mathematical teaching and practice in games is a challenge, but one that games are well suited for.

One game, Dimenxian from publisher-developer Tabula Digita, puts players in an action setting that designer Robert Clegg describes as "a combination of the movies *The Fly* and *The Pelican Brief*."[4] Using first-person 3D technology, the game simultaneously immerses players in a movielike story and, through the story situations, guides them through learning and practice of basic algebra. And although the game looks and plays like a typical first-person game, the principles of its design are all well researched and geared to allow players to achieve the knowledge necessary to pass their basic algebra requirements in school. Used in conjunction with teaching settings in school, this game is already proving that games can teach academic subjects, not only effectively but with the full and willing participation of students, who will keep playing even after class is over, if they can.

Critics say that the lessons learned in a game like Dimenxian could take nearly an hour to learn, but that using other educational methods, they might take five or ten minutes. In terms of efficiency, this might be true, but that doesn't take into account the very real possibility that kids might play games like Dimenxian at home, in their spare time, and, with help from teachers, they could be learning even more efficiently. Moreover, if some of our discussion in previous chapters about the effects of game chemistry on learning are true, possibly students playing a game to learn these principles could be incorporating the learning even more deeply.

SCIENCE

Simulation games like SimEarth and SimLife, even SimAnt, have already proved that scientific subjects can be taught in simulation-style games. Each of these games was based around very well-researched science, modeling reasonably accurately such diverse subjects as earth science, climate change, atmospheric composition, evolution, and ant behavior.

Practical scientific principles appear in other games, such as those that require some knowledge of basic physics in solving puzzles. Simple puzzles involving reflected light are common, as are others that involve various properties of liquids, gasses and solids. Some games have helped people learn various aspects of geography, while others have taught some basic principles of astronomy, biology, and genetics. Most games feature the effects of gravity, although some allow players to experience different types of gravity.

What has been done barely scratches the surface of what can be done. Principles of biology, chemistry, geology, archaeology, physics, astronomy, medicine, forensics, computer sciences, and even nanotechnology can all be incorporated into video game experiences in various ways.

IMMERSIVE HISTORY

Video games are remarkable history teachers. They don't usually require students to memorize cart loads of facts or write essays on obscure events that happened in the past. With some exceptions, they have no real curriculum at all. What they do provide is the opportunity for players to find out what happened in history by taking part in historical events. They must take on the roles of people engaged in diplomacy or battle. They might be pilots flying in World War I or World War II (e.g.,

Combat Flight Simulator, Red Baron, Battle of Britain, Secret Weapons of the Luftwaffe, and many others). They might be driving a boat through the Mai Lai Delta in Vietnam (Battlefield Vietnam) or leading a Union or Confederate formation in one of the significant battles of the Civil War (Sid Meier's Civil War Collection). They might be Roman legionnaires or even gladiators (Rome: Total War), or Palestinians and Israelis (Peacemaker, Global Conflicts: Palestine), or figures in any historical period (e.g., Mikhail Gorbachev in Crisis in the Kremlin). Or they might play combatants or even ordinary citizens at the time of the Revolutionary War (Revolution, Colonization, Age of Empires III) or in ancient Japan (Shogun: Total Warlord Edition) or China (Romance of the Three Kingdoms, Dynasty Warriors).

Players might also take on the roles of the leaders of countries in times of great political tension, making decisions that lead to peace or war, prosperity or ruin. For instance, they might even play Abraham Lincoln or Jefferson Davis in the Civil War, or Ulysses S. Grant and Robert E. Lee. Or Castro and Kennedy during the Bay of Pigs crisis. They might allow players to imagine what they would do in a leader's place. What would players do if they were allowed to play George Bush today? In video games, the players get to decide policy and action, and they must accept the results, learn from failure as well as success, and gain a personal perspective on the challenges of leadership.

In addition to games like Civilization and the many other historically based war games, history can be even more interesting when it deals with the real dilemmas and decisions made by people in historical times. One game called Revolution was a mod using a mod editor from Never Winter Nights, a fantasy role-playing game. Students at MIT, under the guidance of Professor Henry Jenkins, used the mod editor to create a version of the game that depicted the times of the Revolutionary War in America. Players had to decide, based on the arguments and evidence available at the time, whether to support the fledgling revolution or side with the British. In doing so, they learned more deeply what the real historical context was and what the issues surrounding our Declaration of Independence really were.

What makes a great historical video game is the research the designers do to create it. When a game is well researched, players will learn something from the experience—something they can't learn effectively from books, lectures, or movies. Even if they were to physically reenact some event from history, the experience would necessarily be far more limited than the experience offered in a game, because in games there's no physical risk or danger, and the possibilities are practically endless.

SOCIAL ISSUES

Many people already accept the use of video games in more traditional learning environments, but can they also help teach, model, simulate and inspire people's social skills and understanding? The following section presents some thoughts on how they might do just that.

MODELING DIVERSITY, TOLERANCE, AND HUMAN POLARITIES

I take the position that tolerance and acceptance among different groups of people is a good thing. I also believe that when we have positive encounters with members of human groups that are different from our own, we can come to appreciate what we have in common. When we role-play or interact with people of different cultural or social groups in well-designed video games, we have an opportunity to understand what they believe, why they believe it, how they perceive other groups, and what motivates them to behave or act in specific ways.

By picking roles that create positive role models for different sub-groups, even in subtle ways, video games can send positive messages without any overt statement or preachy lesson. Simply "living" in a culturally diverse game world and interacting with or observing people of different groups in positive, or at least fair and realistic roles, promotes tolerance. Of course, the power or effectiveness of this message may vary, depending on the player's position and real-life experience and background.

When a player actually takes on the role of someone from a different culture, experiencing the world and making choices from that character's point of view, the opportunities for learning are even greater. Without stereotyping, it would be very instructive, say, for a male player to role-play a female in a business-oriented game, in which real societal issues are taken into account. Or imagine playing a female character in the same business-based game, but sometimes playing a pretty and appealing young woman, other times playing an older woman or one whose sex appeal is not an asset or impediment. What difference might you expect to experience in such a game? Imagine playing a video game in which you were playing a black African trying to escape slave traders in the eighteenth century. Imagine switching roles and playing the slave trader as well. Or imagine playing different people whose lives were turned upside down by Hurricane Katrina. (See also the game Real Lives discussed in Chapter 8.) Games offer the opportunity to delve into the disparity between our idealized and our shadow selves, and one area in which this can take place is in the characters we play in games and how characters are depicted, not only by their actions and their statements, but also by their ethnicity, religion, gender or sexual orientation, skin color, weight, beauty, socioeconomic status, or other defining factors we all use to judge others. There's no reason why games can't do more to offer us experiences of the gray areas and ambiguities so prevalent in life in the modern world and so representative of human nature in general.

DEALING WITH MORAL AND ETHICAL DILEMMAS

Some games have presented players with moral and ethical dilemmas, and for many players, those were among the most memorable games they ever played. I would like to see more games that deal with challenging issues and encourage players to consider their actions and the consequences of their actions, and not in easy terms. I want to see more games that offer the kinds of difficult choices involving moral decisions about life and death, about accountability and honesty in all kinds of situations, about politics, ethics in business, environmental concerns, religious choices, and many others.

I can imagine more games involving politics, war and diplomacy, social issues, business ethics, and personal morality—games that challenge us to make choices and deal with realistic consequences of those choices can be both challenging and fun, while allowing players to explore their values and beliefs and decision-making skills. As an example, in many youth offender programs, people talk about "thinking errors," basically errors of judgment and perspective that young people made before they committed a crime. Video games could easily create situations in which players address situations similar to those many people are facing today, and they could explore the consequences and results of different decisions in a safe, game environment. If such games are created with effective game structures and situations, good research into how human behavior works, and an eye on the learning opportunities, they could be, at the same time, great games and great growth experiences for players.

EMOTIONAL INTELLIGENCE

Emotional intelligence is basically a person's ability to deal effectively with emotions in their lives. There are more complex and scholarly definitions of the term, but ultimately it is about effective emotional life. Emotional intelligence involves the ability to recognize, understand, and manage one's own emotions, as well as communicate them effectively and to recognize emotional states in others.

For younger players, learning to deal with frustration (which is common when playing video games) and finding appropriate ways to express that frustration can be beneficial, especially with some parental guidance. It might help to know that especially good video game players are calm and concentrated, and with younger kids, offering them role models of great players who keep their cool can be an effective deterrent to overreaction.

Another way that video games can affect emotional intelligence is through identification. When players take on the identity and goals of characters in games, they become affected by the complex emotional trinity of their own emotions, the emotional state of the character they role-play, and the synthesis of the emotions they may feel about the emotions the character feels. In other words, they feel their own emotions about a situation or event in the game, but they also have an emotional response based on how the character in the game experiences the event, which may be different.

We learn about our emotions because we care about a situation or outcome. We feel strongly when our self-interest is involved. We also feel strongly when our sense of fairness or justice is stimulated. With well-designed video games, we can have experiences in games that challenge our emotions and allow us to explore different feelings and reactions. Having emotionally charged events occur in games, and having players make choices in those emotional moments, with appropriate consequences, or even with scenes in which players are given the opportunity to assess their responses might offer many players opportunities to become more emotionally intelligent, particularly where they may be having problems in that area.

As always, these ideas would have to be carefully blended into good game play, but I think it's entirely possible to do so. The effect of using games to help people learn more about themselves can only be good for the games, the players, and their friends and family.

FAMILY DYNAMICS

Experts have studied families for most of the last century, and many theories have emerged, but still there seem to be many families who do not get along, who fight and argue and feud and fail again and again to communicate well with each other. Divorce rates consistently hover around 50 percent, and sadly, many children are neglected, abused, or, often, ignored.

As discussed in the previous chapter, through role playing and through modeling and inclusion, video games can help demonstrate or provide practice in good family dynamics and communications. Examples of effective or ineffective family dynamics can be incorporated into social games in which players find out what works best by experimentation. Perhaps players could actually play the game from the perspective of different family members, or families could even play together in a multiplayer environment. Existing essentially social games, such as The Sims, could be adapted to incorporate such scenarios and dynamic environments.

In another approach, players might find themselves coming into contact with virtual people and virtual families who are effective or ineffective, functional or dysfunctional, and simply by observing the differences they might learn something about what works and what doesn't. The bottom line is, where there's a will there's a way. If game designers are clever and they want to do something to present models of family dynamics, they can do so without affecting the fun aspect of the game—possibly even adding new elements to make it even more fun.

DOMESTIC VIOLENCE

Domestic violence is a pretty concrete behavioral aspect of family dynamics and one that is often ignored or even condoned in various societies. I take the position that it is an unfortunate and, hopefully, avoidable problem. And, like many human behavioral problems, part of the solution is to become aware that the problem exists, and part is to understand both how and why such problems occur and how they can be avoided.

I won't go into the details of domestic violence and its causes and solutions here, but in games, with a little knowledge and effort, players could role-model the participants in family situations where domestic violence can take place. Or, they might witness scenes in which domestic violence erupts. Most such events take place behind closed doors and within the walls of people's homes where nobody but the families can see what is happening. Anytime we are in a position to witness such events, we feel very uncomfortable. Emotions may range from anger or protectiveness to shame, embarrassment, or disgust.

What games can do, if designers decide to incorporate such information in them, is to allow players to be witnesses to abusive behaviors and to feel the emotions that result. Even better, games might allow players to take some kind of effective action and provide feedback for what actions are likely to be effective and what actions are likely to fail or to escalate a situation.

As an example, in a police game in which the player is a member of the force, a domestic violence call might place the player in the role of mediator between angry family members. By varying scenarios and characters involved, the player might gain some specific knowledge and experience about the causes of and solutions to domestic violence.

In other games, the player might actually be one of the participants, or, using the "Rashomon effect" I mentioned earlier, they might even play several different roles in the same situation. Imagine if the player could play the person being abused and then the abuser, understanding the roles and responses of each. The player might even be an innocent observer, such as a child witnessing violence between his or her parents, or a mother watching an angry husband "discipline" the children.

PERSONAL ISSUES AND GROWTH

COMMUNICATION SKILLS

One of my personal areas of study outside video games is human verbal and nonverbal communication. I have spent a lot of time studying, learning, and observing communication styles and techniques and have worked as a mediator, a personal counselor, and a city councilor. In each of these roles, I have observed how a little care and practice can substantially improve people's lives and effectiveness. At the same time, I observe how poorly most people understand effective communications, and how often problems and misunderstandings arise as a result.

Although video games today do not explicitly address communications problems and solutions for the most part, through role playing, inclusion, and modeling, I believe they still can do so. One of my favorite experimental programs is called Façade, which attempts to create a realistic conversation system on a computer. The developers of Façade did not necessarily think of it as a game, but in fact that's what it is.

In Façade, you play a dinner guest of an urban, sophisticated, but terribly dysfunctional couple. As the guest, you get embroiled in their arguments and disagreements. If you are clever, you can bring them to a greater level of understanding with each other. If you are not so clever, they will escalate into a full-fledged argument in front of you and, ultimately, kick you out of the apartment.

Façade is only an experiment in artificial intelligence, but it is promising in its ability to create an engaging situation where the player is dealing with realistic human emotions and situations. It is not a completed project or a completed game, but it suggests that games could also model communication-related challenges and rich stories and adventures could rely not only on combat skills, but smart communications as well.

Clever designers may find ways to create compelling conversation models in games and allow players to experiment within the context of the game with effective and ineffective communications. If people were given the opportunity to learn to communicate effectively—and there are many ways to do so—their lives and those around them would improve. I think video games could help through role modeling, role playing, and skills practice.

PROBLEM SOLVING AND CRITICAL THINKING

Video games do an excellent job of creating problem-solving environments. Good game design almost always presents problems and challenges players to find one or more ways to solve them, often with a variety of desirable or undesirable consequences. The problems may vary from how to get all the red triangles lined up together to how to move an army safely through enemy territory.

Video games present big problems and small problems, but big or small, there are always problems. On the other hand, game players don't necessarily think of them as problems the way they would when trying to study for a test or when having trouble at school or at work. If they think of video game problems at all, they think of them as challenges or as opportunities—a significantly more positive view.

Critical thinking is also very common in video games, but less obvious. What is critical thinking? Essentially, it is the ability to observe and acquire information, evaluate it for relevance to a situation, and use the resulting conclusions and information as a guide to belief and action. In shorter terms, it might be described as "the ability to make good decisions."

One of the factors that distinguishes critical thinking from simple knowledge acquisition is that information and skills obtained are practiced and reinforced, and the results are also evaluated, processed, and understood. In this way, critical thinking is an ongoing process of evaluation, decision, and more evaluation— which sounds very much like the scientific method and also like what players do continually while playing video games. In his book *Everything Bad Is Good for You*, Steven Johnson describes the way video games work in contrast with other forms of entertainment.

> Novels may activate our imagination, and music may conjure up powerful emotions, but games force you to decide, to choose, to prioritize. All the intellectual benefits of gaming derive from this fundamental virtue, because learning how to think is ultimately about learning to make the right decisions: weighing evidence, analyzing situations, consulting your long-term goals, and then deciding.[5]

As I see it, that's another way of saying, "Video games teach you to think critically."

The challenge for video games is to empower players to transfer the kinds of critical thinking they do in games to other areas of their lives. I don't know of any studies that show to what extent players already are able to transfer critical thinking skills to other aspects of life, but I suspect that such skills are part of what Beck is writing about in *Got Game?* (see Chapter 6). Furthermore, I suspect that such transfer could be improved through context. What I imagine are games in which the situations carefully consider puzzles and opportunities for critical thinking that directly affect real-world skills and values.

Games like Zoo Tycoon do this by offering players decisions directly related to what people in business must do all the time. For younger players, this may provide them with sophisticated concepts way beyond their years—or at least what prevideo game generations would have expected of kids. But when six-year-olds are playing games that involve economic decisions around resource allocation and budgeting, customer service, and economic trade-offs, we have definitely entered a new era that is probably taking a lot of people by surprise.

In other areas, games could still improve the impact they offer. For instance, people must use critical thinking to assess the risks and rewards of real-world actions such as investing in real estate or the stock market, using or selling illegal drugs, going to school or going to work (and which school or which job), sending troops to a foreign country, declaring war, voting for a particular political candidate, determining which foods are most healthy, and so forth. Wherever we are faced with decisions requiring evaluation and consideration of multiple factors, we must use our critical thinking skills. Video games can provide scenarios and opportunities for practicing these skills.

NEGOTIATION

Negotiation isn't just about big confrontations between business and labor unions or political leaders on different sides of an issue. Negotiation is a skill that is useful in all areas of life, from dealing with your children's impulses and desires versus your parenting goals to seeking a raise or change in your work life. Yet negotiation skills are not taught in public schools, and neither are they modeled very effectively or consistently in much of society or in many families. Negotiation, like all communication techniques, is learned through practice.

Video games have not often presented negotiation simulations or models, but they could do so. In single-player games, where the computer would have to represent the "other side," the limits of artificial intelligence today might affect how interesting and rich the experience would be. However, with humor or cleverness in the writing and design of interactive negotiation "scripts" for a video game, and the inclusion of an interesting and meaningful context and reward, players would happily engage in negotiations practice without even realizing it, or caring.

In multiplayer situations, there is much more opportunity to present negotiation practice. Nonvideo games like Diplomacy often feature negotiation aspects as part of their overall game structure. Players must effectively negotiate alliances, cease-fires, and other mutual agreements. Diplomacy is far more than simply a game of negotiations, but that is a big part of its appeal. In multiplayer video games, similar situations can be set up so that players must negotiate with each other to succeed at the game. Scenarios such as the political Diplomacy game model certainly would work well, but other situations can also work effectively in video games.

Suppose different players in a multiplayer game are in charge of resources that other players need. But the other players also have resources they might need. Negotiation is necessary to create trade agreements, set prices and quantities, and determine the durations of the agreements. Multiplayer versions of SimCity involve exactly these kinds of negotiations where one city might supply water to another in exchange for money or perhaps excess power.

Negotiation can occur even in very ordinary game circumstances. Certainly some games allow players to haggle with shopkeepers over price. This is a very simplistic form of negotiation. Suppose, on the other hand, players encounter characters with more complex motivations, goals, and needs. Scenarios in which characters must understand each other's viewpoint and find ways to get what they want through negotiation could easily fit into various kinds of games. In simplistic form, they already do.

In many role-playing games, the hero (player) needs something from another character, but the second character, whom I'll call the gatekeeper, is not necessarily going to hand it over without asking something in return. In some cases, the price of the item is too high, and an alternative method of payment must be found, perhaps by performing a service for the gatekeeper. In any event, in a simplistic form, players sometimes negotiate with gatekeepers to achieve their goals. Unfortunately, such scenarios often are very simple, not requiring any real negotiation. With small changes in the game and the characters, however, a much richer negotiation model could be easily incorporated.

The trick in a scenario such as this is to make the negotiation meaningful, present options that are unacceptable to either side, and have more than one potential outcome. In such situations, players will learn to think creatively in dealing with people and find acceptable solutions in difficult circumstances; in essence, they will learn negotiation skills that could carry over into real life.

CONFLICT RESOLUTION

Conflict resolution is a term that can describe any way that someone resolves conflict, including running away, surrendering, using violent means, using the legal system, negotiating, or simply communicating effectively. Literally and simply, conflict resolution is about resolving conflict.

In certain circles, conflict resolution refers to "alternative" methods—in other words, nonviolent solutions and sometimes solutions that avoid the legal system. Mediation is a good example.

When I think of conflict resolution and video games, I think about games that offer alternatives. For instance, while it is common in games to resolve a conflict or to overcome obstacles using violent means, it is also possible in some games to go around the obstacle or avoid the conflict altogether. It may also be possible to change the conflict into a cooperative situation through some effective communication that gets an opponent to come over to your side in the conflict, or by offering something through negotiation that sways the opponent.

In game terms, all solutions are equal, and it is the one that is the most fun, or the one that accomplishes goals and leads to the best rewards, that is generally the most desirable. However, players also like feeling clever and finding obscure and difficult ways to accomplish tasks. They may find the obvious way easily, and although some players may be satisfied with easy solutions, many will look for the path less traveled. Games where rewards for finding alternative methods of resolution are substantial and valued by the player might send an effective message that flexibility in situations can lead to positive results. If showing nonviolent conflict resolution is a goal, then offering players meaningful, satisfying, and realistic alternatives with similarly satisfying rewards can reinforce that message.

Suppose you play a character in a game and you have just caught a young thief entering your house, apparently intent on stealing something. In the game, you probably have the ability and right to attack the thief and attempt to kill him or her. But is this the best solution?

Suppose instead of attacking you ask the thief what he or she needs. Or you call the police. Or you offer to help in some way. In the real world, such decisions can net very real and sometimes surprisingly good or very tragic results. But in a well-designed game, it might be possible to find something good within the thief and turn him or her into an ally or someone who will go forward in life with a better attitude and more options.

Such a scenario is not as outlandish as it may seem. For example, the famous rock-and-roll promoter Bill Graham entered his office on the night of one of his shows at the Fillmore Auditorium only to encounter a young Latino youth with a harmonica breaking in through the window. The youth was trying to find a way to sneak into the show for free. For some reason, Graham didn't immediately turn the kid over to security. Instead, he took the time to talk to the intruder. Eventually, Graham became the kid's manager. The kid's name was Carlos Santana.[6]

PATTERN SHIFTING

People from time to time complain that they are "stuck in a rut." We often find that we continually approach situations in the same way, even when that approach does not make us happy or successful. Our lives seem to be run by habits, inflexible beliefs, and ingrained patterns of behavior and thought. One way people change is by breaking out of patterns—shifting their point of view or belief systems.

Through the TMSI model (see Chapter 5), video games can help players experience different realities and encourage experimentation with different approaches to situations. In fact, many video games require us to make such changes in order to succeed. Our "normal" way of seeing things does not work within the game. We can shift patterns by taking on the role of someone who could not possibly think like we do—for instance, being a woman playing in a man's identity or vice versa; being an Israeli playing an Arab or vice versa. When we change the way we approach problems and situations in our lives, we are effectively shifting patterns and allowing new patterns to form and be evaluated.

What I hope to see are more games that stretch our identities and help us see from different perspectives and have experiences that differ sufficiently from what we are used to, so that we begin to think differently and consider our views critically.

What types of patterns do we hold onto, even when they don't necessarily serve us well? For the future of video games, it would be interesting to include different types of game opportunities to shift patterns of belief and behavior and to seek more openness in our views of politics, religion, economics, and other factors in addition to our personal issues in life.

FINANCIAL AND BUSINESS SKILLS

There are already many examples of video games that help people learn new skills with finances and business, such as in the many "tycoon" games I've previously mentioned, like Railroad Tycoon, Rollercoaster Tycoon, Zoo Tycoon, and others. In the Serious Games field, which is discussed in the next chapter, various aspects of business and training are becoming more and more common, as business owners begin to appreciate the power of video games as training tools.

I expect that mainstream business simulation games will continue to be popular and become even more sophisticated and realistic. At the same time, running businesses is sometimes also a part of a side element of larger games. For instance, in a game like Fable, where players primarily explore the nature of Good and Evil in a fictional world, it is possible to buy and sell houses, and even rent them out for profit. In Ultima VII, you could run a small shop or a bakery business; several other games today feature elements that allow players to be entrepreneurs. Many multiplayer games allow players to be crafters, taking raw materials and turning them into finished goods, and then selling them to shopkeepers or to other players.

Quite a few video games feature merchants and cash, and players must budget their money to be able to afford the items they want or need but currently can't afford. Therefore, budgeting, planning, saving, and even investing are all parts of many games where commerce exists. I don't know of any studies that show whether gamers are better at managing their own money, but suspect, all things being equal, that they could be.

Effective game design can accentuate financial learning by offering goals, challenges, and rewards more specifically tailored toward achieving good budgeting and personal financial goals. If these games carefully incorporate budgeting into an otherwise fun game, the possibility that players will learn good financial skills should increase.

Game designers don't think of everything, and one of the most powerful areas in which games are teaching financial matters arose from the creativity of the game players themselves. Games like the very popular massive multiplayer game EverQuest have developed thriving player-driven outside economies where many items, and even whole accounts, are bought and sold on the Internet. According to Edward Castronova, a leading expert on the phenomenon of online economies, the "gross national product" of EverQuest in 2004 was higher than that of many real countries on a per capita basis.[7] In various player-driven economies, staggering amounts of money are changing hands, and the players of these games and the members of these virtual worlds are learning real-life lessons on finances and, in some cases, on running their own businesses.

One limitation of business models depicted in most video games is that they focus on a sort of "godlike" view in which the player makes all the ultimate decisions. Few, if any, have placed the player within the structure as a role-playing participant, employee, or executive, where decisions are made more like they are made in the real world. One clear, and perhaps accidental, exception occurs in the world of massive multiplayer games where player guilds immerse players in virtual but very realistic issues of cooperation, competition, leadership, and goal achievement. In an article in *Wired* magazine, John Seely Brown and Douglas Thomas discuss how people learn from video games and, specifically, how guild leadership provides excellent and practical training for leadership in business situations. To run a large guild, "a guild master must be adept at many skills: attracting, evaluating, and recruiting new members; creating apprenticeship programs; orchestrating group strategy; and adjudicating disputes." These skills, they contend, "provide real-world training a manager can apply directly in the workplace."[8] Leadership is only one of the useful skills we need for modern life. Looking at video games from the perspective of twenty-first-century skills, listed earlier, there are opportunities to learn, practice, and experience leadership, effective communications, global awareness, collaboration skills, self-direction, and so forth. Whether players are the godlike overseers of businesses, whether they learn commerce in multiplayer worlds or play within a specific role and context in the business world, they can learn these skills and more.

POLITICS AND GOVERNMENT

Video games have sometimes included political and government-related elements, allowing players to engage in political campaigns and even role-play government leaders, such as the 1990s game Crisis in the Kremlin, which placed the player in the role of Mikhail Gorbachev. In The Sims, a virtual election took place in 2004 for the leadership position of one of the areas called Alphaville. This user-driven event involved a political campaign among several candidates, including primaries and a final election. Several other games have also modeled a presidential campaign based on recent U.S. elections. One of my own conceptual designs involved forming and running virtual governments in a massive multiplayer world.

Politics at the national and international levels is complex, yet real civic awareness and global awareness require that we understand our own political system and how we interact with the governments of other countries. Games that feature political and governmental aspects can be based in current realties, historical situations, or totally fictional settings. Whatever the setting, learning and experience can help players be more informed and sophisticated about political as well as economic issues.

While most video games with political or governmental themes place players in high positions, as candidates for office, as leaders already in office, or as famous people from history, other approaches might place people in situations involving local politics and government. In fact, political and governmental issues can incorporate well into games with other, larger themes, becoming only a part of the game player's experience. For instance, players might receive one or more quests in a role-playing or adventure game that require them to seek political solutions, or they might have to help feuding factions to resolve difficulties by taking political steps and engaging in the governmental process.

I often imagine multiplayer games that allow players to experiment with different political systems of government and different economic systems as well. Because politics is about people—leaders and followers—there is tremendous range to be explored.

LEGAL ISSUES

Video games have previously dealt with legal issues through courtroom simulations and games that involved police work. Some games have done a very good job of modeling not just the sensational aspects of these legal themes, but also ethics, training, and proper procedures. It's always fun to play Perry Mason or some equivalent in a game, or to be a member of an elite SWAT team or a CSI investigator on a crime scene. Games have done all that and more.

Legal issues on both the justice side and the enforcement side are often complex and require good judgment and critical thinking skills. Also, there are gray areas to both sides, such as corruption, bigotry, and simple mistakes that can have profound effects on people's lives. The door is wide open for games to tackle more interesting and complex issues relating to police and detective work as well as defense, prosecution, and trails of accused criminals. Using ethical and moral dilemmas and working with ambiguity, games can go further toward presenting players with issues that resonate closely with reality. In fact, creating games based on real, but complex legal cases might be very interesting, especially if they followed the lead of popular TV shows like *Law and Order* and the CSI series. Such games, if they didn't involve lots of shooting and breaking down doors and car chases, might not appeal to all players, but I can think of games set in open and lively worlds in which crime prevention, investigation, and trial could all be incorporated. Surprisingly, a game series like Grand Theft Auto, as maligned as it has been by the press and other opponents, could provide a perfect backdrop for such a game.

One of the problems we encounter—and it is well exemplified by Grand Theft Auto—is that it's often more fun to play our shadow selves than our upright and moral selves. In a game, we get to fantasize. The trick at making legal issue games successful is to make playing the "good" guy as interesting as it is to play the "bad" guy. For today's game audience, this might work if the cop is an edgy type of guy who is not altogether on the straight and narrow, but has a shadowy side—something like the noir heroes of Dashiell Hammet, Mickey Spillane, or Philip Marlow. Modern movies give us clues about modern cultural trends, and the darker hero who still fights for justice is probably a role better suited for older players.

Younger players can also learn about legal issues of all kinds, but in their case the heroes might be cute animals or less threatening and realistic characters like those found in the Carmen Sandiego series. There are many possible approaches, but the opportunities exist to engage players in learning about legal systems while exercising their critical thinking abilities and having fun in the bargain.

LOGISTICS AND PROJECT MANAGEMENT

One of the most important areas of life is how we organize events and projects. Some games, such as war games and business simulations, do tackle issues such as supply chains or resource management and project planning. Real-time strategy games, which involve constant multilevel decisions relating to resources, exploration, building, defense, and offense, offer excellent experience for players at planning and implementing winning strategies under pressure and competition. So do various war games in which players must be the commanders and decision makers.

Simulations such as SimCity and Civilization, among others, also provide practice in long-range planning and logistical decision making, allowing players to try different approaches and to assess the effectiveness of each approach they try. Any game that requires players to think ahead and plan for long-range results or manage resource and supply chains will teach players some of the elements of good project management and logistics operations. Creating games in which various elements of the long-range plan are dependent on others, while some are on specific time lines, can make even more impression and teach more about project planning. The goal is to avoid players thinking, "I'm doing project management" or "This game has cool logistics." They just think, "I want to achieve that goal; now let's see what I have to do next."

Although games that involve such planning and logistics don't replace college courses in those subjects, players with video game experience have developed at least an unconscious competence in these areas, as they do in many skills gained from video games.

ANCIENT WISDOM

Today a group of thirteen elders, women of ancient traditions from all parts of the earth, have gathered to share their collective wisdom with the world before it is all gone. They come from the Arctic Circle; North, South, and Central America; Africa; and Asia. They call themselves the Thirteen Indigenous Grandmothers. Their mission, to remind people of the wisdom of ancient cultures, involves books, speaking events, and videos. But why not video games as well? Indigenous knowledge could easily be modeled in video game situations in which players were put into worlds where they could experience, learn, and practice the skills of their elders, ancestors, and others with ancient wisdom.

Ancient people lived in close harmony with the earth and natural forces. They understood the curative powers of plants and the cycles of the seasons, how to prepare food for the winter, and many other useful skills.

Aggie Baker Pilgrim of the Takelma tribe in southern Oregon is the leader of this international group. "Scientists took until the twentieth century to recognize that everything was connected," she says. "My people knew that from time out of mind. We're such a throwaway society. There should be no hunger in the world. We teach balance and moderation and reciprocity . . . how to give back when you take. These are all ancient lessons."[9]

Video games sometimes show the results of unbalanced use of resources and occasionally model principles similar to those of indigenous peoples, but I have not seen a game that puts players directly into worlds and cultures that understand nature and that live in close-knit village societies in which everyone is part of the whole. I think much of modern life removes us from appreciation of our place in the world, our role as stewards of nature, not just users and abusers.

There is a lot we modern folk could learn from ancient peoples and their traditions. I think a video game based around the combined wisdom of elders such as the Thirteen Indigenous Grandmothers would be highly instructive and transformational for many players, especially young ones who, through role playing and identification, might establish new connections with themselves and with nature. I hope such a game comes to pass before these grandmothers do, taking their understanding and wisdom with them. "Just because you are getting old doesn't mean you don't have some wisdom to offer to other people."[10]

WHAT'S MISSING?

This chapter has left out a lot of other areas in which video games can teach, model, simulate, or inspire—for example, modeling excellence in life or living with ambiguity. What about wilderness survival, emergency medicine, or activism? Consider this chapter as a suggestion of new ways to think about video games. We have barely scratched the surface of what may turn out to be a huge opportunity, but like all significant social movements, this one will start with small steps. Chances are, with creativity and desire, these themes, and more, can be manifested and their positive potential unleashed through video games.

Chapter 8

SERIOUS ENTERTAINMENT

I never did a day's work in my life. It was all fun.

—Thomas A. Edison

This chapter is about a relatively recent rediscovery of the teaching and inspirational potential of fun through video games. I call it a rediscovery because there was a short-lived attempt to use video games for teaching that really started in the early 1980s but reached its peak in the early 1990s. *Edutainment*, as it came to be called, just never quite caught on, and most of the emphasis during the first thirty-odd years of the video game era was on pure entertainment alone. In the past few years, however, video games have been "rediscovered" by a growing group of game designers, businesspeople, military leaders, academic researchers, health professionals, and public policy and political experts, as well as religious groups and various subcultures, who have realized that video game principles can be applied to more "serious" subjects and purposes.

If you have followed the progression of information in this book to this point, then you know that video games can be very powerful tools for learning—the Magic Edge, again. But for the first few decades of the video game era, people considered all video games to be "kid stuff." They were rarely taken seriously, and they only began to approach anything remotely resembling legitimacy when they were able to make the claim that they were making more money than Hollywood. Suddenly, people sat up and took notice. Maybe these games weren't a passing fad but were, in reality, a new form of entertainment as well as a mighty profitable business. Meanwhile, the first generation of game players has grown up—and many still play—and people from various walks of life have begun playing, studying, and using games. Games have become a worldwide phenomenon and continue to grow internationally.

Slowly people have begun to notice that the very strengths of video games, what makes them so popular with an ever-older population of players, might also be used for specific purposes such as teaching educational subjects, training soldiers, helping and healing people with medical problems, and even training people in business. It began to dawn on people that video games were not just fun to play but that they were based on a technology of sorts—a technology that worked on the human mind. Video game designers, it turns out, have been perfecting that technology for more than thirty-five years now—a long time in modern technological terms.

Sure, there is always talk about the evils and dangers of video games, but now people are also exploring how and why they work and what positive values they may offer. Academic researchers have written books about video games, often examining their positive qualities. More game designers have started working with businesses, with the military, and with health care professionals. People have developed a new perspective on games, and today the movement toward video games designed for serious purposes is well underway.

THE SERIOUS GAMES INITIATIVE

One of the most significant indicators of the new movement toward games with serious purpose is the Serious Games Initiative, cofounded by Ben Sawyer. Sawyer says, "We have reached a technological and cultural moment with games where all of a sudden whole new possibilities exist. What we used to think could happen, can happen."[1]

Serious games are not games that are serious but games that are made for serious purposes. They are still games, and they still aim to be fun and entertaining. So what, really, is a "serious game"? According to some authors and researchers, including James Gee, Ben Sawyer, and Marc Prensky, all games are serious, because all games teach or in some way impart skills or information we wouldn't get otherwise. "To me," says Sawyer, "Electronic Arts, which is the largest commercial game company, has been producing serious games all along. I mean, look at their sports games. When I want to teach my son about baseball, for instance, I'll be able to use one of their games, not just to tell him, but to demonstrate the difference between, say, an 0–2 pitch and a 3–2 pitch." Other researchers point out various benefits that come from entertainment-focused games and say that they are all providing value to players on many levels. But there is also a more narrow definition of *serious* in this context, which Sawyer describes as "purpose driven."

One way to look at this distinction is that games in the mainstream commercial world are meant to entertain and make a profit. If they have any other purpose, such as to teach or include some moral value, it is secondary to the entertainment goal. In contrast, a "serious" game starts with a purpose and uses the techniques and technology of games (the Magic Edge/TMSI) to make the experience entertaining. The purpose is the priority and the entertainment value is the method for transmitting the purpose.

AMERICA'S ARMY

Many so-called serious games are very entertaining; some are even quite successful. One of the most impressive and best funded examples is America's Army, a serious game designed and funded by the U.S. military originally as a recruitment tool, although it has become much more than that. This game, which is available free, uses state-of-the-art technology and graphics to simulate training and military operations in a realistic setting. The game has several remarkable aspects. To begin with, after their basic training, players actually perform tasks and missions together with other players online. They are rewarded by a scoring system called "honor," not for killing and committing random violence, but for accomplishing missions and working as a team. While this game does not have all the wild and sensational fictions and magical realities, characters and settings of many commercial games, with seven million registered players, it has to be considered a success by any standard.

America's Army is an ongoing effort, with new updates approximately every four months. Moreover, where many games in the same first-person shooter genre as America's Army prevent you from shooting people on your side, or at least clearly mark them so it's easy to tell which side they are on, America's Army does not do so. "We teach soldiers to think before they fire," says Major Bret Wilson, the game's chief technology officer. "People playing the game get it. They learn that they are accountable for their actions."[2] In fact, America's Army is so dedicated to these principles that only players who have earned high honor points through their actions can enter into certain missions and maps. And for those who transgress? "They are sent to a virtual version of Leavenworth Prison to consider their actions. They are given a ten-minute time-out with nothing to do but stare at a little cell."

Because America's Army is played online and is constantly updated with new missions and new material, some of it borrowed from real military training programs developed from the America's Army technology, players have "careers" in the game, and they can rise in rank and gain new skills as they play. This in part explains why the game has such a large following.

America's Army proves that people can learn within a game context. "The players learn the army's principles," says Major Wilson. "They learn to distinguish lawful from unlawful orders, and they learn the nobler principles of honor and sacrifice and being a member of a team. And they discuss it in forums and over online chat connections. It's clear that the game works to convey our message and our principles."

THE EXPANSION OF SERIOUS GAMES

Not all serious games are as slick and technically impressive as America's Army, but many have achieved success in other ways. There are now games that help teach lawyers how to perform in courtrooms, customizable for any state, and in some states players can even receive law school credit by playing the game. (I've known some lawyers who consider their whole practice of law a game, so this doesn't come as a surprise.) Other games help teach how to invest in the stock market or how to be effective in business meetings.

Video games with standard educational goals range from teaching algebra to physics, Shakespeare, history, and listening skills. One remarkable program, Real Lives, lets you virtually live out the life of someone born in any part of the modern world. The game is based on volumes of statistical data so that whatever life you live in whatever country or region of the world, including the opportunities and events that take place during that life, is likely to be statistically accurate. It's an amazing experience to live the life of someone in Rwanda or Chile and compare it with a life lived in Great Britain or Japan. Once again, through the Magic Edge, particularly the ability to form an identification with the character in the game, you learn and absorb much more by "living" these experiences with all their life-changing and emotional impact, than you would by memorizing the statistics behind them.

Serious games are being used in large businesses now for a variety of purposes—such as at the ice cream franchise Cold Stone Creamery, where it is used to help train employees, and at Canon, where a game helps train people how to repair copiers, with still more training games in the works. In all, corporate training games are a good deal. They are far cheaper to produce than commercial games, having budgets sometimes only 5 percent of major commercial budgets, yet they save a great deal of money over alternate training methods. Best of all, employees will often play training games at home and in their free time. Why? Because they are fun.

Serious games have serious purposes, and, to a large extent, their designers consider video game technology to be a tool. Just as a hammer is used to drive a nail into a board, video games can be used to reinforce a message or provide an effective learning environment in a variety of serious settings. And it is because of the efforts of the commercial game developers that this tool has been refined and perfected.

GAMES AS TOOLS

Throughout history, people have developed tools to accomplish the important tasks of life and leisure. We invented weapons to hunt and to defend ourselves. We invented mortars and pestles to grind grain and plows to till the earth. We invented the printing press and the telephone and the Internet. Some of these inventions were clearly focused on a primary task, but some had unintended consequences and uses beyond what the inventors had originally intended, often leading to new discoveries as well.

Video games were conceived almost as soon as video technology became available. Even as early as the 1950s, Ralph Baer, a television technician, was writing diagrams of TV sets that played games. (Baer was also the creator of the first home game system, the Odyssey, in the early 1970s, as well as the inventor of Simon and other games. He is considered by many to be the true "father of video games.")

Yet, because video games were games and therefore seen as a form of entertainment, they were not initially seen as tools to be used toward any other purpose. Over the years, as we have learned more about video games and realized their power and potential for learning, we have begun to expand our understanding of what games are and what they can be. Today, it's safe to say that video games have more than one identity. They are still entertaining. They are still controversial at times. And they are seen, more and more often, as tools and technology that can be used in a variety of ways.

Ben Sawyer compares the game industry to a privately funded NASA.

> Whatever you may think of individual games, this industry and its innovation and learning has provided us the opportunity to create these games. People wonder if the games they are buying off the shelf are good or not. They really need to understand that those games and the unencumbered growth of the game industry are empowering us all. Games you might personally not agree with are fueling the technology, knowledge, and experience that are being applied to new purposes. We should be careful how we deal with the game industry.

Sawyer and others involved in the new game movements also contend that there's money in these fields, and because the money will come, so will the legitimacy of serious approaches to games. The games will get better and will be more accepted. If these proponents of serious games are correct, then the movement toward games with positive impact on players is well on its way, led largely by pioneers whose vision combines purpose with play.

GAMES FOR HEALTH

Affiliated with the Serious Games Initiative, Games for Health focuses on games that promote health, healing, and medical training. Remarkable results are already being obtained by combining games with various aspects of medical practice. Games are helping people deal with pain, recover from mental and physical trauma, and create a positive self-image in combating diseases such as cancer and leukemia. Simulations are also being used to train doctors and surgeons, not only in very direct medical practices such as surgery, but also in emergency medicine, patient care, and other related tasks such as the management of a medical facility. As game technology becomes more and more realistic, it can be applied successfully to training with higher levels of realism and accuracy. As our understanding of how games work improves, designers can apply that understanding better toward improving the lives of medical patients and improving the performance of medical practitioners, as well as helping already-healthy people become healthier.

Much of what is going on in health fields relating to games is still in research phases, but the results are highly encouraging. Games like Virtual Vietnam have been remarkably successful at rehabilitating veterans of the Vietnam War who suffer from posttraumatic stress disorder (PTSD). Dr. "Skip" Rizzo at the University of Southern California is modifying a commercial game program to create Virtual Iraq, which is designed to help soldiers returning from Iraq. His use of virtual reality and game scenarios in a therapeutic setting is proving far more successful at eliminating PTSD symptoms than other, more traditional therapies.

On the other side of the coin, Dr. Anuradha Patel has been successfully reducing trauma in young patients undergoing serious and painful medical procedures by using the ability of games to immerse patients. The medical term is *distraction therapy*, and it is based on the fact that the human brain can only track so much information at once. By presenting very compelling information to patients' brains, they simply don't have room for the pain in their consciousness anymore. Distraction therapy is being used in many settings, with many different types of distractions. Among the most promising media for certain age groups are video games. In this sense, video games are more powerful than pain, at least in the young people Patel is treating. And it's a good thing because children who go through such difficult medical procedures without mediating processes often are traumatized, and the effects can last their entire lives.

Another game that deserves mention here was created by a nine-year-old leukemia patient named Ben Duskin. With a little help from the Make-a-Wish Foundation and a game developer from LucasArts, Ltd., Ben was able to create a game in which he could imaginatively combat the multiplying disease cells in his body in a virtual environment. The game plays like an arcade game and is simple and fun. What is remarkable is that Ben's Game, as it is known, is in its fourth version and is being used in many hospitals to help patients in their recovery.

Recently media reports have highlighted the concept of improving your brain or keeping it "young." Certain kinds of cognitive activities do seem to have a beneficial effect on the brain and its ability to keep function as we get older. Games like Sudoku have become wildly successful, especially in Japan, but also in the United States and elsewhere. Sudoku is a mathematical puzzle game that requires a lot of brain work. Last year, the game giant Nintendo came out with Brain Age, a game whose purpose is, similarly, to exercise the brain and help keep it working in tiptop shape. Surprisingly, Brain Age has been a huge seller both in Japan and in the United States, with millions sold. By the standards commonly applied to games—such as stunningly realistic fantasy graphics, lots of action, and complex hand-eye coordination—Brain Age is totally lacking. Yet it appeals to a wide range of players.

EXERGAMING

Games are changing, and audiences are changing. And because the video game audience is changing, new opportunities for game developers seem to appear every year, and new uses of existing games sometimes take unexpected turns. For example, the commercial game world has provided new inspirations for Games for Health in the form of new "exergames."

Exergames are games that promote healthy exercise, and it turns out that some commercial games such as Konami's Dance Dance Revolution and Red Octane's In the Groove, both arcade games that involve physical dance movements, not only get people's hearts pumping in therapeutically approved ways but also help players become more physically fit and lose weight. On the Sony PlayStation, the Eye Toy camera is being used for a variety of games. Some of these games are purely for entertainment alone, but there are others that function as personal exercise and fitness trainers. In the medical world, Eye Toy games help people with physical impairments, such as stroke victims, to regain their mobility and control. It turns out that playing a game during physical therapy not only is more fun but inspires patients to play longer and more often. The same is true with exercise, where people all over the world are discovering the joys of losing weight and gaining fitness while playing games.

The immediate commercial potential of such exergames is being put to good use by the emergence of membership gyms, similar to the popular Curves franchise, but with game technology instead of traditional exercise machines. In personal health and fitness, as well as in medical applications, games have definitely found a home.

Another recent technology that holds promise for "physically interactive gaming" is Nintendo's newest console called Wii, which features two wireless controllers that allow physical motions to translate into on-screen actions.

GAMES FOR CHANGE

Games for Change is another affiliate of the Serious Games Initiative, devoted primarily to supporting games that promote social change, including public policy and politically oriented games. The group helps promote games from all over the world that attempt to shed light on issues related to social justice, international diplomacy, nonviolent protest, waging peace, and other such areas. Many of these games are being produced by government agencies and non-governmental organizations (NGOs).

One of the most successful games in this field is the United Nations game Food Force, which depicts the mission of the International Food Programme to distribute food to the needy all over the world. In the game, players actually deal with the challenges of locating people in need, including formulating healthy foods for specific areas and developing long-term food aid projects, flying food drops, and even driving delivery trucks through potentially hostile territory. The game, which is free to download from www.food-force.com, has attracted millions of fans all over the world, including children who, because of this game, want to enter public service when they grow up. A teacher's lesson plan is also available for use in school settings.

Another game that has created considerable attention is A Force More Powerful. Billed as "a game of nonviolent strategy" and based in part on a documentary film by the same name, A Force More Powerful puts players in the role of nonviolent resisters to oppressive political regimes in ten different scenarios. Working in conjunction with leaders from the Serbian student group who helped overthrow the dictator Slobodan Milošević and a team of political scientists, sociologists, and economists, the developers of this game created a complex and realistic strategy game that allows players to find out what it's really like to organize and run a nonviolent campaign against a powerful and ruthless political force. The game even allows players to create their own scenarios based on whatever situation they would like to model.

These two games are powerful and professionally produced games for change created on very slim budgets by commercial game standards; however, neither game would likely have been created by a commercial for-profit company. However each, in different ways, is able to show some of the range of game possibilities to produce compelling content with real-world significance in an entertainment package.

It's not only governmental agencies and NGOs who have entered the Games for Change arena. In a somewhat surprising collaboration, Reebok (through the Reebok Human Rights Foundation), MTV (through its mtvU organization), and International Crisis Group sponsored a contest to create a game or other use of technology that would help stop the genocide in Darfur. The winner of the contest was Darfur Is Dying, a video game created by students from the University of

Southern California. This simple game depicts the dangers and tragedies of Darfur refugees by putting players in control of a child or adult who must forage for water while armed patrols threaten his or her life. In that role, you must also assist in building and rebuilding homes in the camp, bringing water to grow food, and seeking medical attention to stay healthy enough to keep functioning in an impoverished environment. All the while, your character, along with everyone in the camp, faces threats of death and the destruction of their meager camp by marauding Janjaweed militia. As removed from reality as this game is when we play it in the safety of our own environment on a computer thousands of miles away, the utter futility and mortal danger of our virtual characters can only help us understand the plight of people suffering in these conditions. No news report can have this kind of impact as, through identification with the character, we make their goals our goals. And when we fail, and our characters suffer death, mutilation, rape, and humiliation while seeking those peaceful and survival-oriented goals, we come a small step closer to understanding. Ironically, this game is not, in a strict sense, fun. It is tragic and frustrating, yet somehow it works. It still effectively uses the Magic Edge of games to motivate players to engage in the game's fiction and do their best to help, through their choices and their skills, these virtual victims of genocide and oppression.

THE "NEXT STEP" REVISITED

Does the Serious Games Initiative, along with its related movements, represent the Next Step described earlier? Maybe. It may be that, as serious games related to business, health, social issues, and other topics establish themselves and become legitimate, accepted, and, perhaps most important, profitable, changes in the overall attitudes of game designers and game companies will also occur. If this shift of priorities or vision occurs, games may start to provide more socially relevant and meaningful content while simultaneously achieving their entertainment goals.

I am certain that these games with serious purposes can do a lot to awaken people's enthusiasm about games and remove some of the stigma currently attached to them because of the negative press they often receive. And I'm all for it. I totally support the direction people like Ben Sawyer and all the serious games designers are going.

At the same time, I believe that these serious games have some hurdles to overcome. For one thing, it is very well known that most game players do not want to play a game that openly teaches or is obviously oriented toward learning. The main audience for commercial games seriously plays for fun. They don't mind learning while they play, as long as they don't think of it as learning. Although attitudes may shift, especially with older players who seem more willing to engage in games that they know are also teaching, most gamers will cringe when a game is described as "educational" or "good for you."

So, even as serious games of various types make inroads into the public consciousness and find interested audiences, the chances are that few of them will rival commercial games in sales, partly because by nature they are purpose driven first and entertainment oriented second. Players have a very sensitive nose for fun and for games that try to tack fun onto something that doesn't interest them.

Hopefully, serious games will sell, but will they sell millions of copies and attract literally millions of players? If they do, then great changes can take place among players and in all cultures that are influenced by games. While we wait to find out whether games with purpose can also be games with megasales, I think we ought to be exploring every option, including the one I call the Next Step in commercial game development.

Going the other way—embedding something essentially educational or beneficial into a game primarily oriented toward entertainment—can be effective, though such an approach also has its challenges. If both approaches are attempted, the winners will be the people who play these games.

The approach I'm suggesting, that designers ask, "What more can I do?" and take the Next Step, is getting its first public airing in this book, so as you read this, you are a pioneer. And, as you will see later in this book, I hope to enlist you in the movement toward a new perspective on video games. By now I hope you can see that there's something going on—that the potential of video games is far greater than you thought when you first picked up this book.

Chapter 9

SMART PARENTS, SMART PLAYERS

While we try to teach our children all about life, our children teach us what life is all about.

—Angela Schwindt

Think of this chapter as a self-help guide for the family members of video gamers. If you've ever wanted to burn those games or toss that PlayStation or Xbox in the trash, you're in the right place. Even if you have read the previous chapters and now understand games better, you may still be in conflict with members of your family. Don't despair. Help is on the way.

SPEAKING THE DIGITAL LANGUAGE TO THE DIGITAL NATIVES

One author with excellent advice for moms and pops and teachers is Marc Prensky, an educator who argues persuasively for the role of games as learning tools. His book, *Don't Bother Me, Mom—I'm Learning!*[1] is full of good advice and strategies for parents when dealing with video games.

One of Prensky's most insightful observations is that the modern digital culture has its own citizens, culturally distinct from the pre-digital population. He calls them Digital Natives. The rest of us are Digital Immigrants—visitors to a foreign land with a language all its own.

Prensky believes that the skills needed in a rapidly changing technological world are precisely the skills being learned by video game players today. Most important, they are learning to think on multiple levels, and they do it voluntarily.

In *Everything Bad Is Good for You*, Steven Johnson points out that video games are "hard."[2] They require players to grasp and interpret unstated rules, make order out of many interlocking "fractal" goal-reward structures, focus deeply on short-term challenges as they simultaneously pursue long-term strategies and use intuition to understand the way the game works. No wonder kids get bored at school, where the information is offered in linear bits and facts and theories, where the motivation is weak or missing and the reward is usually to avoid failure and punishment.

I think communication between gamers and nongamers is critical to finding harmony within families as well as in helping kids interpret the sometimes controversial or confusing messages of some video games. Prensky points out, however, that Digital Immigrants speak with what he calls a noticeable accent. Here are some of his examples of that "accent" from *Don't Bother Me, Mom—I'm Learning*:

- Printing out your email. (If you have your secretary print it out for you, your accent is even thicker.)
- Turning to the Internet for information second rather than first.
- Reading the manual for a program rather than assuming that the program itself will teach you to use it.
- Needing to print out a document written on the computer in order to edit it (instead of just editing it on the screen).
- Thinking that "real life" happens only off-line![3]

This last item is often hard for parents to understand. They think there's a clear distinction between what happens in the digital world and what happens everywhere else. For Digital Natives, the world of cell phones, blogs, chat, e-mail, MySpace, iPods, and video games are part of real life. Even though they are keenly aware that video games are fantasies, their involvement with friends and fellow players makes these games often more real, in the sense of relevance, than many other aspects of their lives. So to say to a gamer something like "You have to participate more in real life," assuming a very clear distinction, might not mean the same thing to the gamer that it means to you.

While you may be speaking a slightly different language, as a Digital Immigrant, you can learn to listen and to communicate with the Natives. As you communicate with the Natives, you might be surprised at what you can learn about them, while simultaneously easing the tensions caused by cultural and language barriers. In this chapter, I offer some useful ways to bridge the cultural game between you and your gamers.

ASK A GAMER:
SOLVING VIDEO GAME CONFLICTS

Conflict between family members is a common, but largely avoidable, problem in mixed households. By "mixed households" I mean households with video gamers and nongamers, where conflict most often occurs between parents and kids or between spouses. There is definitely a separation taking place, where some people may be deeply involved in an activity that other members of the family cannot understand or relate to. In many cases, this leads to antagonism, anger and argument in various forms.

Our attitudes about video games, which are based in part on their pervasively negative public image, affect how we respond to the separation. Perhaps you have found yourself thinking or saying the following: "Why do you spend all that time doing nothing? You should be doing something constructive." "Those games are going to rot your brain and make you lazy." "You need to get out and socialize, get exercise and join the real world." "You're not taking care of your [homework/chores/responsibilities]." "You care more for that stupid game system than your own family."

Would you think the same way about something your child or spouse was deeply involved in if you thought it was good for them? Suppose they had a strong interest in intramural sports or spent time at the gym keeping the body firm and flexible. Perhaps they spent hours a day doing homework or earning extra money, or studying medicine in their spare time in preparation for medical school. How would it be different if the video game had some positive value?

Of course, you might respond, "I don't mind that they play these games, but why do they have to play *that* kind of game?" Or you might say, "It's OK to play a game for a few minutes, but they play them for hours at a time. They just disappear into that strange world and don't seem to want to be in this world anymore."

When someone in our family seems to disappear and we don't know what they are doing or why, it's natural to be concerned. How we respond to our concerns can spell the difference between conflict and successful communication. What action do we take, and what attitude is behind that action? We can be upset, angry, or even determined to put a stop to this behavior. Approaching the situation with such confrontational attitudes will, almost inevitably, result in more conflict and it is likely that the game player will become defensive and even rebellious.

Any situation can suggest many responses, and many choices are always available to us. Before the situation reaches the stage of anger and ultimatums, I recommend an alternative approach, which I think is better than any other, at least initially. It's very simple. Instead of being angry, become curious. Curiosity is often a good approach to communication in general and can lead to many discoveries that we miss when our ideas and beliefs are absolute and fixed in place. In communication between gamers and nongamers or authority figures, curiosity can open doors that would otherwise be closed—on both sides.

Curiosity without action won't lead to any answers, of course, so the next step is to question the gamer. For instance, you might say, "I know I've been on your case about your game playing, but I just read this interesting book about video games, and it got me thinking that maybe there's more to the game playing than I thought." What questions might you ask, once the gamer has begun breathing again?

Remember, you are curious, so you really want to know more about the games your family members like, why they like them, and what they are thinking about when they play. Knowing what they are thinking can offer a big clue to what they are learning and what, if any, misconceptions you may have formed about their games. Here are a few questions to ask about any game:

"Would you tell me about the game you're playing? What's the story? What do you have to do to succeed?"

"What are you thinking about when you are playing? What decisions do you have to make?"

"Do you think I could do it?"

Gamers might think it's weird that their parent or spouse suddenly takes an interest in what they are doing, particularly if there has been conflict over the issue, but if the curiosity is genuine, most gamers will be more than happy to tell you all about the game. Pretty soon, your head will be swimming with concepts; ideas; names of items, characters, skills and locations; buttons; decisions; statistics; goals; rewards; strategies and more. If you're brave, ask to try the game. You might be pretty pathetic at it (the gamer would probably say, "You suck"), but even you can learn and improve. (For some guidelines on getting started in video games, see the next chapter.) More important, it allows gamers to share what they know with you. Instead of arguing about the game, suddenly you're collaborators.

If the gamers start telling you which buttons to press and how to play, ask them to tell you instead what the game is all about and what strategies they use, or how they are able to complete the goals of the game. You really want to know what they are thinking—the cognitive side of game play. The "how to play" aspect of many games today is so complex that, without actually spending time doing it, you would get little out of an explanation of which buttons do what. Knowing what the gamers are thinking, what decisions and challenges they face, and how they solve problems is much more revealing than knowing what buttons to push. Often, because so much of what they do is unconscious competence, gamers may even surprise themselves when they try to describe what they are doing.

Sometimes you may see gamers doing things that seem violent or antisocial. Rather than make judgmental statements, perhaps say something like, "I don't think I could do what you're doing. I think it would upset me. But then, I'm not a game player. What is it like for you? Do you ever feel bad about what you're doing?" Or you might ask, "Why is it OK to do these kinds of things in a game, but not in the real world?" This will seem like a really dumb question to a lot of gamers, and they might look at you and say, "Doh! It's just a game, dude." Or something like that. This is a good time to laugh, because from the gamers' point of view, this is not only obvious, but in a way they are sharing a point of view with you—specifically that game playing is not serious in the same way that the physical world is. In a digital world, they're telling you in very simple terms, there's no harm done and, like the Cole Porter song from a time long before most gamers were born, "Anything Goes."

Why should you take this approach, using curiosity and dialogue with gamers instead of simply going in and laying down the law? Curiosity along with nonjudgmental communication helps establish rapport between you and the game player. With rapport, you can express your personal feelings or concerns without any negative, generalized video game baggage. Moreover, you may come to understand more about the appeal of video games from the player's point of view, and if you've read the previous chapters in this book, you may start to recognize the positive aspects in some of these games. With all this new knowledge and rapport, you and your gamers will find it easier to create compromises and strike a balance between play and other aspects of life.

ABSORBED AND UNRESPONSIVE

While I recommend curiosity as the first and most important approach to communication with games, it is not the only approach. There will be times when you just have to be firm, when you have to put your foot down. Video games are, after all, very absorbing, and video gamers are, even with the best of intentions, not always aware of the time it takes between agreement to do something and actually doing it. In other words, when gamers say, "In a minute," they might mean a minute, but more often they mean a half an hour or more.

With healthy people playing video games, such loss of time awareness is common and nothing to worry about. You may want to consider getting agreements ahead of time and setting limits. From experience, I would suggest making time limits somewhat flexible and allow for the possibility of renegotiation. In video games there are frequently moments when, from the gamers' point of view, it's just not "a good time" to stop. Use your judgment as to whether it's really critical that they go to bed at 10 or at 10:15, but set an outside limit and make it clear that they need to wrap up their activities within a set time frame. For instance, they can commit to finding a "good place to stop" at 10 and finish that process no later than 10:15. After that, they will just have to stop, or come up with a really convincing reason why not.

Because parental styles do differ, negotiation and flexibility may not feel comfortable to all parents, but I suggest them because, with otherwise healthy players, compromise and agreements are both possible and can be effective.

ESCAPING INTO UNREALITY

In some cases involving tension around video game playing, there may be other, more troubling issues that affect the situation, as I discussed in Chapter 1 in the "Can Video Gamers Become Addicts?" section. Even when more severe problems exist within a family environment, however, curiosity is a good way to break into the gamer's world. Where depression or traumatic events may lead someone to escape into video game play and isolate himself or herself from the family, it might require more work to establish rapport, but it also can open up the gamer to reveal and admit the larger and more significant problems. Focusing on the video game as the problem itself, on the other hand, instead of as a symptom of the problem, does nothing to find the real challenge.

Understanding that a lot of video game playing and a lack of responsiveness may be a symptom rather than the cause of the problem gives you a perfect opportunity to open doors and allow gamers to express their real feelings. Focusing on the video game with curiosity, and sharing the players' reality, actually allows you both to focus on something that is, in reality, neutral. With this shared focus you give space for the gamers to express themselves in what is a comfortable environment for them.

A PARENTS' GUIDE

When I was writing my first video game book in 1990, I was concerned about the possible impact of the games I was writing about. I was also a father with two children to consider. Obviously I was not worried about games for myself, but how could I be sure they were all right for my kids and, more important, as an author, for the people who read my books?

At the time, there were far fewer researchers in the field of video games than there are today, but I did find Patricia Greenfield, whose 1984 book, *Mind and Media: The Effects of Television, Video Games and Computers*, is still referenced today by writers studying video games. With her advice, I created a chapter, which I included in my first few books, called "A Parents' Guide to Video Games."[4]

Although I wrote that chapter in 1990, its material is still relevant today. I've revised and expanded the simple guidelines originally presented there for coexisting with kids and video games, with information and ideas from several additional sources.

SET CLEAR LIMITS AND EXPECTATIONS

Tell your children just what is expected of them. Make it clear that the homework must be done, the grades kept up, and the lawn mowed (or whatever they do around the house). Make sure they know that playing games is OK, but it is a privilege that can be revoked if they don't keep a sense of responsibility about their lives. Suggest that they have responsibilities in life, just like you do, and ask them to imagine what it would be like if you played video games instead of doing what you do to maintain the family, whether it is earning money or maintaining the household. Remind them that they have responsibilities, too, and that the video games are not their primary job in life but rather their leisure-time activity.

ENCOURAGE PHYSICAL ACTIVITY

Physical exercise is important to health, and, with some exceptions (see Chapter 8), games do not offer much physical activity. You want to encourage kids to engage in physical activities, and sometimes they may resist. Games can be very compelling. "Come on, Mom, I'm in the middle of a quest. I can't stop now." Make agreements with kids that they will monitor their time, but have a little flexibility as well. Realize that the games are sometimes very important to players, and allow some negotiation, as long as the kids follow through on their agreements.

One argument that may go a long way toward motivating kids to keep in shape is that healthier people make better game players. Professional game players who compete in highly charged tournaments actually keep in shape just like athletes. They call themselves "cyberathletes." The top-ranking competitive game player in the world today, Jonathan Wendel, who goes by the handle Fatal1ty, plays games for hours a day, but he also runs, plays sports, and works out every day. Why does he keep in top physical shape if all he's doing is pressing buttons and moving a mouse around? "Playing at the level I play requires more than just eye-hand coordination," he says. "I need split-second reflexes, stamina for long tournaments, and the ability to make smart decisions. I think of myself as an athlete, just like any other athlete, and being physically fit and healthy gives me a huge advantage over any opponent who is not in good shape."[5] Tell your kids what Fatal1ty says, and maybe they'll get off their butts and get in shape, too, if they want to be the best players.

ENCOURAGE SOCIAL ENGAGEMENT

Some games are very social, while others are played in isolation. It is not always obvious which ones involve other real players and which ones do not, so it's a good idea to ask. In any case, I believe that people need to have physical interaction with other people, so if your children tend to spend a lot of time alone playing games, work with them to find activities that interest them and that include other people.

USE THE DESIRE FOR GAMES AS A MOTIVATOR

Most kids who play video games are never satisfied. They'll master one game but already want to buy new ones. Kids know that games cost money, so you can use their desire for more games to motivate them to earn money or do more chores around the house. I'm not suggesting using games as a bribe but rather as a moti-vator and a way to trade value for value. With a positive attitude, kids will see it as a fair trade where everybody gets something from the deal: they have earned their game, and you have acknowledged the game's value to them.

ASK THE GAMER

I already covered this tip earlier in the chapter, but it bears repeating: instead of standing on the sidelines wondering what the heck they are doing in there, talk to the kids playing the games. Be curious. Ask them what they are doing and how they do it. Once you get them talking about a game, you'll be surprised at the complex details they will offer of how they play. Many parents find their children less than communicative, especially when they are teenagers, but get them talking about the latest game they are playing, and they'll talk up a storm.

Getting involved is also your opportunity to discuss your concerns. When kids tell you all about the game, you can ask what it means to them. "Don't you feel bad when you blow that guy away with the rocket?" "Why do you need to get to the top of that building?" "Why are you fighting these people?" With younger children, ask them questions that reveal their ability to distinguish fantasy from reality. For instance, "Do you know that it's OK to do that in a game but that you could hurt someone if you did it for real?"

If you really want to be cool, let go of your inhibitions and ask to try it. Ask them to show you how to play. You might be the world's worst player, but you also might be amazed at how much fun some of these games can be. And your kids will definitely appreciate that you gave it a try.

REACTION VERSUS RESPONSE

In *Killing Monsters*, Gerard Jones suggests that parents are the single-most important role models in a child's life. Parents can influence children not only by how they behave in their lives, but also by how they react to the types of entertain-ment a child is enjoying. Because children will often choose types of entertain-ment that push limits and go counter to what parents think is appropriate, Jones contends that a parent's response is sometimes more influential even than the source of entertainment, itself. He suggests that parents do not need to like every-thing their children like. "Effective modeling can certainly involve telling children what we don't like," he writes. "We can get so caught up in the debate about whether entertainment is 'harmful' that we forget our right to an opinion." Jones goes on to state that honesty and clearly stated opinions model decisiveness and moral courage. "It's far more useful for a child to see a parent calmly stating an opinion than dithering in worry. The kids, of course, will learn from their parents' example and start declaring their own tastes with equal strength."[6]

AFFIRMATION

Jones also suggests that parents affirm who their kids are, trust their desires, pay attention to how they are using their fantasies, and encourage them to tell stories. He suggests that parents give them the tools to take control, help them distinguish fantasy from reality, allow them their own reactions, intervene carefully when necessary, and help them make their fantasies work positively in their lives. Each of these bits of advice is accompanied in Jones's book by a very good discussion and, often, with real-life examples. For parents interested in understanding the role of fantasy entertainment, including video games, in the lives of their children, *Killing Monsters* can be very helpful.

DELVING DEEPER

In *Don't Bother Me, Mom—I'm Learning!* Prensky suggests that parents can engage in a much deeper level of learning and exploration with their kids. Once you have established some sort of dialogue with gamers, you can use the video games themselves as an educational opportunity—for both of you.

Prensky suggests that you can ask players to think about what they are learning from the games they play. You can also examine with them the experiences of the game and how they relate to other useful skills. As an example, Prensky suggests that you can help kids appreciate the value of self-evaluation—something they learn in games but may not have applied to their other activities. Because they are regularly using learning principles and self-evaluation in their game playing, they can become more effective learners, less intimidated by outside measures such as tests, and more self-directed and confident.

Prensky also suggests understanding what kinds of games your kids like and using those games to spark more learning in various areas, depending on the game. His Web site, www.gamesparentsteachers.com, lists many current games and the possible areas of interest they offer. I will provide some suggestions in the next chapter as well.

Finally, Prensky suggests working with your kids' teachers to integrate what they can be learning at home with what they are doing in school and to let the teachers know how you are working with your kids.

BECOMING A MEDIA ANALYST

What do I mean by a "media analyst"? Do I expect you to appear on CNN and report on the media or write a column for the local newspaper? Well, not exactly. A media analyst, in this context, is someone who examines and critically considers the media they consume and the media their kids consume. Not only parents but kids, too, can become media analysts.

Media is everywhere in our lives today. We consume it, and it influences us. Television programming and news, movies, music, art, books and comics, video games, and, increasingly, Web sites and blogs all contend for our attention. In fact, some experts describe our culture as an "attentional economy" because we have limited time to focus on anything in particular and we have to decide where to "spend" our attention. Time is limited. Our choices sometimes seem unlimited.

Imagine that you have a limited amount of "attention points" to spend in the same way that you might have a limited amount of money to spend in the supermarket. When your food budget is limited, you pick more carefully what you buy, making sure to have the staples and the most important items before you start piling luxury items into your cart. You probably also consider which are the healthiest foods and how to create the most balanced diet. Likewise, in an attentional economy, some of your attention points have to be spent on the necessities of life, whether it's doing your job, attending school, or just making sure the dishes get done. The rest is up to you.

You become a media analyst when you recognize that you are making informed decisions about where you spend your attention points the same way you make careful decisions about spending your money on goods and services.

There are different ways to understand media. One way is to read reviews and articles about products. You may find ratings a useful starting point, especially for television, movies, and video games, although ratings systems will not tell you everything you might want to know about a product, and certainly not any positive value the media may offer. Relying entirely on ratings and reviews, while convenient and quick, may not provide you with the information needed to be a true media analyst.

Harvard professor and author Kimberly Thompson suggests that consumers learn to "deconstruct" the media they consume. She suggests asking the following questions, which were developed by kids at the Boston YWCA Youth Voice Collaborative:

- ◆ "Who made this media product?"
- ◆ "What motivated the producer (selling a product or idea, education, entertainment)?"
- ◆ "What are the main messages?"
- ◆ "What values and preferences come with the messages?"
- ◆ "How might other people interpret this message differently?"
- ◆ "How does the producer attract and hold your attention (appealing to your emotions, shocking you)?"
- ◆ "What information does the media producer omit and why?"[7]

By far the most important part of being a media analyst if you have young children is to examine the media with them. As noted earlier, this means discussing and questioning the media, explaining how you see it and asking kids what they are getting from the kinds of media they enjoy.

What do you gain from becoming a media analyst? The obvious answer is that you can help protect your children from negative influences, and, where they are choosing media that has controversial material, you can be there to help interpret that material in healthy ways. The less obvious answer is that, by looking critically at the media you and your children consume, you also make more conscious choices about spending your attention points. You and your children are also far more likely to gain knowledge and understanding by thinking about media rather than just approaching it as a way to kill time. Active participation with active reflection make the experience we gain from our media, including video games, far more rewarding and rich.

How Useful are Video Game Ratings?

In 1994, largely in response to political pressure over what was seen as a rising tide of realistic violence in video games, the video game industry created the Entertainment Software Rating Board, known generally as the ESRB. The ESRB consulted with many child development and academic experts, studied other ratings systems and conducted nationwide research with parents, ultimately creating a system that works much like the movies to rate video games for age appropriateness based on content such as violence, language and sexual themes.

Responding to the feedback from parents, ESRB ratings offer both age-based categories and detailed information about the types of content a game contains.

There are seven rating categories, which are printed on the outside of every game box sold at retail:

 EARLY CHILDHOOD: Titles rated EC (Early Childhood) have content that may be suitable for ages 3 and older. Contains no material that parents would find inappropriate.

 EVERYONE: Titles rated E (Everyone) have content that may be suitable for ages 6 and older. Titles in this category may contain minimal cartoon, fantasy or mild violence and/or infrequent use of mild language.

 EVERYONE 10+: Titles rated E10+ (Everyone 10 and older) have content that may be suitable for ages 10 and older. Titles in this category may contain more cartoon, fantasy or mild violence, mild language and/or minimal suggestive themes.

 TEEN: Titles rated T (Teen) have content that may be suitable for ages 13 and older. Titles in this category may contain violence, suggestive themes, crude humor, minimal blood, simulated gambling, and/or infrequent use of strong language.

 MATURE: Titles rated M (Mature) have content that may be suitable for persons ages 17 and older. Titles in this category may contain intense violence, blood and gore, sexual content and/or strong language.

 ADULTS ONLY: Titles rated AO (Adults Only) have content that should only be played by persons 18 years and older. Titles in this category may include prolonged scenes of intense violence and/or graphic sexual content and nudity.

 RATING PENDING: Titles listed as RP (Rating Pending) have been submitted to the ESRB and are awaiting final rating. (This symbol appears only in advertising

The ESRB rating icons are registered trademarks of the Entertainment Software Association.

ESRB Content Descriptors

- Alcohol Reference - Reference to and/or images of alcoholic beverages
- Animated Blood - Discolored and/or unrealistic depictions of blood
- Blood - Depictions of blood
- Blood and Gore - Depictions of blood or the mutilation of body parts
- Cartoon Violence - Violent actions involving cartoon-like situations and characters. May include violence where a character is unharmed after the action has been inflicted
- Comic Mischief - Depictions or dialogue involving slapstick or suggestive humor
- Crude Humor - Depictions or dialogue involving vulgar antics, including "bathroom" humor
- Drug Reference - Reference to and/or images of illegal drugs
- Edutainment - Content of product provides user with specific skills development or reinforcement learning within an entertainment setting. Skill development is an integral part of product
- Fantasy Violence - Violent actions of a fantasy nature, involving human or non-human characters in situations easily distinguishable from real life
- Informational - Overall content of product contains data, facts, resource information, reference materials or instructional text
- Intense Violence - Graphic and realistic-looking depictions of physical conflict. May involve extreme and/or realistic blood, gore, weapons and depictions of human injury and death
- Language - Mild to moderate use of profanity

- Lyrics - Mild references to profanity, sexuality, violence, alcohol or drug use in music
- Mature Humor - Depictions or dialogue involving "adult" humor, including sexual references
- Mild Violence - Mild scenes depicting characters in unsafe and/or violent situations
- Nudity - Graphic or prolonged depictions of nudity
- Partial Nudity - Brief and/or mild depictions of nudity
- Real Gambling - Player can gamble, including betting or wagering real cash or currency
- Sexual Themes - Mild to moderate sexual references and/or depictions. May include partial nudity
- Sexual Violence - Depictions of rape or other violent sexual acts
- Simulated Gambling - Player can gamble without betting or wagering real cash or currency
- Some Adult Assistance May Be Needed - Intended for very young ages
- Strong Language - Explicit and/or frequent use of profanity
- Strong Lyrics - Explicit and/or frequent references to profanity, sex, violence, alcohol or drug use in music
- Strong Sexual Content - Graphic references to and/or depictions of sexual behavior, possibly including nudity
- Suggestive Themes - Mild provocative references or materials
- Tobacco Reference - Reference to and/or images of tobacco products
- Use of Drugs - The consumption or use of illegal drugs
- Use of Alcohol - The consumption of alcoholic beverages
- Use of Tobacco - The consumption of tobacco products
- Violence - Scenes involving aggressive conflict

In addition to the symbols, which are printed on the front of each box, specific content descriptors are also printed on the back of each video game package.

ESRB ratings are based on a detailed questionnaire filled out by each video game producer plus recorded footage of the game, including all pertinent content (as defined by the ESRB) and any extreme examples in categories such as violence, language, sex, controlled substances, and gambling. According to the ESRB, recorded material, the questionnaire, and any other submitted materials are reviewed by at least three specially trained ratings experts who typically have experience with children. Ratings experts do not necessarily have advanced game-playing skills; their job is to determine the age-appropriateness of the content.[8]

Do THE ESRB RATINGS WORK?

ESRB ratings aren't perfect. They do attempt to inform the public about the content of the games. Almost all video games sold at retail in the United States and Canada are rated by the ESRB, and while many major retailers will only stock ESRB-rated games, enforcement of the ratings is voluntary. Some critics claim that younger children are easily gaining access to M-rated titles on a regular basis. Other critics claim that some information should be included about criminal activities—specifically where young players can engage in criminal actions without consequences. Another problem with the ESRB ratings is that they cannot inform people about games obtained from the Internet or other nonretail sources.

One possible failure of rating systems occurs when parents don't pay attention to what their kids are getting. Many M-rated titles are actually purchased by parents for their children, and increasing numbers of young parents are playing video games themselves. It's possible that they are purchasing M-rated titles for their own enjoyment, but ultimately the kids gain access to them as well.

Although the incidence of younger children playing M-rated titles is not known, according to a study by Peter D. Hart Research, most parents with video-gaming children are aware of the rating systems, and about 74 percent of them do refer to those ratings all or most of the time when purchasing video games for their children. More than 50 percent of parents said they "never allow" their children to play M-rated games, while another 41 percent say they "sometimes allow" their kids to play such games after checking the ratings descriptions and making a specific determination.[9]

The ESRB rating system attempts to inform consumers about the content that will be found in the games they rate. Other groups and Web sites offer advice as well, often tinged with judgment and, from what I can tell, unproven assertions about the effects of games and a good deal of strong rhetoric. Chapter 1 took a hard look at some of the most volatile issues surrounding video games, and I don't think anyone can state with absolute certainty that they understand how video games affect players. The only agreement I find among experts is that video games are highly effective learning environments, but not that they are necessarily harmful, even when violent or antisocial in theme. Therefore, I prefer to focus on rating systems that intend to inform without attempting to use unproven facts to convince people of the evils of video games or that use hyperbolic language to inflame fear or revulsion.

Rating systems are always a suggestion or guideline, rather than a strict requirement, and each parent can choose how to define appropriate media for his or her children. With good parental involvement, even games that might not seem age appropriate can be fine. Without any parental involvement, any rating system is probably going to be ineffective.

KEEPING KIDS SAFE IN ONLINE GAMES

> While online computer exploration opens a world of possibilities for children, expanding their horizons and exposing them to different cultures and ways of life, they can be exposed to dangers as they hit the road exploring the information highway.[10]

One of the greatest online dangers facing children and adolescents comes from people who attempt to victimize them through sexual interaction. Although sexual predators appear far too commonly in chat rooms and other social areas on the Internet, they can appear also in online games where children may be playing.

There are many ways to help protect children from falling victim to such sexual predators, but the first and foremost is, as always, to communicate openly with them about the possible dangers and ways they can recognize and avoid such people. Several organizations and Web sites, including the FBI and Wired Kids, offer a lot of very good information (see the Resources at the end of this book). Wired Kids is especially good to share with children because it is very kid-friendly.

Here are a few basic guidelines to share with your kids when they are online, whether it is in a video game, a friendship, or chat environment like MySpace or Friendster. If you don't know what these services are, ask. There's a good chance that your kids are aware of them. Whatever your kids are doing, share the following guidelines with them:

- Never arrange a face-to-face meeting with someone they met online.
- Never respond to sexually explicit communications. If someone persists in making sexual comments, use the Block feature of the game or site to prevent any future contact.
- Never respond to messages or bulletin board postings that are suggestive, obscene, belligerent, or harassing.
- Never upload (post) pictures of themselves onto the Internet or online service to people they do not personally know.
- Never give out identifying information such as their name, home address, school name, or telephone number.
- Never download pictures from an unknown source, as there is a good chance there could be sexually explicit images.
- Be aware that whatever they are told online may or may not be true.

These guidelines are especially important to consider with younger children. It is important to remember, however, that most people in online chat environments and in video games are normal people who are often seeking legitimate friendships. Many people have met online and become friends in the real world. To go overboard and reject all possible friendships because of some possible dangers may deny your children very meaningful relationships. In the end, I think it comes down to communication and clear boundaries.

It is also important to remember that adolescents in particular are moving away from the total control of their parents and beginning to explore more adult aspects of life, including sexuality. The best way to prevent them from falling prey to sexual predators or from obtaining false and misleading sexual messages is to keep the lines of communications open. Although some technologies may allow you some degree of control over what kids are exposed to, none are absolute.

While the dangers of sexual predation may not be as common in video games as they are in other Internet contexts, the same precautions are advisable. Kids who are there to play in a game world often find overly personal approaches from strangers to be a "turn-off," but some of the online sexual offenders can be quite clever and can gradually establish relationships with kids. Again, informed kids and informed parents, working together, are the best defense.

PHYSICAL RISK FACTORS FROM VIDEO GAMES

Video games are frequently criticized for being too violent or antisocial, for being possibly addictive and, at times, sexually inappropriate (see Chapter 1). Less commonly, you may hear that video game playing can cause physical problems such as eye strain and repetitive motion injuries.

Physical issues arising from video game playing are easily corrected, at least in theory, by taking breaks, using good ergonomics, keeping fit, and, in some cases, doing simple exercises. For instance, the Web site www.medicineonline.com recommends that players take periodic breaks at half-hour or hourly intervals and do some simple stretches for the fingers, wrists, shoulders, and neck. Further recommendations include looking away from the screen at intervals, improving posture, and paying attention to symptoms such as pain in joints, eye irritation, headaches, and so forth. To prevent eye strain, focus the eyes at varying distances every fifteen to twenty minutes.

These are all good suggestions, and would almost certainly help prevent common physical side effects of video game playing. However, they do require the game player to monitor time while playing and to take frequent breaks, neither of which most gamers are likely to remember to do without practice and, in many cases, outside motivation in the form of a family member or some sort of reminder system. Of course, typical video gamers won't be much inclined to take preventative measures until they actually develop symptoms, so again, if we are talking about children, it may be up to the parents to suggest—or enforce— healthy game-play habits.

Marc Rizzaro, a sports physiotherapist, has studied problems associated with video game playing such as tendonitis in the thumbs and wrists plus a variety of neck and upper- and lower-back problems due to bad posture. He suggests that the most important ways to prevent problems from occurring are staying healthy and fit, strengthening forearms and fingers by stretches and moderate amounts of squeezing a tennis ball or "stress" ball, and employing healthy ergonomics. "Use the 90-degree rule," he says. "You can avoid most problems if you keep knees, hips, hands, and elbows all at 90 degrees, with wrist support if you can. Avoid looking up at the monitor, keep wrists flat and not flexing downward, and have good back support."[11] Rizzaro also suggests taking periodic five-minute breaks and avoiding a sedentary lifestyle.

One piece of advice not generally mentioned is to play relaxed, as really good game players do. Tension in the hands, back, neck, or arms makes you play more poorly. To be the best, players need to learn to relax when playing, both physically and mentally, and when players are relaxed, they are less prone to injuries and other unpleasant effects. Just relaxing when playing, while it won't replace good healthy game-playing habits, will certainly make the player better at the game while reducing potential negative physical effects.

Also, as mentioned previously, the best gamers—the ones who compete on the professional circuits—treat themselves as athletes and exercise regularly, keeping their bodies and minds in top shape. People who play a lot of video games should definitely consider including good stretching and exercise as part of their lifestyle. If they want to combine their game playing with their exercise, no problem. They might consider getting a dance pad and playing one of the dance video games such as Dance Dance Revolution or getting Sony's Eye Toy for the PlayStation and trying one of the exercise games available for that system.

Chapter 10

GET IN THE GAME

You can discover more about a person in an hour of play than in a year of conversation.

—Plato

Perhaps you're curious. Perhaps you're thinking, "What if I wanted to try playing a video game?" You might also be thinking, "OK. So games aren't all bad for my kids, but which ones should I get, and why?"

In this chapter, I offer a game beginner's primer. A game beginner is often called a *newbie*, so it will be your newbie primer. I will also suggest some video games that might interest you once you get your game on. I won't overwhelm you with long lists of games; a few examples of games with positive, useful or inspiring content will do. Hopefully, experience with these suggested games will help you evaluate other games that might interest you, and you will know what characteristics to look for.

Because the landscape of video games is constantly changing, this chapter is focused primarily on video games that you can find in video game stores. However, I may mention some older titles that also deserve your attention. Older titles can often be purchased through the Internet long after they have ceased to appear on retail shelves, so if you're particularly intrigued by an older title described here, search for it on eBay or Google it. There are also businesses that specialize in buying and selling older games, and often you can find great older games for great prices at such stores and sites. Note also that some older games also require older machines or technology, but some are available with "emulators" that can imitate older technology on newer machines.

WHAT'S IN A GAME?

Back in the early to mid-1970s, during the first few years of video game history, it was pretty fair to say that all video games were substantially alike. They certainly featured subtle differences, but in a broad way they were almost all very similar. When someone said "video game," it generally referred to a game of action that involved eye-hand coordination and minimal strategy, viewed on a video screen.

By the late 1970s, however, video games began a steady process of expansion, not only into people's homes by way of video game consoles and home computers, but also in terms of variety. New types of games appeared year after year, differing sufficiently from previous types of games to merit new classifications or categories. Where the original video games were generally classified as "arcade" games, today there are many identifiable categories and subcategories of games, such as real-time strategy games (RTSs) and turn-based strategy games, first-person shooters (FPSs), adventure, role-playing games (RPGs) and action RPGs, sports, puzzle, and various types of online games.

CATEGORIES OF VIDEO GAMES

Categories in most entertainment media, including literature, movies, and television, refer generally to the content or story. For instance, a movie might be a drama, a horror flick, a buddy movie, or a comedy. Video games are unique in that they are categorized more specifically by game play elements and, sometimes, by player's point of view. For example, in first-person shooters, players see as if from the eyes of their character (first-person view). The game is a "shooter" primarily because it involves various hunter and hunted situations with, generally, a lot of shooting. In contrast, in a third-person game, players see the action generally from above and behind their character. Another game type, the strategy game, can be recognized (simplistically speaking) by elements such as resource management, long- and short-range planning, and specialized "units" that perform operations under the player's control.

Although video games, like movies, can feature humor, horror, adventure, action, and, in fact, just about any kind of experience available in movies, the way they are categorized is still by game play elements. You can have a science fiction, an urban action, or even a humorous shooter game (yes, they exist), and each would still be called a shooter. You can have historical, science fiction, or even humorous strategy games, but they are still primarily categorized as strategy games. All video game genres are similar in this respect; it's the style of game play that determines its category.

ARCADE GAMES

The original video games were all arcade games, so called because they were first introduced in pinball arcades and other public places. Although home game systems became popular in the 1970s and early 1980s, the earliest days of video games were dominated by arcade games such as Pong, Breakout, Gun Fight, and Tank. Even as home video games began their rise to popularity, arcade games thrived with hits like Space Invaders, Pac-Man, Centipede, Asteroids, Missile Command, Defender, and Tempest.

The main characteristic of arcade games is action, and though they vary in style, complexity, and sophistication, they all involve quick reflexes, eye-hand coordination, and, generally, pattern recognition. Always popular, arcade-style games are becoming more so with the emergence of huge new markets through casual and mobile games.

SHOOTERS

Players call these games "shooters" because there is generally a lot of shooting going on. Two subcategories of shooter games are worth noting: the first-person shooter (FPS) and the arcade-style shooter. Naturally, all shooter games contain some degree of violence, and some contain very bloody and gory graphics in dark futuristic or supernatural environments. Some shooters, on the other hand, feature interesting storylines and minimal or no blood or gore.

FPS

First-person shooter games are among the most popular types of games in the commercial game market, and they have been since the mid-1990s when they became an overnight sensation in the mainstream game world with the release of Doom. FPS games are characterized by the point of view, which always is seen from the main character's eyes. Generally, the screen opens up in front of the character, showing possibly his (the main characters are usually male) hands and weapon(s).

First-person shooter games are full of action and strategy. In addition to fast reflexes and quick decision making, they often involve cunning tactics. All current FPS games allow players to play against each other, either individually, in free-for-all games, or even in team games both online and over local networks. In the context of multiplayer competitive play, the context of FPS games changes from a fictional world to something more akin to an individual or team sport, like paintball, for instance.

Current FPS examples are games in the Quake, Halo, and the Unreal series. Some of the best FPS games also offer editors that allow players to create sophisticated versions of their own, as mentioned in previous chapters.

Arcade Shooters

Once one of the dominant game genres, especially in the 1980s and early 1990s, arcade shooters often involve a spaceship or plane moving through an essentially two-dimensional landscape, shooting waves of enemies in the air and ground or in space. Arcade shooters also sometimes depicted a side view of a well-armed character in a platform game.

Arcade-style shooters tend to be pretty mindless and provide very limited context for the action. It's sufficient to know that whatever attacks you or gets near you, for that matter, is an enemy, and you want to take it out in a hail of bullets or laser beams or bombs, or whatever you have.

Arcade shooters celebrate eye-hand coordination, quick reflexes, and, often, the ability to track multiple targets and enemies, along with reward items (called power-ups), simultaneously. Also important is the ability to make hair-trigger decisions that often mean the difference between high scores and dismal defeats (a quality shared by all shooter games and most arcade-style games).

Arcade shooters can also be learning environments that reward good vision, technique, and strategy, although these skills are often practiced intuitively. However, those who think and observe patters can still prevail in such games. There's a famous story that illustrates this principle.

When J. W. "Wild Bill" Stealey, a real-life jet pilot, was challenging all comers in an arcade shooter based on World War I aircraft, he was king of the hill. That is, until a little computer systems analyst, after watching him play a while, took up the challenge. This systems analyst proceeded to dominate the game and beat Wild Bill's score easily. "What kind of flight experience do you have?" asked Stealey in amazement. The newcomer answered, "None at all. I just analyzed the responses of the computer pilots and anticipated what they would do." The newcomer was Sid Meier, now one of the most famous game designers in the world. Stealey and Meier subsequently went into business and formed Microprose, one of the early video game success stories.

The story of Stealey versus Meier suggests that even in the simplest games, there is often more than meets the eye and that gamers, whether consciously aware of it or not, probably are seeing and understanding patterns and behaviors and making predictions in order to effect better strategies. What's important here is that, even in these apparently simple games, gamers may be learning, thinking, problem solving, and becoming better observers of phenomena in general.

THIRD-PERSON ADVENTURES

The third-person view appears as if a camera were following the main character, usually from just above and behind. In some games, the view is adjustable, allowing the player to determine how close or far and at what angle the camera follows the character. Players may also have the option to change to first-person by turning the camera view off.

Third-person games are very common and come in many forms. A few are essentially shooter games, like first-person shooters, but from the third-person perspective. Others are what might be called "action adventures" in which violence often plays a part, but other elements, such as puzzle solving and greater levels of story development, are also included, such as in the Tomb Raider series.

Third-person games may also feature arcade-style action with, at most, cartoonlike violence, such as the landmark game Mario 64, the first 3D version of the famous Mario Bros. franchise. Three-dimensional arcade games have gone far beyond the simple arcade games of the past and often feature different types of activities, complex puzzle solving, and free exploration along with plenty of action. As complex as 3D arcade games are, young children love them and will focus on them for long periods, finding all the secrets and solving all the puzzles with an intensity they rarely show for other activities.

Other 3D third-person video games are more adult yet also involve very sophisticated decision-making options. Some, such as the Metal Gear games, Silent Hill, or Deus Ex, may even contain storylines with emotional intensity and challenging mysteries to solve.

ONE-ON-ONE FIGHTING

Once the most popular video game category, one-on-one fighting games have lost some of their dominance to first-person shooter games over the past decade, but they have not disappeared by any means. One-on-one fighting games generally involve two combatants who fight with fists and feet and weapons, sometimes magic as well. This genre gained special popularity in the mid-1990s with Street Fighter 2 and later gained even more notoriety with Mortal Kombat.

With some exceptions, fighting games are most often devoid of story. They tend to be simple contests of skill, although the skills required can get pretty complex. Many fighting games have secret moves that involve complex combinations or sequences of game controller operations. Often these secret moves are not documented, and players are expected to discover them on their own. In other games, special moves are given as rewards for notable accomplishments. Players may work very hard to earn these abilities.

Although most one-on-one fighting games involve fantasy characters in fantasy game experiences, more traditional sports games such as boxing, wrestling, and various types of martial arts also fall into this category as well as in the sports category.

STRATEGY GAMES

Strategy games primarily originated from computerized versions of strategy board games. In fact, early computer strategy games looked and played a lot like those old board games. Since then, they have evolved considerably, and they continue to become more complex and realistic graphically.

Today there are two types of strategy games, each with its unique qualities and game play experience. The main difference between the two is a matter of time.

Real-Time Strategy (RTS)

The clock never stops in real-time strategy games, which have become so popular that they have their own acronym—RTS. One important characteristic of RTS games is time pressure, which requires fast thinking and quick responses to situations. Whereas in turn-based games, which I will describe next, players can take lots of time to consider their options—akin to playing chess—RTS games leave very little time for reflection.

In an RTS game, players deal with resource management and technology advancement, troops and machines for attack or defense, exploration, and territory control—all at once. They also must deal with budgets and trade-offs. RTS players must learn how to assess situations quickly, making instant decisions on how to deploy their resources to be most effective, and they must learn to do everything simultaneously because *multitasking* is the watchword for RTS players. They must often be both offensive and defensive at the same time. Anyone who wants to win has to see the whole picture at once and be taking action on several fronts at the same time. If a player has not planned well early, it may be too late to implement a winning strategy.

RTS play can be quite challenging against a computer opponent, which can be set to play in different difficulty modes, from easy to godlike. For even greater challenge, playing against online human opponents controlling rival civilizations or groups requires added flexibility because real players introduce uncertainty and surprises. In either case, RTS games are about extreme situational awareness, quick thinking, and sound strategic and tactical decision making.

Turn-Based Strategy

Turn-based strategy games still retain some connection with their board game roots by allowing players and opponents to alternate—to take turns at implementing their strategies. Time in the game stops during each turn, and players can make any moves they like before deciding to end their turn. Turn-based strategy games can get very complex, but they generally start with fairly simple options and grow in complexity over time. Perhaps the most famous turn-based strategy game series is Civilization.

Like all strategy games, turn-based games involve resource allocation and strategic thinking. They often allow different approaches to a situation. Civilization, in particular, allows players to choose war, diplomacy, technology, culture, or dominance (by controlling most of the available land and resources in the game) as winning strategies, though not all strategy games offer as many options.

ROLE-PLAYING GAMES (RPGS)

The idea behind an RPG is that the player controls a character in the game and, through that character, plays its roles in the game's fictional world. In that sense, all character-based games are role-playing games, even the shooters and arcade games in which the player controls an in-game character, but the category of games known as "role-playing" games originated live and online as role-playing in which people talked and acted within these roles like actors. Most players today simply play characters as extensions of themselves, however, and don't attempt to play, speak, and act as if they really were those characters.

Video game RPGs have evolved to include some specific and recognizable elements, and although they may vary in complexity and specific style, they share these features:

- In RPGs, the player's character usually has a specific class, chosen by the player, that helps define the character's role in the game.
- The player's character also has statistics that govern the character's effectiveness in a variety of situations. These statistics generally change as the game is played, sometimes automatically and other times through specific assignment by the player.
- In most RPGs, the character also can have, learn, or acquire specific skills, and it is the player who decides what skills to develop for the character.
- RPG characters often can attain "levels" of experience in which they become stronger and often improve their stats or skills or acquire new abilities.
- RPGs always involve some kind of exploration of the game's world, meaning that players can spend a lot of time just looking around, uncovering the features and the secrets of that world.
- In order to further the story of the game, RPGs rely heavily on quests, missions, and tasks given by nonplayer characters (NPCs). Quests, missions, and tasks provide focused activities in the form of goals, challenges and rewards for the player.
- Many RPGs include teams (called *parties*) of player-controlled characters or nonplayer allies who often represent different character classes and skill sets. By combining their abilities and using teamwork, players can be more effective in exploration and combat. Typical RPG classes include Warrior, Mage, Archer, Thief, and Healer/Priest/Cleric, with variations of each.

RPGs are among the most complex types of games because they deal with characters, stories, statistical abilities and skills, and, generally, very big game experiences that can last for dozens or even hundreds of hours. In the case of RPGs played in massive multiplayer worlds (discussed later), the game experience is ongoing and only ends when the player decides to stop playing the game.

It is worth mentioning that many games incorporate elements of the RPG systems. For instance, while there are many "pure skill" games, many shooter and adventure games have incorporated RPG elements, as have some action games and other types. In this sense, they are hybrids that use statistics, levels, upgradable skills, and sometimes character classes—all elements generally associated with RPGs.

Along with the cross-pollination of RPGs into other types of games, there are also different styles of RPGs. They all have character classes, statistics, and skills, but they may differ in play style, depth of story, and range of human interaction.

ADVENTURE GAMES

Next to arcade games, adventure games rank among the oldest styles of video games ever made, but they have changed dramatically since their inception with text-only games like the original Adventure: Colossal Caves in the 1970s and the very popular text adventure Zork. When graphics were added to adventure games, they earned the nickname "pick up the stick" games by many players because they involved a lot of elements of finding objects and then finding where they were used in the game to solve puzzles.

Today, adventure games are much like RPGs, but often without the changing statistics and skills and with more emphasis on 3D world action than most of their 2D predecessors. The prototype for this sort of game is probably Tomb Raider, but games such as Resident Evil or Silent Hill also qualify. (Ironically, all three of these titles have also inspired one or more Hollywood films. Also ironically, all three of these titles feature female heroes, and although Resident Evil games can feature male or female leads, it is Milla Jovavich who has played the lead in both Resident Evil movies.)

Adventure games today often feature deep stories and plots, though generally not as convoluted as certain "big" RPG plots. Like RPGs, they are most often focused on exploration but also rely more on action skills than typical RPGs. Tomb Raider's heroine, in particular, is very athletic and can climb, jump, and do acrobatic moves that you would not generally see in an RPG hero—and that most of us could never imagine doing.

In some ways, I am using the adventure category to describe just about any third-person 3D game that isn't either an arcade game (like Mario) or a shooter (like Gears of War) or a war game (like Call of Duty). To be fair, war games deserve their own category, but also they can be seen as variations of other genres, such as FPS, strategy, or adventure games, as well as, in some situations, vehicle simulators.

Like RPGs, adventure games can encompass a wide range of storylines and settings. They can be historical, modern, or futuristic. They can rely on violence more or less, depending on the type of game. Adventure games can be thrillers, horror stories, action stories, comedies, or even romantic adventures.

SIMULATIONS

A simulation is an attempt to re-create something from the real world, or based on scientific principles, in a computer program. Just about anything can be simulated, from surgery to duck hunting, from flying commercial and military aircraft to running a business, from managing a city to a social life in a virtual world.

Because simulations are based on real-world skills and situations (or sometimes scientifically plausible fantasies), they have great potential to teach by encouraging experimentation. Simulations are like living laboratories that allow us to be the scientists who delve into their secrets. They are also like entertaining classrooms where we can learn new knowledge and skills while having fun.

Simulations sometimes have very explicit goals or sets of goals for players to accomplish, such as successfully flying an airplane through a storm and making an emergency landing in a flight trainer simulation. However, many simulations have only subtle goals that are implied by the type of simulation it is and the kinds of tools available. For instance, a game like SimCity has few stated goals, and players can decide what kinds of cities they want to create and how to run them. On a subtler level, however, certain features of the game can only be "unlocked" when the player's city has attained certain milestones of population or wealth. Where such rewards are available only as a result of specific accomplishments, goals are strongly implied, if not enforced.

SPORTS GAMES

Calling this group "sports games" sounds somewhat redundant. They are, after all, video games about games. But they are also among the most popular and enduring game genres in the video game community.

Early sports video games were essentially arcade games that required good timing and good eye-hand coordination. Today, sports games contain incredible detail and accuracy, often using real sports stars for physical models and as consultants. Sports games have become so sophisticated and accurate that most of them can teach players more about any given sport and its subtle strategies and rules than they ever get as spectators, and possibly even as participants.

Sports games continue to increase in realism, detail, accuracy, and even story elements. For many years now, players have been able to play not only the players themselves but also the team managers who deal with line-ups, injuries, drafting new players, and the overall management of the teams. In their perennially popular John Madden football series, Electronic Arts has introduced something called "Superstar Mode," which allows players to role-play an NFL hopeful, beginning with choosing the right parents and passing through fame, fortune, agents, and the responsibilities of success. Among other things, the Superstar Mode offers some small look at the life of an athlete before (and after) he or she becomes famous, as well as the hard work it takes to become a "hall of famer."

GOD GAMES

Some games allow players almost unlimited control over a game world, but only a limited ability to influence the behaviors of the residents of that world. In this way, SimCity was not only a simulation of city planning but a god game that allowed the player to raise and lower land, determine zones, and build streets, bridges, and more, but not directly tell any of the residents of the city (the "sims") what to do. Only through indirect influence could the player affect the sims.

This godlike role creates specific game-play opportunities while at the same time offering very definite learning opportunities. Because these games provide an overview of the world but little intimate involvement at the individual level, they are great for creating puzzles involving systems, cause and effect, and multiple interacting influences. In a sense, most real-time and turn-based strategy games are similar to god games, but they allow players the ability to direct individual units—people or machines—in the game. On the other hand, most god games are strategy games—more so if they are very directed about goals (such as in the prototypical "god" game, Black & White) or less so in games where the goals are less well defined (as in SimCity).

MASSIVE MULTIPLAYER PERSISTENT WORLDS

Online video gaming has expanded steadily since the mid-1990s. Although earlier games were meant to be played by a single player or by more than one player in
the same location, today's games regularly feature online options for players to
join each other and play either cooperatively or competitively over the Internet.
One particular type of game that deserves special mention is the massively multiplayer online game (typically abbreviated as MMO). MMOs are sometimes
referred to as massively multiplayer online role-playing games (MMORPG) or
even "persistent world" games.

MMOs, by any name, are virtual worlds inhabited often by many thousands of
players through their in-game characters, called *avatars*. In these worlds, people can
socialize, play in groups of various kinds, compete or cooperate, explore, do commerce, and often craft and sell items. These worlds are operational 24 hours a day, 7
days a week, 365 days a year—which is why they are also called "persistent worlds."

It may seem odd that people actually speak of visiting these worlds or even
inhabiting them through their proxy avatars. After all, there is no there there.
There is nothing but programming and pixels lighting up a screen, or so it seems.
In reality, these virtual worlds combine ideas, adventures, and people. Just
because the people in these worlds are not in their own bodies does not mean that
they are not "there." Wherever their bodies may be, their minds and their personalities are fully in the online world, and people often find each other's company
in these virtual worlds very satisfying, making friends and even, in some cases,
finding love and marriage.

People of all generations play in these game worlds, including men and
women, children and adults, and people from different geographic and social
backgrounds from all over the world. Player-run organizations, often called
guilds, are common in MMOs, and they function like other groups of human
beings, with leaders and cooperative tasks and group goals—plus the usual sorts
of squabbles and personality clashes that you might see in any group. In this way,
MMOs are interesting places to learn social skills and to interact with a far wider
variety of people than most of us would normally meet or interact with.
Moreover, the playing field is even, in that issues such as age, gender, or national-
ity do not affect a player's opportunities in the game since the avatar is an idealized simulacrum—a placeholder for the person behind the screen.

MMOs generally use role-playing techniques, such as classes, skills, and "levels" of achievement. A few MMOs are more action oriented, and some are even based around first-person shooters.

While MMOs occasionally seem to involve players so much that they may become overly obsessed (see Chapter 1), most MMO players enjoy an entertaining adventure space and a social space all at once. At their best, MMOs provide fun, adventure, challenge, puzzles, financial challenges and opportunities, stories, social opportunities, notoriety, and a place to go where there are always other people willing to share.

OTHER GAME TYPES

CASUAL GAMES

Certainly one of the big surprises when it comes to the potential of games for positive impact comes from what are called "casual games." Many of you probably play casual games. In general terms, these are games we play for leisure and relaxation, for short duration sessions, or sometimes for social purposes that are as important to the game experience as the game itself. In the digital world, *casual games* has a slightly more specific meaning, but still the term refers to games with smaller scope, smaller budgets, and generally shorter unique game sessions than the megablockbuster commercial games targeted toward what we think of as the primary video game audience.

Casual games are card games, board games, puzzle games, word games, and even arcadelike games played on computers, game consoles, personal digital assistants (PDAs), and cell phones. And that's just the beginning. Already these games can be found in-flight on major airlines, on demand on hotel TVs, through interactive television channels, and even in Vegas-style slot machines and gambling devices.

Casual games are designed for leisure time. Jason Kapalka, cofounder and creative director of PopCap Games, told me, "We are looking for games you can play while, at the same time, talking on the phone with someone."[1] Of course, that is only one vision of casual games, but it does sum up many of them, which require only a part of the brain and some eye-hand coordination. I think of it as something similar to driving a car, which, once you have mastered it and gained enough experience, is almost automatic. While you are driving, you can listen to music, talk on a phone, or do any number of other activities while your hands and eyes are busy managing the driving process. Likewise, some casual games can be as automatic, but generally much more fun. In contrast, some casual games, for all their simplicity, can be very absorbing and can require considerable concentration and skill, particularly if you want to beat your high score or master the system.

What is remarkable about casual games, which were never intended to do anything more than entertain, is that along with their increasing sophistication and creative ideas, they also seem to be having significantly positive physical and mental impacts on those who play. And if you think this is some trivial statistic, consider who is playing. Regular casual game players now number, by different accounts, anywhere from a safe estimate of one hundred million to as many as three hundred million active players. With more than a billion game-ready cell phones out there, it's certain that these numbers will increase.

Moreover, more than two-thirds of those playing are thirty-five and older. Women number more than half the players—a statistic not typically associated with most mainstream video games. According to David Cole of DFC Intelligence, one of the most respected analysts in the field, the casual game market is expected to grow from $700 million in 2005 to over $13 billion by 2011.[2]

So what benefits are players reporting in the letters and testimonials they are sending to casual game companies?

- Stress relief
- Cognitive (brain) exercise
- Pain distraction/relief from pain
- Positive affirmations and building confidence
- Mood lifting
- Manual dexterity
- Learning through pattern recognition, resource allocations, spelling, word recognition, and typing skills

People writing these testimonials range from sufferers of debilitating diseases to ambulance drivers, from students to professional musicians. Even famous big-budget game designers. . . . In particular, people who never considered playing a video game before have discovered the enjoyment, along with some unexpected positive benefits of playing casual games.[3]

Once again, the benefits that come from casual game play are largely unintended. Some casual games are based around word play and even vocabulary, and it's arguable that they were designed to benefit people's literacy skills to some degree, but overall the positive benefits that players are reporting are a secondary effect of the games and not by any stretch their primary purpose.

Once again, this is an example of how games can positively impact players without even trying. Once again, I'm going to suggest that they can do so much more.

MOBILE GAMES

Mobile phones today have become an everyday appliance in many people's lives all over the world. They keep our schedules, take pictures, make home movies, store and play popular music, browse the Internet, send and receive text messages and e-mail, play video games, and, yes, even make phone calls. I'm surprised people aren't brushing their teeth with their cell phones. At a 2006 industry event, Microsoft chairman Bill Gates stated that one of Microsoft's primary targets in its Xbox Live service included "more than a billion game-ready cell phones."[4]

Industry pioneer Trip Hawkins sees cell phone games as immensely important. He predicts that there will be more than three billion cell phones within a few years and that games on cell phones will play an important role in society. He talks about the changes in social life that occurred during the Industrial Revolution, where families began to splinter and husbands went away to work and ultimately women entered the workforce, too. "Changes in society have contributed to the breakup of families and the small villages that used to exist," he says. "We now live in one place and then drive to work, to shop, to eat. People are in transit, and this contributes to a rootlessness."[5]

Hawkins describes mobile technology as a ubiquitous social computer. "You know that everyone else has one, and you have a way of being members of a community and of finding like-minded people or reaching out to find new friends." He believes that games and other activities on mobile devices can bring people together as no other technology has in history, and his company, Digital Chocolate, is geared toward that goal.

Another game pioneer, John Carmack, is also entering the cell phone game arena. Considered one of the greatest technical geniuses of the game industry, Carmack was the guy who revolutionized real-time 3D graphic games, with Doom and Quake among his notable accomplishments. Now he, too, is eyeing the mobile world. His first entry was a mobile version of his hit game Doom, but that was followed by his first original title in ten years, Orcs and Elves. Carmack dreams of doing something to connect people through cell phones in a massive multiplayer environment, something that has yet to be done but that would connect possibly thousands of players simultaneously through their cell phones in a shared environment with shared experiences.

Though most mobile games are crude by comparison with their console and computer-based big brothers, there is reason to expect that mobile games may spawn an even bigger business than any other medium. Already there are experiments in using cell phones and global positioning system (GPS) data to create games that take place in the real world. The opportunities are immense and growing rapidly. The question of how games on mobile devices can provide players with positive impact is yet to be seen. Only time will tell.

VIDEO GAME SUMMARY

Many of the game types described in this chapter have evolved over the years to become the major categories in the commercial game world. These are the games people refer to most often when they are talking about video games. Other relevant categories of games, such as the casual and mobile games as well as physical games like Dance Dance Revolution, Eye Toy, and Nintendo Wii, are categorized differently because of their audience, their purpose, or their mode of delivery. Serious games, as discussed in Chapter 8, are likewise separately categorized because of their intended purpose.

Games in every category, however, almost always fit into one of the main game categories. For instance, many casual and mobile games fit into puzzle or arcade categories, though some are word games, and others may be predominantly social interaction games somewhat different from those described in this chapter. Physical games are often arcadelike, though there are some action and adventure games now using physical movement as part of the game play. Serious games may use any and all game genres, differentiating themselves not by style of game but by the intention behind the design.

At this point, you know quite a bit about games and something about their positive potential. You probably have some idea what kinds of games you'd like to see out there and what you'd like to see them do for you, your kids, or other players around the world. Now it's time to consider how you can get in the game, too.

THE NEWBIE PRIMER

When I speak with nongamers about the positive potential of video games, they sometimes say, "Listening to you, I'm curious to try playing a video game, but I wouldn't know where to start. I'm sure I would be terrible at it or just get embarrassed and frustrated." Because there are literally thousands of video games and new ones arrive each year, it's not easy to know where to start. In this section, I'll suggest a progressive method of becoming comfortable with video games.

STEP 1

Think about the games you already play, such as card games, board games, or sports. These games all offer rules of play, goals, challenges, and rewards. You are already familiar, then, with how games work.

STEP 2

There are many online sites for so-called casual games that offer games that are not intimidating. I recommend PopCap's Bejeweled or Bookworm as good starting games. Bejeweled is a good puzzle/arcade game in which you try to move colored shapes to make patterns of three or more in a row. By making clever choices, you can cause additional "matches" to occur, gaining even higher scores. You can play Bejeweled in various modes, ranging from an untimed mode that allows you to experiment and learn without any danger of losing, to an "expert" mode that will challenge your ability to recognize patterns quickly and even develop some good strategies while working against the clock.

Bookworm is similar in some ways to Bejeweled, except that it involves forming words out of scrambled letters. Again, there are different modes of play. Other casual games that might get you into the spirit of games without being too challenging are Tradewinds Legend, Diner Dash, and Plantasia. Each of these three games offers different types of game play and can introduce you to more game elements, types of challenges and strategies. Check them out online using your favorite search engine.

After casual games, you can try some more complex video games. If you're interested in the role-playing genre, you can download a simple RPG called Fate from Wild Tangent. You can even try the first few levels for free. (Hint: Fishing is a great way to get free stuff in this game.)

If you think you are ready to try other kinds of complex game experiences, I recommend looking at games like Civilization or SimCity and starting slowly to build up an idea of how the game works. For a more active challenge (and if you have plenty of time), try Kingdom Hearts 2 (PlayStation only) or Elder Scrolls: Oblivion (Xbox 360 or Windows PC). After you have done some experimentation with one of these games, try looking in game stores or online for walkthroughs, FAQs, or commercial strategy guides for these games, but be forewarned: detailed strategies for these games can get quite complex. Go slowly to enjoy the discovery and learning these games provide. If you have kids to play with, let them help. Chances are they'll pick it up quickly or already be familiar with some aspects of the games. If you're especially brave, try playing the games your kids like, with them or perhaps on your own at first. Remember, video games are all about learning. Try to view learning to play that way. Relax and enjoy the ride.

Another way to learn about playing video games is to join a massive multiplayer world. The advantage of such worlds is that they are full of experienced players, many of whom would be delighted to tutor a newbie. Games like City of Heroes are particularly simple by comparison with most MMOs, but even in complex games like World of Warcraft, Guild Wars, or EverQuest, you can often find very helpful people by simply asking. In most of these games, you can create a character to test with very easily. Don't worry too much about your first character—just create one. Then go inside the game and type in a request for help, something like "Complete newbie looking for help getting started." You should be able to get the basic keys and commands from the product manual. Learn the methods of movement, how to send a message, and how to reply. From there on, you can experiment on your own or ask for help as much as you like. Be honest, and you'll probably find someone to help you.

GAMES TO CONSIDER

The games listed in this section are often complex and challenging. Also, they have something to offer by combining excellent entertainment with opportunities to think and to learn. Each offers advantages in different ways—for instance, through puzzle solving or role playing or through learning history, science, or skills. Some inspire through stories or by introducing players to new ideas.

Age of Empires (Microsoft Games)

Genre: Real-time Strategy

Rating: T

Platform: Windows PC

So far there have been three Age of Empires games, each set in a different historical period. Age of Empires starts in the Stone Age and spans ten thousand years of human evolution. Age of Empires 2 takes place in the Middle Ages, and Age of Empires 3 is set in the European colonization of the New World. Age of Mythology introduces players to the world of Greek and Roman mythology. (Also, look at Sid Meier's Gettysburg and Civil War Collection for game-oriented views of American history.)

Animal Crossing (Nintendo)

Genre: Role Playing

Rating: E

Platform: Nintendo DS

Animal Crossing puts players in a world of their own, complete with in-game friends and friends they can contact via wireless connection. Both social and instructive, this game allows players to engage in a number of tasks and activities, including designing their own clothing, buying and selling, collecting, and decorating. Great for any age.

Black & White 2 (Microsoft Games)

Genre: God Game

Rating: T

Platform: Windows PC

Black & White 2 is a complex game in which the player literally plays the god of a world. Players have the power of life and death over the "little people" and can even teach and train a monstrous "pet" creature who can wreak havoc or help and assist the world's inhabitants. As "god," players decide whether to be naughty or nice, and the world itself, and its people, respond to those decisions. A "good" god ultimately creates a paradise, where an "evil" god's world slowly evolves into something hellish. Like Fable (by the same designer), Black & White 2 allows players to explore their own morality and see the effects in a fascinating strategy/god game.

Chemicus: Journey to the Other Side (Tivola Publishing)

Genre: Puzzle Game

Rating: N/A

Platform: Windows PC

Chemicus is a puzzle-based, first-person adventure game that happens to teach chemistry. Chemicus plays like some other video games, using various items as components to create magical potions, except in this case the magical potions are actual chemical compositions created with real materials.

Civilization IV (Take 2)

Genre: Turn-Based Strategy Game

Rating: E10+

Civilization IV is the latest installment of one of the most popular video games of all time. Although there are many modes and options of play, in the standard game you play the leader of a nation that begins its existence in 4000 B.C. Develop your cities and explore the world while dealing with your neighbors through diplomacy or through warfare. There are many ways to play Civilization IV, and many ways to win. Civilization IV helps teach not only various levels of thinking, planning and strategy, but something about the relationships and evolution of technology and different approaches to conflict. This game is infinitely replayable. (For a real-time strategy game with similar themes, try Rise of Nations.)

Elder Scrolls: Oblivion (Take 2)

Genre: Third-Person RPG

Rating: M

Platform: Windows PC/Xbox 360

Elder Scrolls: Oblivion is set in a fantastically rendered world, full of trees and flowers and rivers and lakes. Just running around the countryside in this game is rewarding. The game itself is complex, often involving human interactions with computer-controlled characters who have personalities and lives of their own. There is a main storyline, which is interesting in itself, but players can explore the world at will and discover all kinds of side plots, quests and surprises. A very deep and complex world, often violent.

Fable/Fable 2 (Microsoft Games)
Genre: Adventure

Rating: M

Platform: Xbox and Windows PC

Fable is a third-person adventure game that allows players to explore the consequences of good and evil offering constant opportunities to choose through actions, which path to take in this virtual life. Not necessarily recommended for young children, this game could nevertheless be a great opportunity to explore with older kids the consequences of our decisions, to explore our darker natures, or to question why we live the lives we live. Use with discretion.

Kingdom Hearts 1&2 (Buena Vista Games/SquareEnix)
Genre: Action RPG

Rating: E10+

Platform: PlayStation 2

From the makers of the highly successful Final Fantasy series of RPGs, the Kingdom Hearts games feature Disney characters, such as Mickey Mouse, Donald Duck, and Goofy (and many more), in complex and engaging adventures. The Kingdom Hearts games offer quite diverse experiences, ranging from challenging fighting to exploration and quests to designing and building your own custom rocket ships—all wrapped up in a complex story frequently acted out with characters from famous Disney movies. Great for all ages.

Madden 2006/2007 (Electronic Arts)
Genre: Sports

Rating: E

Platform: PlayStation 2, Xbox, Xbox 360, Windows PC

The Madden series is the most successful video game sports franchises ever, and with the 2006 version, it introduced the Superstar Mode of play, which allows players to create a superstar from the ground up and deal with all the challenges of being a famous player. Combining the superstar role-playing element with an already complex football simulation makes this a breakout sports title.

Mario (Nintendo)

Genre: Arcade/Adventure

Rating: E

Platform: All Nintendo systems

Mario is the hero of numerous games from Nintendo, all of them fabulous fun for kids and adults alike. Mario games range from strict arcade games to racing games, party games, and complex 3D action-adventures. If you have access to older Nintendo consoles such as the Nintendo Entertainment System, the Super NES, Nintendo 64, or GameCube, you can play Mario games of many styles. The latest Mario games are found on the handheld DS and the Wii console.

Katamari Damacy/Me and My Katamari (Namco)

Genre: Arcade

Rating: E

Platform: PlayStation 2

Katamari Damacy was a relatively obscure Japanese game until it was "discovered." The game is hard to explain because it is truly one of a kind. The main character pushes a rolling device, something like a carpet sweeper, which picks up items from the surrounding environment—common items such as thumbtacks, mice and children's toys. The items stick to each other and form a ball, which the player's character continues to push. As the ball gets larger, the items it can pick up get bigger, too, until players might be picking up cats or dressers or whatever strange items the designers put in the world. Katamari Damacy and Me and My Katamari are delightful games at any age, and they might also be a great way to help teach the names of common household items to preschoolers.

Legend of Zelda (Nintendo)

Genre: Action RPG

Rating: Various ratings, none higher than T

Platform: Nintendo consoles and handheld players

The Legend of Zelda for the original Nintendo Entertainment System was, by many people's assessment, one of the best games ever created. Since that first "Zelda" game, Nintendo has released many products in the series. They are all highly imaginative and full of puzzles, strategies, and challenges. The later versions in the series are all set in imaginative 3D worlds and sometimes involve complex storylines, with time travel and even some emotional moments.

Metal Gear Solid (Konami)

Genre: 3D Adventure

Rating: M

Platform:

There are many games in the Metal Gear series, and what makes them unique is the depth of design and the clever game play, which most often involves stealth and intelligent choices over brute strength and violence. Metal Gear games are about conflict and are sophisticated in themes, so they are probably more appropriate for older children and adolescents, but they are excellent games both from an entertainment perspective and also from the puzzle-solving perspective.

Nintendogs (Nintendo)

Genre: Simulation

Rating: E

Platform: Nintendo DS handheld

Take care of a very cute little puppy, train it with voice and gesture commands, and play mini games with it. Pick from among several species. Excellent and imaginative.

SimCity IV (Maxis/Electronic Arts)

Genre: Simulation

Rating: E

Platform: Windows PC

SimCity IV is the most recent version of the famous city simulation that has inspired players since the early 1990s. All SimCity games are about learning, experimentation and creativity, planning, and many of the practical challenges of city planning and development. As counterintuitive as this may seem, SimCity games are popular with children as young as six.

The Sims (Maxis/Electronic Arts)

Genre: Simulation

Rating: T

Platform: Windows PC and handhelds

The Sims is unlike any other game. There are several versions of The Sims, including The Sims Online. Each person who plays The Sims approaches the game differently. It can be a "life" simulation, a social game, or a chance to create your ideal family life and home environment. The Sims is a product that often appeals to people who have never played games before, although it is probably less popular with young boys, who crave more action or who may not thrive on the social aspects of the game.

Spore (Maxis/Electronic Arts)

Genre: Mixed

Rating: Unknown

Platform: Windows PC

Spore is a vast game that actually encompasses many categories of games, from arcade to real-time simulation, city building simulation, and space exploration. Spore encourages creativity, problem solving, planning, and lots and lots of experimentation, along with some good foundation in micro- and macro-scale events, complex ecosystems, and the long-range repercussions of early decision making.

Toontown Online (Disney Online)

Genre: Online Multiplayer RPG

Rating: E

Platform: Windows PC

Toontown Online is Disney's massive multiplayer game for youngsters, though I have known some adults to enjoy it as well. The environment is very safe for young players, and the content is heavy on imagination, humor, and safe social interaction and light on violence.

Viva Piñata (Microsoft Games)

Genre: Simulation

Rating: E

Platform: Xbox 360

Viva Piñata is an unusual game that combines simulation elements with great imagination in a colorful world ideal for young players. The game has many features, including taking care of living piñatas of various kinds and protecting them from enemies and other dangers, while tending and building a beautiful environment. Players can even trade piñatas with friends or visit each others' piñata gardens. Viva Piñata is a simple game on the surface but gets more complex as you play it.

Zoo Tycoon (Microsoft Games)

Genre: Simulation

Rating: E

Platform: Windows PC

Zoo Tycoon is a simulation game that allows players to manage and build a zoo. In some ways, Zoo Tycoon is like SimCity, but in addition to the management, planning, and financial aspects of the game, it also includes learning about the animals of the world, including many endangered species in the special "Endangered Species" edition of the game. Unlike SimCity, players get a much closer view of how well they are doing by the feedback they get from the zoo patrons. Zoo Tycoon is only one of several "tycoon" types of games, such as Railroad Tycoon, Rollercoaster Tycoon, Pizza Tycoon, and, without the "tycoon" title, but with all the fun and challenge, The Movies. The Movies is one of my favorites, because it lets you be a movie mogul and guide the rise of your studio, manage the actors, and determine the types of movies you create, not to mention landscaping and designing the movie lot itself.

GAMES YOU CAN PLAY AS A FAMILY

You can play any game together. In fact, I encourage it, but here are a few that might especially lend themselves to good family fun without controversy:

- Dance Dance Revolution (Konami)
- LEGO Star Wars: The Video Game (LucasArts)
- Mario Kart (any version) (Nintendo)
- Mario Party 7 (Nintendo)
- Nintendo Wii games (several) (Nintendo)

Chapter 11

DIGITAL ADVOCACY

We believe that a rich, fulfilling, and healthy life of play provides the greatest happiness to human beings, and that helping make this life a reality is our most important mission.

—Kyushiro Takagi, president and CEO, Namco, Inc.

I had two purposes when I wrote this book. The first was to offer you an opportunity to turn your understanding of video games on its head. I hoped to present you with the positive perspective of what video games are and what they can be.

My second purpose in writing this book was to enlist you in advocacy for the future of video games as positive social influences. While I do my best to offer this message to the community of video game designers and producers, I believe that you can be the most effective advocates for this seminal idea. What it boils down to is that video game designers have an opportunity to take seriously the impact—in game terms, the emergent impact—that occurs while the players are having fun playing.

I think it's fair to say that video games in most cases have something useful to offer, and in some cases they offer very specific benefits to their players. It's also fair to respect the fact that the video game industry is a commercial business industry, and that the games it produces need to be profitable to justify the time and cost of development.

What am I suggesting, then? Merely a change of attitude and focus that allows video game producers to consider new ways to design games so that they can expand their range. There are many ways to accomplish creative expansion of any medium, and game designers are always seeking those ways that video games can expand. My suggestion is small in terms of game innovation and won't compare favorably with the next great 3D engine or technology. On the other hand, my suggestion could lead to improvement in the lives of players and the people around them. In terms of overall impact, helping people learn to communicate better, be more tolerant of each other, and become more prepared for the challenges of their school, work, and family lives reaches deeper and might promise more lasting impact on the players themselves, even if the new technology is what brings them to play.

The suggestions and ideas in this book are not radical or particularly new. Many people have thought about these ideas, have written and talked about them, and, in some cases, have even implemented them in video games. What I hope to do is bring this message to those of you who have not previously considered video games from this perspective.

My approach is not intended to result in weak and uninteresting games. Quite the contrary, history suggests that games with a net positive influence on players can be among the most popular, successful, and memorable games of all time. Whenever people talk about the best games ever, Civilization and SimCity are among them. Civilization has inspired many players to be more curious about history, human innovation, and technology—not to mention strategy, diplomacy, and culture. It is being used in schools as a teaching aid as well. SimCity, which was rejected by every major game company when it was first developed, has become the model of simulations for learning and fun in video games. Playing SimCity allows players to take the role of a city's mayor, manager, and engineering staff all in one. They determine zoning, taxes, and policies. They build roads, move earth, and establish sewer systems and emergency services. Before this game, managing a city never sounded like much fun to most people. Since SimCity was released, millions of gamers have discovered both the challenges and the rewards of managing a complex system like a city.

A full discussion of how to design video games with positive impact would be more detailed than the scope of this book allows, and it would consist of lengthy discussions of different types of game situations illustrated through dozens of specific design examples. To put it simply, when I describe games with positive impact, I mean games that empower players by teaching, modeling, simulating, and inspiring using the principles of context, inclusion, role modeling, and the other techniques described in Chapter 6.

Chapter 7 more specifically described some educational, social, and personal areas in which video games could have a positive impact. That chapter represents the real core of what I am proposing. The other chapters describe the method. If you grasp that video games can help people learn more about mathematics or can model family dynamics, help people learn to negotiate or even how to think more critically, then you understand what I am suggesting.

Video game designers know they are impacting the people who play their games. Many take their role as communicators seriously. At the same time, they are aware that they are creating entertainment opportunities first and foremost. Their focus is on making games fun and appealing to their audience—a specific group of players who are going to be attracted to the games they create.

Having to appeal to a specific audience does not prevent game designers from creating deeper and more meaningful experiences in their games, or from considering the inclusion of material and experiences that can teach, model, simulate, and inspire in positive ways.

If you believe that video games can be better and that they can be intentionally created with positive impact in mind, then you can do something to see more such games.

ADVOCACY IS SIMPLE

Advocacy is how we let others know what we believe in and what we want them to consider. To me, advocacy is quite the opposite of being afraid of something, criticizing it, or opposing it. To be an advocate for video games means to see their positive reality or potential and to stand up and make that opinion known.

This book gives you the information and understanding you need to make very specific recommendations and requests. Too often, people without real knowledge of video games can only say, "I don't like this" or "This is bad" or "I am concerned for my kids." Now you can do more. You can say specifically what kinds of games you want and, if you are a parent, what you want your kids to come away with.

There are several effective ways to advocate for the kinds of video games you want to see. First, you advocate by what you purchase. This is the clearest and simplest message you can send to the game companies. However, game purchase decisions are somewhat complicated for parents, given the fact that what your kids want is not always what you think they ought to have. If you are a parent, you must make a judgment call in such cases, but if you stay involved and consider the suggestions offered in Chapters 9 and 10, you may come to understand what your kids are playing and what they are taking away from it. Moreover, if there is something controversial in the game, you have the opportunity to discuss it with your kids and ensure that the messages received from the game are clear.

The other easy expression of advocacy is simply to communicate. Send a fax, make a call, write a letter, or hire a skywriter. Send e-mails to the company, to the CEO, or to the designers themselves. (Contact information for major video game companies and distributors is provided in the Resources.) According to Louis Castle of Electronic Arts, "At EA everybody opens their own mail and reads their own e-mail. Any communication, from a player, a fan, or a concerned parent, has a huge impact."[1] Even if other companies are not as conscientious, they do pay attention to the communication they get. If that communication is clear and offers positive suggestions, it will have greater impact than an ambiguous or entirely negative message.

In addition, most game companies host game-related discussion sites on which anyone can post a message. Game companies hire community managers to facilitate those discussions and to pay close attention to what is being written and discussed. As I said, anyone can go to a fan site and post a message. That means you, too.

TALKING POINTS: WHAT YOU CAN SAY THAT WILL MAKE A DIFFERENCE

Maybe video game concepts like TMSI and Magic Edge are still somewhat unfamiliar to you. You may be wondering how you can advocate for something that perhaps you only partially understand.

To help you make your communications with game companies more effective, I offer a few useful talking points. Consider these short sentences and paragraphs as basic examples, and use them for inspiration. Feel free to mention this book and the concepts you like. There's a good chance that the persons you're contacting will be familiar with this book, and if they are not, perhaps they'll be inspired to find out more about TMSI and the other concepts outlined here.

GENERAL STATEMENTS

Here are some statements you can make that generally describe the kinds of video games suggested in this book:

> "I understand that there are many types of games for different players. I would support game companies that think about the overall impact of the games they make on their players."

> "When I go to buy a video game, I am looking for something that has some depth and possibly has something to teach or in some way enriches my life."

> "Show me games that teach, model, or inspire players or simulations that help us learn and explore different subjects."

> "Please produce games that are fun to play but that also present opportunities for players to explore values and beliefs, to understand that actions come with consequences, and to become good decision makers in areas of life where it really counts."

COMPARATIVE STATEMENTS

For comparative statements, find games you like or games that have the kinds of impact you are looking for, and let the company know what you like about them. Simply fill in the specifics in the following statements:

> "I want to see more games like [name]."

> "Games like [name] do [effect], and I believe this provides an overall positive impact on people."

DESCRIBING CONCEPTS

These statements can help you describe the concepts in this book, such as the Magic Edge, TMSI, and others:

> "Because video games are so good at motivating players, I am interested in games that use that motivation to inspire players in some way—to learn, to understand more about life or to practice useful skills."

> "I believe in the power of video games to be a positive force in my kids' lives, and I am interested in seeing more games that teach useful skills. They might also model important attitudes or abilities or even inspire the kids to learn more about subjects like math, history, communications, business, and other useful skills and knowledge."

THE FUTURE OF VIDEO GAMES

For the past thirty years, video games have grown, changed, evolved, and reached a level of sophistication few of us imagined possible back at the beginning. Then, games were simplistic novelties made by amateur artists and hackers in garages and bedrooms. Today, video games are a big business, and games have turned into the new epics of entertainment. Perhaps the most compelling aspects of video games for me are their ability to engage me in a world where I am exploring and learning constantly, to entertain me in ways that no other media can offer, and to connect me with other people in a shared environment, with shared goals and experiences—people I would never have encountered any other way. Video games are providing new technologies, new careers, new university programs and are having a growing impact on politics and education. More important, video games are contributing to a new and evolving culture, primarily fueled by our youth, but spilling over into people of all ages.

Even with so much demonstrable progress, many observers see the current state of video games as equivalent to the state of Hollywood filmmaking in the 1930s. If so, then there is much more to come.

At their best, video games can spread knowledge and insight, and connect people in new and stimulating ways. What does the future of video games have to offer? It's entirely up to us to decide.

◆ ◆ ◆ ◆ ◆

If there is radiance in the spirit, it will abound in the family.

If there is radiance in the family, it will abound in the community.

If there is radiance in the community, it will grow in the nation.

If there is radiance in the nation, the universe will flourish.

(Adapted from the *Tao Te Ching*.)

Resources

Major Game Company/Distributor Information

Acclaim
Web site: www.acclaim.com
Contact page: www.acclaim.com/contact.htm

Activision
Web site: www.activision.com/en_US/home/home.jsp
Phone: (310) 255-2000

Atari
Web site: www.atari.com/us
Send comments to Atari, Inc. 417 Fifth Ave., New York, NY 10016 Attn: Bruno Bonnell

Bioware (Canada)
Web site: www.bioware.com/bioware_info/contact
Phone: (780) 430-0164

Blizzard
Web site: www.blizzard.com/support/?id=msi0281p#Phone_Support
Phone: (949) 955-1382

Capcom
Web site: www.capcom.com
Phone: (408) 877-0500

Electronic Arts
Web site: www.ea.com
Phone: (650) 628-1500

Funcom
Web site: www.funcom.com
E-mail contact: pr@funcom.com

Koei
Web site: www.koei.com
Phone: (650) 692-9080

Konami
Web site: www.konami.com
Contact via online form at
https://www.konami.co.jp/inquiry/cgi-bin/inquiry02.cgi?PAGE_NAME=index.
Also, read the "Message from CEO" at www.konami.co.jp/en/corporate/

LucasArts

Web site: www.lucasarts.com

Mail to LucasArts, P.O. Box 29908, San Francisco, CA 94129-0908

Microsoft

Web site (games): www.microsoft.com/games/default.aspx

Phone: (425) 882-8080

Namco

Web site: www.namco.com

Phone: (408) 235-2000

Fax: (408) 235-2005

Also read the CEO's statement at www.namco.com/pane_single.php?res=company_info

NCSoft

Web site: www.ncsoft.com/eng/index.asp

Phone: (512) 498-4000

Nintendo of America

Web site: www.nintendo.com/home

Phone: (425) 882-2040

Sony Corporation of America

Web site: www.sony.com

Contact: SCEA Attn: Correspondence, PO Box 5888, San Mateo, CA 94402-0888

Take 2 Interactive

Web site: www.take2games.com

Phone: (646) 536-2842

Tecmo

Web site: www.tecmoinc.com

Phone: (310) 944-5005

THQ

Web site: www.thq.com

Phone: (818) 871-5000

Ubisoft

Web site: www.ubi.com/US/default.aspx

Phone: (888) 824-7038

GAME INDUSTRY ORGANIZATIONS

Academy of Interactive Arts & Sciences
Web site: www.interactive.org
Located in Los Angeles, the Academy of Interactive Arts & Sciences (AIAS) is an official professional academy of the $7+ billion interactive entertainment software industry. AIAS is supported by the industry's leading companies.

Entertainment Software Association (ESA)
Web site: www.esa.org
The Entertainment Software Association (ESA) is the "U.S. association exclusively dedicated to serving the business and public affairs needs of companies that publish video and computer games for video game consoles, personal computers, and the Internet."

Entertainment Software Rating Board (ESRB)
Web site: www.esrb.org
The Entertainment Software Rating Board (ESRB) is a self-regulatory body established in 1994 by the Entertainment Software Association (ESA). ESRB independently applies and enforces ratings (www.esrb.org/ratings/ratings_guide.jsp), advertising guidelines, and online privacy principles adopted by the industry.

International Game Developers Association (IGDA)
Web site: www.igda.org
The International Game Developers Association (IGDA) is a nonprofit membership organization that advocates globally on issues related to digital game creation. The IGDA's mission is to strengthen the international game development community and effect change to benefit that community.

Video Game Voters Network
Web site: www.videogamevoters.org
The Video Game Voters Network, a project of the Entertainment Software Association, is a means by which American adults who play computer and video games can organize and take action on important policy issues affecting the computer and video game industry.

LINKS TO OTHER ORGANIZATIONS AND RESOURCES

del.icio.us/tag/gaming2learn (gaming2learn)
glsconference.org (Games+Learning+Society)
info.americasarmy.com/home.php (America's Army home page)
libertus.net (site dealing with free speech issues)
terranova.com (Edward Castronova's site on massive multiplayer words)
www.21stcenturyskills.org (Partnership for 21st Century Skills)
www.apa.org (American Psychological Association)
www.casualgamesassociation.com (site for casual game players)

www.computeraddiction.com (Maressa Orzack's site)
www.fbi.gov/publications/pguide/pguidee.htm (FBI guidelines for online child safety)
www.fepproject.org/factsheets/mediaviolence.html (Free Expression Policy Project article on media violence)
www.gamepolitics.com (articles about games and politics)
www.gamesparentsteachers.com (Marc Prensky's site)
www.henryjenkins.org (MIT professor Jenkins's site)
www.kidshealth.org (site devoted to children's health issues)
www.kidsrisk.harvard.edu (information and advice about media and kids)
www.kotaku.com (game news and commentary)
www.mediaed.com (Media Education Foundation)
www.mediafamily.org (National Institute on Media and the Family)
www.mediawise.org (media advisory site, with a yearly video game report card)
www.medicineonline.com (general site for medical information)
www.pogo.com (casual games site)
www.popcap.com (casual games site)
www.safekids.com (children's safety)
www.sagepub.com (Sage Publications, for *Games and Culture: A Journal of Interactive Media*)
www.seriousgames.org (The Serious Games Initiative)
www.stevenberlinjohnson.com (Steven Johnson's Web site)
www.trainingplace.com (learning technologies)
www.wirekids.org (kid-friendly media awareness site for parents and children)
www.ywcaboston.org/programs/yvc (Boston YWCA Youth Voice Collaborative)
zone.msn.com (casual games site)

GAMES

America's Army (info.americasarmy.com/home.php)
Darfur Is Dying (www.darfurisdying.com/)
Façade (www.interactivestory.net)
Food Force (www.food-force.com)
Peacemaker (www.peacemakergame.com/)
Real Lives (www.educationalsimulations.com/products.html)

Notes

Chapter 1

1. Associated Press, "Clinton Seeks 'Grand Theft Auto' Probe," *USA Today*, July 14, 2005.
2. C. Everett Koop, comments delivered in a 1982 speech before the Western Psychiatric Institute as cited in the *Journal of Applied Social Psychology* 16, no. 8 (1986).
3. Ronnie Lamm, interview with Robert MacNeil, *MacNeil/Lehrer NewsHour*, PBS, December 29, 1982.
4. Senate Subcommittee Hearing. "Testimony from Software Industry and Opponents on Content of Video Games," CBS News Transcript, December 10, 1993.
5. Steven Fink, interview with Robert MacNeil, *MacNeil/Lehrer NewsHour*, PBS, December 29, 1982.
6. Elizabeth Carll, interview with author, September 19, 2006.
7. American Academy of Pediatrics, "Policy Statement on Media Violence," Pediatrics 108, no. 5 (November 2001): 1222–26, http://aappolicy.aappublications.org/cgi/content/full/pediatrics;108/5/1222.
8. Senate Commerce Committee, "The Impact of Interactive Violence on Children," March 21, 2000, Government Printing Office Online, www.gpoaccess.gov.
9. David Grossman, statement before the New York State Legislature, October 1999, and as quoted by Aaron Ruby, "It's Addictive! Or Is It?" *Business Week*, September 15, 2006.
10. Mothers against Videogame Violence and Addiction, www.mavav.org/resources, October 11, 2006.
11. Harold Schechter, *Savage Pastimes* (New York: St. Martin's, 2005), 59.
12. Ibid., 25–26.
13. Rowell L. Huesmann, as quoted by Richard Rhodes in "The Media Violence Myth," *Rolling Stone*, November 23, 2000.
14. Jib Fowles, *The Case for Media Television Violence* (Thousand Oaks, CA: Sage, 1999), 37.
15. Jib Fowles, interview with author, September 7, 2006.
16. Rowell L. Huesmann, interview with author, September 19, 2006.
17. Fowles, *The Case for Media Television Violence*, 28.
18. Jonathan Freedman, interview with author, September 15, 2006.
19. Ibid.
20. Fowles, ibid., 28.
21. Senate Commerce Committee, "The Impact of Interactive Violence on Children."
22. Dmitri Williams, interview with author, August 22, 2006. All of Williams's quotes cited in this chapter are from this interview.

23. Marjorie Heins et al., "Brief Amici Curiae of Thirty-three Media Scholars in Support of Appellants, and Supporting Reversal," United States Court of Appeals for the Eighth Circuit, September 2002, www.fepproject.org/archives, accessed October 11, 2006.

24. Congressional Public Health Summit, American Psychological Association et al., "Joint Statement on the Impact of Entertainment Violence on Children," July 2000, www.aap.org/advocacy/releases/jstmtevc.htm, accessed October 11, 2006.

25. Ibid.

26. Henry Jenkins, "The Values in Video Games," *Religion & Ethics Newsweekly*, Episode 639, May 30, 2003.

27. Albert "Skip" Rizzo, presentation at Games for Health conference, May 9, 2006.

28. Gerard Jones, *Killing Monsters: Why Children Need Fantasy, Super Heroes, and Make-Believe Violence* (New York: Palgrave Books, 2002).

29. Henry Jenkins, "Lessons from Littleton: What Congress Doesn't Want to Hear about Youth and Media," *Independent School Magazine*, https://nais.org/publications/ismagazinearticle.cfm?ItemNumber=144264, accessed October 11, 2006.

30. United States Circuit Court of Appeals, opinion accessed at www.ca7.uscourts.gov/tmp/X20YAKHQ.txt, October 11, 2006.

31. Data compiled from Bureau of Justice Statistics data, version 08/07/02; historical data on video game releases courtesy of J. L. Sherry, and console numbers supplied by David Cole of DFC Intelligence, Inc.

32. Peter Vorderer, interview with author, October 10, 2006.

33. Craig Anderson, interview with author, April 12, 2006.

34. Huesmann, interview with author.

35. Associated Press, "Korean Man Dies after Computer Games Binge," October 10, 2002, www.theage.com.au/articles/2002/10/10/1034061292187.html.

36. Anthony Faiola, "When Escape Seems Just a Mouse-Click Away," *Washington Post,* May 27, 2006.

37. Maressa Orzack, interview with author, September 7, 2006.

38. Ibid.

39. Nick Yee, speech at the Palo Alto Research Center (PARC), July 20, 2006.

40. Ibid.

41. Ibid.

42. Maressa Orzack, interview with author, June 2005.

43. Nick Yee, interview with author, June 2005.

44. Ibid.

45. Eugene Provenzo, *Video Kids: Making Sense of Nintendo* (Cambridge, MA: Harvard University Press, 1991), quoted on the Media Awareness Network Web site: www.media-awareness.ca/english/index.cfm.

46. Ben Macklin and James Becher, "Video Games: Where to Now?" *eMarketer*, March 2006.

47. Shannon Prather, "Judge Throws Out Minnesota Video Game Law," *TwinCities.com Pioneer Press*, August 1, 2006, quoting State Senator Sandy Pappas.

48. James Ivory, interview with author, September 22, 2006.

49. Johan Huizinga, *Homo Ludens* (Boston: Beacon, 1938; reprinted 1955, 1971).

50. Henry Jenkins, "Testimony Before the U.S. Commerce Committee," May 4, 1999, http://commerce.senate.gov/hearings/hearin99.htm.

CHAPTER 2

1. "Usage over Time" spreadsheet, May–June 2005, Pew Internet & American Life Project (www.pewinternet.org), http://207.21.232.103/trends.asp#activities, accessed October 11, 2006.
2. Ibid.
3. Ben Macklin and James Becher, "Video Games: Where to Now?" *eMarketer*, March 2006.
4. Entertainment Software Association, "2006 Sales, Usage and Demographic Data," www.theesa.com, accessed October 11, 2006.
5. Michael Cai, "Electronic Gaming in the Digital Home," Parks Associates, September 1, 2005.
6. Ibid.
8. Information Solutions Group survey conducted for PopCap Games, September 2006, PopCap Games press release.
8. Matt Richtel, "Relying on Video Game Sequels," *New York Times*, August 8, 2005.
9. Macklin and Becher, "Video Games."
10. Kathy Schoback, "The Economics of a Next-Gen Game," presentation at the 2005 Game Developer's Conference, San Jose, CA.
11. Ibid.
12. Will Wright, keynote speech at the 2006 Game Developers Conference, San Jose, CA.
13. Louis Castle, interview with author, June 14, 2006. All of Castle's quotes cited in this chapter are from this interview.

CHAPTER 3

1. Anne Pellowski, interview with author, May 25, 2006.
2. M. R. Lepper and T. W. Malone, "Intrinsic Motivation and Instructional Effectiveness in Computer-Based Education," in *Aptitude, Learning and Instruction: III. Cognitive and Affective Process Analyses*, ed. R. E. Snow and M. J. Farr (Hillsdale, NJ: Erlbaum, 1987), 223–53.
3. Mihaly Csikszentmihalyi, *Flow: The Psychology of Optimal Experience* (New York: Harper & Row, 1990).
4. Ibid., 1.
5. Acetycholine effects: http://en.wikipedia.org/wiki/Acetylcholine.
6. See www.medical-library.org/journals5a/neurochemistry.htm; http://people.eku.edu/palmerj/200/neurons.htm; www.library.oit.edu/ereserves/data/PSY339Powers7.pdf.
7. Norepinephrine and focus: http://en.wikipedia.org/wiki/Norepinephrine.
8. For dopamine and Parkinson's, manic depression, and Alzheimer's, see Duane E. Haines, ed., *Fundamental Neuroscience* (London: Churchill Livingstone, 1997), 22. For more on dopamine, also see http://en.wikipedia.org/wiki/Dopamine.

9. Jeffrey Goldstein, "Effects of Electronic Games on Children," Department of Social & Organizational Psychology, University of Utrecht, The Netherlands, March 2000: "Positron emission tomography (PET) scans were taken while healthy men played a video game. The neurotransmitter Dopamine, thought to be involved in learning, reinforcement of behavior, attention, and sensorimotor coordination, was released in the brain during play." See also James E. Zull, "What Is 'The Art of Changing the Brain?'" *New Horizons for Learning*, May 2003.
10. Carl Jung, *Alchemical Studies* (Princeton, N.J.: Princeton University Press, 1983), vol. 13, 470.
11. Bruce McEwen, *The End of Stress as We Know It* (Washington, DC: National Academies Press, 2002). See also www.naturalhealthweb.com/articles/McEwen.html.
12. Margaret Martinez, interview with author, May 27, 2006.
13. Attributed to Wu-tsu Fa-yen (1024–1104).

CHAPTER 4

1. Steven Johnson, *Everything Bad Is Good for You: How Today's Popular Culture Is Actually Making Us Smarter* (New York: Riverhead Books, 2005).
2. *Concise Oxford Dictionary* (Oxford: Oxford University Press, 1999).
3. Virginia Overdorf, "Learning and Performance," William Paterson University, November 21, 2000, www.wpunj.edu/cos/ex-movsci/mllearn/sld003.htm, accessed October 11, 2006.
4. Eric R. Kandel, James H. Schwartz, and Thomas M. Jessell, *Principles of Neural Science*, 4th ed. (New York: McGraw-Hill Medical, 2000).
5. Marc Prensky, *Don't Bother Me, Mom—I'm Learning!* (St. Paul, MN: Paragon, 2006).
6. Ibid.
7. Cognition and Technology Group at Vanderbilt, "Anchored Instruction and Its Relationship to Situated Cognition," *Educational Researcher* 19, no. 6 (1990): 2–10. See also "Learning and Transfer," in *How People Learn: Brain, Mind, Experience, and School,* ed. John D. Bransford, Ann L. Brown, and Rodney R. Cocking (Washington, DC: National Academy of Sciences, 1999), chap. 3, http://darwin.nap.edu/html/howpeople1/ch3.html.
8. James Paul Gee, interview with author, May 30, 2006.
9. Constance Steinkuehler, "Cognition & Learning in Massively Multiplayer Games: A Critical Approach," University of Wisconsin, 2005.
10. Anne Pellowski, interview with author, May 25, 2006.
11. James Paul Gee, *What Video Games Have to Teach Us about Learning and Literacy* (New York: Palgrave Macmillan, 2003).
12. Gerard Jones, interview with author, June 17, 2006.

CHAPTER 5

1. Steven Johnson, *Everything Bad Is Good for You: How Today's Popular Culture Is Actually Making Us Smarter* (New York: Riverhead Books, 2005).

2. "A series of meaningful choices" is often attributed to game designer Sid Meier, but it is now in common use by many writers and designers.
3. Department of Defense, "Data Administration Procedures," DoD 8320.1-M, March 29, 1994, authorized by DoD Directive 8320.1, September 26, 1991.

CHAPTER 6

1. Bruno Bettelheim, *Uses of Enchantment: The Meaning and Importance of Fairy Tales* (New York: Vintage Books, 1977); and Gerard Jones, *Killing Monsters: Why Children Need Fantasy, Super Heroes, and Make-Believe Violence* (New York: Palgrave Books, 2002).
2. See, for example, Jean Lave and Etienne Wenger, *Situated Learning: Legitimate Peripheral Participation* (Cambridge: University of Cambridge Press, 1991).
3. Trip Hawkins, interview with author, June 23, 2006.
4. Joseph Campbell, *The Hero with a Thousand Faces* (Princeton, NJ: Princeton University Press, 1949).

CHAPTER 7

1. Rusel DeMaria and Johnny Wilson, *High Score: The Illustrated History of Electronic Games*, 2d ed. (Emeryville, CA: McGraw-Hill/Osborne, 2004).
2. Partnership for 21st Century Skills, www.21stcenturyskills.org, accessed October 11, 2006.
3. John C. Beck, interview with author, October 9, 2006.
4. Robert Clegg, interview with author, June 30, 2006.
5. Steven Johnson, *Everything Bad Is Good for You: How Today's Popular Culture Is Actually Making Us Smarter* (New York: Riverhead Books, 2005), 41.
6. A favorite personal story of Bill Graham, told to the author several times on different occasions.
7. Edward Castronova, "Virtual Worlds: A First-Hand Account of Market and Society on the Cyberian Frontier," CESifo Working Paper No. 618, December 2001.
8. John Seely Brown and Douglas Thomas, "You Play World of Warcraft? You're Hired!" Wired, April 2006.
9. Aggie Baker Pilgrim, interview with author, June 30, 2006.
10. Ibid.

CHAPTER 8

1. Ben Sawyer, interview with author, May 5, 2006. All quotes from Sawyer cited in this chapter are from this interview.
2. Major Bret Wilson, interview with author, May 8, 2006. All quotes from Wilson cited in this chapter are from this interview.

CHAPTER 9

1. Marc Prensky, *Don't Bother Me, Mom—I'm Learning!* (St. Paul, MN: Paragon, 2006).

2. Steven Johnson, *Everything Bad Is Good for You: How Today's Popular Culture Is Actually Making Us Smarter* (New York: Riverhead Books, 2005).

3. Prensky, *Don't Bother Me, Mom*, 28–29.

4. Rusel DeMaria, *Nintendo Games Secrets* (Roseville, CA: Prima, 1990).

5. Jonathan Wendel, aka "Fatal1ty," interview with author, June 20, 2006.

6. Gerard Jones, *Killing Monsters: Why Children Need Fantasy, Super Heroes, and Make-Believe Violence* (New York: Palgrave Books, 2002), 186.

7. KidsRisk, www.kidsrisk.harvard.edu.

8. Federal Bureau of Investigation (FBI), "A Parent's Guide to Internet Safety," www.fbi.gov/publications/pguide/pguidee.htm, accessed October 11, 2006.

9. Peter D. Hart Research Associates, "Parents' Awareness and Use of the ESRB Rating System Based on a National Survey of Parents Conducted on Behalf of the Entertainment Software Rating System," March 27, 2006 (1724 Connecticut Avenue, NW, Washington, DC 20009).

10. FBI, "A Parent's Guide to Internet Safety."

11. Marc Rizzaro, interview with author, October 4, 2006.

CHAPTER 10

1. Jason Kapalka, interview with author, July 10, 2006.

2. DFC Intelligence, "The Online Game Market," 2006; also e-mail correspondence with author.

3. PopCap surveys, www.popcap.com/press/?page=press_releases&release=casual-games_survey, accessed September 13, 2006.

4. Bill Gates, Electronic Entertainment Expo, Microsoft press conference, May 2006.

5. Trip Hawkins, interview with author, June 23, 2006. All quotes from Hawkins cited in this chapter are form this interview.

CHAPTER 11

1. Louis Castle, interview with author, June 14, 2006.

RECOMMENDED READING

GAMES AND THEIR EFFECTS

Beck, John C., and Mitchell Wade. *Got Game? How the New Generation of Video Gamers Is Reshaping Business Forever*. Boston: Harvard Business School Press, 2004.
Are video gamers better prepared for the twenty-first century? This book provides some intriguing answers.

Fowles, Jib. *The Case for Television Violence*. Thousand Oaks, CA: Sage, 1999.
A clear analysis of the literature on the effects of television violence, including an analysis of the Eron/Huesmann studies.

Freedman, Jonathan L. *Media Violence and Its Effect on Aggression: Assessing the Scientific Evidence*. Toronto: University of Toronto Press, 2002.
A thorough assessment of the literature on media violence.

Gee, James Paul. *What Video Games Have to Teach Us about Learning and Literacy*. New York: Palgrave Macmillan, 2003.
Gee's groundbreaking academic analysis of video games helped open the doors for video game academic studies and the realization that something called "learning" was going on.

Huizinga, John. *Homo Ludens*. Boston: Beacon, 1938; reprinted 1955, 1971.
Fascinating study of the role of play in human life.

Johnson, Steve. *Everything Bad Is Good for You: How Today's Popular Culture Is Actually Making Us Smarter*. New York: Riverhead Books, 2005.
If you think popular culture is a vast wasteland, check out this book. Johnson has a knack for seeing what others miss.

Jones, Gerard. *Killing Monsters: Why Children Need Fantasy, Super Heroes, and Make-Believe Violence*. New York: Palgrave Books, 2002.
Especially helpful for parents to understand the purpose of our children's fantasies, particularly those dark and violent ones.

Prensky, Marc. *Don't Bother Me, Mom—I'm Learning!* St. Paul, MN: Paragon, 2006.
Prensky helps parents understand the educational value of video games, with excellent analysis and advice.

SOCIAL ISSUES

de Becker, Gavin. *The Gift of Fear: Survival Signals That Protect Us from Violence.* Boston: Little, Brown, 1997.
An expert on violence looks at the causes and contributing effects in high-profile cases.

Goleman, Daniel. *Emotional Intelligence.* 10th ed. New York: Bantam Books, 2006.
An important book for our society, discussing how we can be more emotionally healthy.

LEARNING AND PLAY

Bransford, John D., Ann L. Brown, and Rodney R. Cocking, eds. "Learning and Transfer," in *How People Learn: Brain, Mind, Experience, and School.* Washington, DC: National Academy of Sciences, 1999, http://darwin.nap.edu/html/howpeople1/ch3.html.
An excellent and approachable analysis of learning theories by the National Academy of Sciences.

Csikszentmihalyi, Mihalyi. *Flow: The Psychology of Optimal Experience.* New York: Harper & Row, 1990.
Classic book on the optimal state of being. Has influenced many game designers.

VIDEO GAME ANALYSIS

Bogost, Ian. *Persuasive Games: The Expressive Power of Videogames.* Cambridge, MA: MIT Press, 2007.
How video games influence people, and how they can be used for purposes such as political influence and advertising. A very detailed and thoughtful analysis.

Koster, Ralph, and Will Wright *A Theory of Fun for Game Design.* Scottsdale, AZ: Paraglyph, 2004.
Industry veteran Koster provides an analysis of how video games work and why. Primarily oriented toward game designers, but interesting reading for anyone interested in the subject.

Michael, David, and Sande Chen. *Serious Games: Games That Educate, Train and Inform*. Boston: Thomson Course Technology, 2006.
One of the first studies of the phenomenon of serious games. A good introduction.

Salen, Katie, and Eric Zimmerman. *Rules of Play: Game Design Fundamentals*. Cambridge, MA: MIT Press, 2003.
A very technical and fascinating breakdown of the elements that constitute play. Recommended only for people who want to get down to the details.

CLASSICS OF MYTH AND FANTASY

Bettelheim, Bruno. *Uses of Enchantment: The Meaning and Importance of Fairy Tales*. New York: Vintage Books, 1977.
A landmark book on the meaning of fairy tales and the role of fantasy in our lives.

Campbell, Joseph. *The Hero with a Thousand Faces*. Princeton, NJ: Princeton University Press, 1949.
A classic work that translates myth and fantasy into a roadmap that has been used by writers and filmmakers for decades.

HISTORY AND CULTURE OF VIDEO GAMES

DeMaria, Rusel, and Johnny Wilson, *High Score: The Illustrated History of Electronic Games*. 2d ed. Emeryville, CA: McGraw-Hill/Osborne, 2004.
My book with Johnny Wilson is full of stories of the early development of the video game industry with thousands of pictures to illustrate the history.

Herz, J. C. *Joystick Nation: How Videogames Ate Our Quarters, Won Our Hearts, and Rewired Our Minds*. Boston: Little, Brown, 1997.
One of the first books to analyze the content and culture of video games and video gamers.

Jenkins, Henry. *Convergence Culture: Where Old and New Media Collide*. New York: New York University Press, 2006.
MIT professor Henry Jenkins's most recent book on modern culture. Highly recommended.

Kent, Steven L. *The Ultimate History of Video Games: From Pong to Pokemon and Beyond—The Story behind the Craze That Touched Our Lives and Changed the World*. Roseville, CA: Prima, 2001.
Certainly one of the most comprehensive histories of the video game industry.

INDEX

About the Author

Rusel DeMaria is the author of more than sixty game-related books, including the best-selling *High Score: The Illustrated History of Electronic Games*. He has been a senior editor for several national video game magazines and a columnist both nationally and internationally. He has been a presenter at the prestigious Game Developers Conference and appeared as an expert commentator on the PBS special, "The Video Game Revolution," and several other TV and radio shows. He is also a musician, professional mediator, recreational tree climber, martial artist, and city councilor.

About Berrett-Koehler Publishers

Berrett-Koehler is an independent publisher dedicated to an ambitious mission: Creating a World that Works for All.

We believe that to truly create a better world, action is needed at all levels—individual, organizational, and societal. At the individual level, our publications help people align their lives with their values and with their aspirations for a better world. At the organizational level, our publications promote progressive leadership and management practices, socially responsible approaches to business, and humane and effective organizations. At the societal level, our publications advance social and economic justice, shared prosperity, sustainability, and new solutions to national and global issues.

A major theme of our publications is "Opening Up New Space." They challenge conventional thinking, introduce new ideas, and foster positive change. Their common quest is changing the underlying beliefs, mindsets, and structures that keep generating the same cycles of problems, no matter who our leaders are or what improvement programs we adopt.

We strive to practice what we preach—to operate our publishing company in line with the ideas in our books. At the core of our approach is stewardship, which we define as a deep sense of responsibility to administer the company for the benefit of all of our "stakeholder" groups: authors, customers, employees, investors, service providers, and the communities and environment around us.

We are grateful to the thousands of readers, authors, and other friends of the company who consider themselves to be part of the "BK Community." We hope that you, too, will join us in our mission.

A BK CURRENTS BOOK

This book is part of our BK Currents series. BK Currents books advance social and economic justice by exploring the critical intersections between business and society. Offering a unique combination of thoughtful analysis and progressive alternatives, BK Currents books promote positive change at the national and global levels. To find out more, visit www.bkcurrents.com.

Be Connected

Visit Our Website

Go to www.bkconnection.com to read exclusive previews and excerpts of new books, find detailed information on all Berrett-Koehler titles and authors, browse subject-area libraries of books, and get special discounts.

Subscribe to Our Free E-Newsletter

Be the first to hear about new publications, special discount offers, exclusive articles, news about bestsellers, and more! Get on the list for our free e-newsletter by going to www.bkconnection.com.

Get Quantity Discounts

Berrett-Koehler books are available at quantity discounts for orders of ten or more copies. Please call us toll-free at (800) 929-2929 or email us at bkp.orders@aidcvt.com.

Host a Reading Group

For tips on how to form and carry on a book-reading group in your workplace or community, see our website at www.bkconnection.com.

Join the BK Community

Thousands of readers of our books have become part of the "BK Community" by participating in events featuring our authors, reviewing draft manuscripts of forthcoming books, spreading the word about their favorite books, and supporting our publishing program in other ways. If you would like to join the BK Community, please contact us at bkcommunity@bkpub.com.